Peasants

Praise for this book

'Peasants: Chayanov's recovered essays is packed full with ample evidence that the past is critical to informing the present. This is a book about what peasants are, what they do, how they do it, the role they play in society, and why all of this matters – a lot. The essays, written a century ago, portrayed struggles which are ongoing. The challenges Chayanov described certainly continue but peasants around the world have refused to be disappeared. Bravo Teodor, Alexander, Irina and Jan Douwe for reminding us – in numerous and nuanced ways – all of the power and wisdom that can be garnered by looking carefully at history as we collectively envision and work towards a world with more, not fewer peasant communities.'

Annette Aurélie Desmarais, former Canada Research Chair in Human Rights, Social Justice and Food Sovereignty (2013–2023), University of Manitoba

'These 'lost' essays by Chayanov are a joy to read. They enlighten and enrich the roots of a tradition that still has a lot to impart. They grapple with the central questions of 'modernization': what elements of the past can help build a flourishing future? And what needs to be done to ensure such a future? Chayanov's answers aren't always as Chayanovian as one might think! But they are always based on a wealth of empirical data, and the 'peasant economy' continues to have a major role to play in his vision of the sane society.'

Julien-François Gerber, International Institute of Social Studies, The Hague

'It is an amazing fortune that this book has finally come to light. If this work had been published at the time the essays were written by Chayanov (1920s), it is likely that the course of the contemporary history of agronomy, cooperativism, the agrarian question and rural development would have been different. I can only say to all interested in rural, food and agrarian issues that this book must be on your shelf.

This book needs to be incorporated into the lexicon of those that struggle for a more sustainable agriculture in the 21st century.'

Sergio Schneider, Professor of Sociology of Rural Development and Food Studies at the Federal University of Rio Grande do Sul (UFRGS), Porto Alegre, Brazil

'This book will unveil A.V. Chayanov to any kind of reader. Those who get to read Chayanov for the first time will get a good insight into Chayanov's thoughts and will find into one piece a broad overview of his work. These include the agrarian question, processes of differentiation, the role of cooperation or a description of social agronomy. Those who are familiar with Chayanov's work will find unpublished writings and letters. All, will be delighted to read how up-to-date is his work, particularly for those working in the construction of food systems based on agroecology. I fully recommend this book not only to those interested in critical agrarian studies but also to agronomists who really want to understand how relevant the profession is and why they need to work with and for people. In Chayanov's words: Like any social work, social agronomy relies on people and can influence agriculture only through people.'

Marta Rivera, Research Professor, Spanish National Research Council (CSIC)

Peasants

Chayanov's recovered essays

Edited and translated by
Teodor Shanin, Alexander Nikulin, Irina Trotsuk
and Jan Douwe van der Ploeg

Practical
ACTION
PUBLISHING

Practical Action Publishing Ltd
25 Albert Street, Rugby,
Warwickshire, CV21 2SD, UK
www.practicalactionpublishing.com

A catalogue record for this book is available from the British Library.

A catalogue record for this book has been requested from the Library of Congress.

ISBN 978-1-78853-249-5 Paperback
ISBN 978-1-78853-250-1 Hardback
ISBN 978-1-78853-251-8 Electronic book

Citation: Shanin, T., Nikulin, A., Trotsuk, I., and van der Ploeg, J.D., (2024) *Peasants: Chayanov's recovered essays*, Rugby, UK: Practical Action Publishing <http://doi.org/10.3362/9781788532518>.

Since 1974, Practical Action Publishing has published and disseminated books and information in support of international development work throughout the world. Practical Action Publishing is a trading name of Practical Action Publishing Ltd (Company Reg. No. 1159018), the wholly owned publishing company of Practical Action. Practical Action Publishing trades only in support of its parent charity objectives and any profits are covenanted back to Practical Action (Charity Reg. No. 247257, Group VAT Registration No. 880 9924 76).

Cover photo shows a portrait of Alexander Chayanov by Jim Scott, with deep gratitude from the editors and translators for its reproduction on the cover.

Cover design by Katarzyna Markowska, Practical Action Publishing

Typeset by vPrompt eServices, India

Agrarian Change and Peasant Studies Series

Class Dynamics of Agrarian Change
by Henry Bernstein 2010

Peasants and the Art of Farming: A Chayanovian Manifesto
by Jan Douwe van der Ploeg 2013

Food Regimes and Agrarian Questions
by Philip McMichael 2013

Sustainable Livelihoods and Rural Development
by Ian Scoones 2015

Political Dynamics of Transnational Agrarian Movements
by Saturnino M. Borras Jr. and Marc Edelman 2016

Agrarian Change, Migration and Development
by Henry Veltmeyer and Raúl Delgado Wise 2016

Agroecology, Science and Politics
by Peter M. Rosset and Miguel A. Altieri 2017

Speculative Harvests: Financialization, Food and Agriculture
by Jennifer Clapp and Ryan Isakson 2018

Counterrevolution: The Global Rise of the Far Right
by Walden Bello 2019

Agriculture and the Generation Problem
by Ben White 2020

Scholar-activism and land struggles
by Saturnino M. Borras Jr. and Jennifer C. Franco 2023

Agrarian Change and Peasant Studies

Little books on big issues

Open Access ebook edition

Sponsors of the Open Access ICAS small ebook book series
[Logos: ICAS, PLAAS, Steps, RLS, ISS, TNI, ERC]

Contents

List of tables

Book Series Foreword

Peasants: Chayanov's Recovered Essays is the twelfth volume in the Agrarian Change and Peasant Studies Series from icas (Initiatives in Critical Agrarian Studies). The first volume is Henry Bernstein's *Class Dynamics of Agrarian Change*, followed by Jan Douwe van der Ploeg's *Peasants and the Art of Farming*, Philip McMichael's *Food Regimes and Agrarian Questions*, Ian Scoones' *Sustainable Livelihoods and Rural Development*, Marc Edelman and Saturnino M. Borras Jr.'s *Politics of Transnational Agrarian Movements*, Henry Veltmeyer and Raul Delgado Wise's *Agrarian Change, Migration and Development*, and Peter Rosset and Miguel Altieri's *Agroecology: Science and Politics*; *Speculative Harvests: Financialization, Food and Agriculture* by Jennifer Clapp and Ryan Isakson is the eighth volume in the series, followed by Walden Bello's *Counterrevolution*, Ben White's *Agriculture and the Generation Problem*, and Jun Borras and Jennifer Franco's *Scholar-Activism*.

Together, these twelve books reaffirm the strategic importance and relevance of applying agrarian political economy analytical lenses in Critical Agrarian Studies today. They suggest that succeeding volumes in the series will be just as politically relevant and scientifically rigorous.

A brief explanation of the series will help put *Peasants: Chayanov's Recovered Essays* into perspective in relation to the icas intellectual and political project.

Today, global poverty remains a significantly rural phenomenon, with rural populations comprising three-quarters of the world's poor. Thus the problem of global poverty and the multidimensional (economic, political, social, cultural, gender, environmental, and so on) challenge of ending it are closely linked to rural working people's resistance to the system that continues to generate and reproduce the conditions of rural poverty and their struggles for sustainable livelihoods. A focus on rural development thus remains critical to development thinking. However, this focus does not mean de-linking rural from urban issues. The challenge is to better understand the linkages between them, partly because the pathways out of rural poverty paved by neoliberal policies and the war on global poverty engaged in and led by mainstream international financial and development institutions to a large extent simply replace rural with urban forms of poverty.

Mainstream approaches in agrarian studies are generously financed and thus have been able to dominate the production and publication of research and studies on agrarian issues. Many of the institutions (such as the World Bank) that promote this thinking have also been able to acquire skills in producing and propagating highly accessible and policy-oriented publications that are widely disseminated worldwide. Critical thinkers in leading academic institutions are able to challenge this mainstream approach, but they are generally confined to academic circles with limited popular reach and impact.

There remains a significant gap in meeting the needs of academics (teachers, researchers and students), social movement activists and development practitioners in the Global South and the North for scientifically rigorous yet accessible, politically relevant, policy-oriented and affordable books in Critical Agrarian Studies. In response to this need, icas has launched this small book series. The idea is to publish "state of the art small books" that will explain a specific development issue based on key questions, including: What are the current issues and debates in this particular topic and who are the key scholars/thinkers and actual policy practitioners? How have such positions developed over time? What are the possible future trajectories? What are the key reference materials? And why and how is it important for ngo professionals, social movement activists, official development aid circle and nongovernmental donor agencies, students, academics, researchers and policy experts to critically engage with the key points explained in the book? Each book will combine theoretical and practical politics-oriented discussion with empirical examples from different national and local settings.

We aspire and work to make the many, if not all, books in the series available in multiple languages in addition to English, namely, Chinese, Spanish, Portuguese, Indonesian, Thai, Japanese, Korean, Italian, Russian, Turkish and Arabic. The Chinese edition is in partnership with the College of Humanities and Development of the China Agricultural University in Beijing, coordinated by Ye Jingzhong; the Spanish edition with the PhD Programme in Development Studies at the Autonomous University of Zacatecas in Mexico, coordinated by Raúl Delgado Wise, Fundacion Tierra in Bolivia coordinated by Gonzalo Colque; the Portuguese edition with the Universidade Estadual Paulista, Presidente Prudente (unesp) in Brazil, coordinated by Bernardo Mançano Fernandes, and the Universidade Federal do Rio Grande do Sul (ufrgs) in Brazil, coordinated by Sergio Schneider; the Indonesian edition with University of Gadjah Mada in Indonesia, coordinated by Laksmi Savitri; the Thai edition with rcsd of University of Chiang Mai, coordinated by Chayan Vaddhanaputi; the Italian edition coordinated by Alessandra Corrado at the University of Calabria; the Japanese edition with Kyoto University, coordinated by Shuji Hisano of Kyoto University, Koichi Ikegami of Kinki Universit, and by Sayaka-Funada-Classen; the Korean edition with Research Institute of Agriculture and Peasant Policy and coordinated by Wongkyu Song; the Russian edition with The Russian Presidential Academy of National Economy and Public Administration (RANEPA), coordinated by Teodor Shanin and Alexander Nikulin; the Turkish edition coordinated by Umut Kocagöz and Duygu Avci; and the Arabic edition coordinated by Hamza Hamouchene of the Transnational Institute (TNI).

Given the objectives of the Agrarian Change and Peasant Studies Series, one can easily understand why we are delighted to have as Book 12 the recovered essays by Chayanov. The first twelve volumes fit together well in terms of themes, accessibility, relevance and rigour. We are excited about the bright future of this important series!

Saturnino M. Borras Jr., Sergio Coronado, Ruth Hall, Max Spoor, Henry Veltmeyer, and Ye Jingzhong
ICAS Book Series Editors
August 2023

Preface: Chayanov's worlds

Alexander Vasilyevich Chayanov was born in 1888. He studied with enthusiasm and success in the gymnasium and at the Moscow Agricultural Academy. He then completed a two-year internship in leading European agrarian research centres in Belgium, France, and Italy. After his return to Russia, Chayanov studied peasant economies in different regions, actively participated in the organization of peasant cooperatives, and taught not only as an associate professor at the university but also as a rural lecturer-activist. He published a number of scientific articles on the peasant economy, agricultural cooperation, and agricultural regional studies, which led to his reputation as a young and talented agrarian scientist. Moreover, Chayanov was known for his exceptionally broad and deep interests in different sciences and arts: mathematics, geography, history, literature, and poetry. Chayanov was especially successful in interdisciplinary studies and easily developed vivid models and metaphors in both scientific writing and works of fiction.

In Chayanov's time, Russia was a great peasant country. Primarily at the expense of the peasantry, Russia conducted large-scale industrialization and the modernization of its economy. However, the peasantry remained the most numerous and disenfranchised class in the country. In tsarist Russia, peasants were not freed from serfdom (a specific form of slavery) until 1861, but the Russian landowners kept most of the land and class privileges. By the early 20th century, in spite of such social-political inequality, the Russian peasants steadily showed their will and ability to develop their economy and unite into cooperatives and public unions.

Meanwhile, in the fertile black earth regions of Russia, the situation of so-called 'agrarian overpopulation' worsened. Demographic growth had determined a sharp increase in the number of peasant economies, while their size had shrunk, leading to poverty and social tension. The tsarist regime was in no hurry to implement the necessary social-economic reforms, which determined the discontent of different social strata. Already in the first Russian Revolution of 1905–1907, the peasantry expressed strong discontent. With great difficulty, the tsarist government managed to suppress numerous peasant uprisings in many regions of the empire.

Thus, the agrarian (or rather peasant) question became the most pressing one in Russian intellectual and political disputes in the early 20th century. Many prominent scientists, politicians, and public figures discussed the ways to solve the agrarian question. It should be noted that the social and economic discussions of the agrarian question in Russia were based on excellent, empirical, statistical data collected by Russian statistical departments. *Zemstvos* (local self-governments of Russia) often opposed the tsarist government on the basis of ideology. Many local statisticians and agronomists considered it their professional and civic duty to scrupulously study the life of the common people, the peasantry. They used such comprehensive data about peasant life and economy to propose and defend projects to solve the agrarian question in Russia.

It was this intellectual, political environment that determined the formation of Alexander Chayanov as a talented agrarian economist. The data of the *zemstvos'* studies of the peasant economy's budgets were the basis of Chayanov's first works proving that the peasant family economy had its own motivation and development dynamics that were different from the capitalist economy. According to Chayanov, the peasantry would be able to effectively defend their social and economic interests in the capitalist world.

The Revolution of 1917 called the 29-year-old professor Chayanov to active, political work. He was one of the co-founders of the political party of Russian cooperators. He was also a leading expert in the League of Agrarian Reforms, which united the best agrarian scientists of all political directions to develop optimal solutions for the agrarian question in the Revolution of 1917.

In his popular science booklet, *What is the Agrarian Question?* (1917), Chayanov primarily emphasized the enormous, regional diversity of the rural worlds of such a huge country as Russia and insisted that the agrarian question should be formulated and solved 'from below', on the basis of specific regional, and local, rural needs. Chayanov called for a wide and careful consideration of the economic and cultural diversity of rural Russia. According to him, agrarian reform had to search for an optimum between high labour productivity on the land and broad democratization of the national income. Chayanov supported the nationalization of the land, which would lead to a system of peasant labour economies under market commodity relations. He emphasized the need to take care of confiscated landlord estates. He proposed the transfer of part of the landlords' property to the peasants on the condition that the state would redeem these lands from their former owners. Part of the highly developed landlord estates had to be converted into special, state economies working on the issues of scientific, cultural, and educational rural development. In fact, in this work, Chayanov sought to synthesize and harmonize various possible approaches to complex agrarian reform in Russia. In 1918, Chayanov published a book on the main directions of agrarian consulting in the early 20th century. The book focused on the interaction of agronomists with peasants and was called *Main Ideas and Methods of Social Agronomy*.

It should be noted that by 1917 the peasantry had already experienced World War I (1914–1918) and had returned home from the front unwilling to delve into the difficulties of the optimal solution of the agrarian question. The peasants dreamed of the immediate expansion of their land allotments through the seizure and liquidation of all landlord estates. In their revolutionary impatience, the peasants welcomed the so-called 'Lenin's Decree on Land', which had literally borrowed the agrarian ideas of the left *Narodnik* parties and their demand for the immediate and free transfer of all the land to the peasants. Critics of Lenin's revolutionary approach believed that it provoked and encouraged the revolutionary anarchy of the peasant masses that mercilessly and recklessly plundered the remains of landlord estates and established their local law of land use that was inconsistent with the rational and national interests of rural development.

In the midst of the Civil War, by introducing central planning and total state control and prohibiting market relations, the Bolsheviks sought to completely socialize and, in fact, militarize the entire social and economic life of the country. For instance, in 1918, the Bolsheviks nationalized the peasant cooperative bank in spite of the protests of the Russian cooperators and Chayanov, who personally met with Lenin to persuade him not to nationalize the peasant cooperative bank.

At first Chayanov had a negative evaluation of the Bolshevik revolutionary experiment. However, already in 1918, he agreed to cooperate with the new Soviet government in the belief that the Revolution could provide the peasantry and peasant cooperation with new and previously impossible opportunities for social development. Despite the horrors of the Civil War, Chayanov worked fruitfully on preserving and developing peasant cooperatives and wrote articles and books on the nature of the peasant economy and peasant cooperation. At the same time, Chayanov critically analysed the theoretical and practical foundations of the new revolutionary, bureaucratic, economic system of Russia, which he called 'state collectivism'.

In 1919, Chayanov published his fiction novel, *My Brother Alexey's Journey to the Land of Peasant Utopia*. In the novel, he combined ironic criticism of capitalism and Bolshevik communism with a positive programme of the victorious, rural development of peasant cooperation to create a new, effective, humane, multicultural, social-political order. Chayanov's utopia is a striking description of a pluralistic and multicultural social order that resists both capitalist and communist dogmas. His criticism of bureaucratic socialism turned out to be prophetic, because, in 1921, Lenin and his party recognized the failure of the so-called 'war-communism policy' – the militaristic, bureaucratic system of governing the country. Lenin and his party announced the start of the New Economic Policy of building socialism on the basis of a flexible balance between the city and the village, market entrepreneurship and state planning, the working class and the peasantry. The hopes of the New Economic Policy were pinned on the development of peasant cooperation. That is why Chayanov's book on the theory and practice of cooperation was on the desk of a dying Lenin.

The 1920s were the apex of Chayanov's organizational and intellectual career. He created and headed the Agricultural Research Institute of Economics and Politics, which became the Russian and, perhaps, the world's leading agricultural intellectual centre. At the same time, Professor Chayanov frequently taught in the Agrarian Academy, embarked on scientific trips to European universities, and was one of the most influential agrarian experts in the People's Commissariat (Ministry) of Agriculture of the USSR. Many Bolshevik leaders listened to his opinion even after Lenin's death. Proof of this is found in a letter from Chayanov to the outstanding Soviet party leader Vyacheslav Molotov, *On the current state of agriculture in the USSR compared with its pre-war state and the situation in agriculture of capitalist countries* (1927).

It was in the 1920s that Chayanov published his main scientific works: *Theory of Peasant Economy* (1926), *Basic Ideas and Forms of Agricultural Cooperation* (1927), *Theory of Differential Optima* (1928), and *Methods of Budget Studies* (1929). Moreover, Chayanov wrote books not only for his fellow professors and leaders of the Revolution, but also and primarily for the peasants. In the 1920s, his *A Short Course on Cooperation* – a small book of 20,000 words reprinted five times – was a course of lectures on the foundations of agricultural cooperation that was extremely popular among literate peasants, rural activists, and agronomists of Russia. Each chapter of this book contains clear and concise definitions of cooperation and its types illustrated by popular, historical, and contemporary examples of the cooperative movement and by specific cases of interaction of peasant economies and different types of cooperatives.

This Chayanov book represents two great genres of world literature. On the one hand, it is a kind of propaedeutic 'ABC of Cooperation' on the model of Leo Tolstoy's *ABC for Children*. On the other hand, it is a kind of 'Cooperative

Manifesto' on the model of the Communist Manifesto by Karl Marx and Friedrich Engels. In it, Chayanov presents a fascinating picture of the struggle of the Russian, and international, cooperative movement for a new, just, social world. In his cooperative studies, Chayanov repeatedly mentioned that peasant cooperation had to constantly overcome, on the one hand, the element of the capitalist market and, on the other hand, the element of state bureaucracy.

In the late 1920s, Joseph Stalin began the centralized expansion of the bureaucratic system of economic management, which allowed him to implement collectivization – the system of brutal state management – by uniting peasant economies into so-called 'production cooperatives' or collective farms. These were agricultural enterprises in which peasant property and labour were often forcibly united into a formal, cooperative property controlled by the party bureaucracy.

The ideas of Chayanov and his colleagues, representing the will and mood of the independently thinking and working peasantry, were surely a main obstacle for such an agrarian reform. In his theory of agricultural cooperation, Chayanov argued that the free, vertical cooperation of autonomous economies 'from below' was more socially and economically efficient than the horizontal, bureaucratic (Stalin's) collectivization 'from above' that doomed Russian agriculture to inefficiency and stagnation.

In 1930, in the midst of Stalin's collectivization, Chayanov and many of his colleagues were thrown into prison and accused of creating the Labour Peasant Party, which, it was claimed, resisted Stalin's collectivization. In reality, it had simply been invented by the secret police. For many decades the name of Chayanov was banned and forgotten in Soviet Russia. His unique system of vertical cooperation was completely destroyed, and a huge horizontal system of Stalin's cooperation was built on its ruins. History proved that Soviet collective agriculture was an inefficient system, which, because of bureaucratic control, constantly suffered from a lack of incentives for free peasant labour. The professional elites of peasants, agronomists, and economist-statisticians were destroyed in Stalinist purges, and, in 1937, Alexander Chayanov and many like-minded people were executed.

In the diverse legacy of Chayanov, his work *On the Theory of Non-Capitalist Economic Systems* is of particular importance as a kind of intellectual testament. It was published in 1926 in German in Germany, because, already at that time, it was impossible to publish this work in Soviet Russia due to political censorship. Chayanov considered the world (national) economy not as a single whole, like in the classical, political economy, but as a conglomerate of various economic forms based on different organizational principles. According to Chayanov, each economic form has a specific purpose manifested in the search for profitability and cost-effectiveness. They form the basis of the economic balance of the system; such an economic balance determines the organizational plan of the economy as a detailed model of its economic activity.

Thus, Chayanov developed his famous table of national economic systems, in which slavery and communism and family economy and capitalism coexist historically and logically, despite their differences in time and scale of economic activity. In the comments to the table, Chayanov emphasized the impossibility of expressing the mode of existence of one economic system in the elements or categories of any other system, because every national economic system is a complex combination of its own internal connections and phenomena. The size and shape of each system are determined by organizational-production and cultural-historical processes. For instance, in the manufacturing industry, under certain technical and social conditions, the capitalist economy is beyond competition, whereas in agriculture, capitalist relations undergo significant difficulties because of the social problem of the optimal concentration of production.

However, Chayanov recognized that in the 19th and 20th centuries, capitalism played a leading role in the development of the world economy despite its serious flaws. According to Chayanov, capitalism 'does not need' any social-economic realities beyond the limits of capitalist profitability, which determines the place of the peasantry in the calculations of agricultural profitability. Moreover, the intermittent, impulsive development of capitalism violates the economic balance and leads to crises in the system, which has a dangerous impact on the entire national economy. The attack of capitalism on the national economy creates system elements that oppose it with their economic essence and start a serious rivalry with capitalism. Chayanov considered the peasant family-cooperative and socialist movements to be the two most important anti-capitalist phenomena.

Why is Chayanov's legacy still of such great importance? Why are his ideas even more relevant today than 100 years ago? Of optimal importance are Chayanov's interpretation and analysis of the peasant economy 'from below'. Second, is his anti-Stalinist and, at the same time, anti-capitalist programme of peasant cooperation. Finally, we are indebted to his explanation of the necessity of a model of diverse and parallel economies. This idea is consistent with the contemporary desire to organize an effective and fair social life 'from below' (through the initiatives of individuals, families, and communities) with the solidarity of cooperatives and local, public organizations that contribute to the further expansion of the cultural diversity of large and small social worlds.

T. Shanin, A. Nikulin, and I. Trotsuk

INTRODUCTION

On interpretation and relevance: an introduction to 6 recovered essays

Jan Douwe van der Ploeg

This book contains six, highly valuable, essays written by Alexander Chayanov. These essays have been recovered and carefully translated through the admirable efforts of Sasha Nikulin, Irina Trotsuk and Teodor Shanin of the Russian Presidential Academy of National Economy and Public Administration (RANEPA) in Moscow. They are highly valuable in that they help to give a more complete and better balanced overview of the works of Chayanov, but also, or maybe especially, since they offer analytical tools and insights that are highly useful, I think, in grasping and understanding the complexities of today's agriculture.

Highly valuable, but not easy

However, reading the essays is not that easy. The problem is partly that they refer to times and places that are no longer familiar to most of us. Today's world differs in many respects, and sometimes decisively, from Russia in the early 20th Century. But there is more. The difficulties in correctly interpreting these essays also stem from them being rooted in debates that have evolved considerably in the meantime. The complexity of the essays also reflects the intellectual struggle in which the author himself was engaged in at the time of writing. As he wrote in another text, the world economy, centres of capitalism and peasant agriculture were "literally changing before our eyes" (1925/1986:257). Dealing with these complex and, at that time, contingent processes, was no walk in the park – for one thing it required the development of a new language apt to grasp what was occurring 'before his eyes'. This inevitably provoked one of the troublesome aspects of these essays – which reflect a search for the right words, a process that evidently passes through sometimes confusing modifications. I will illustrate this further on.

Confusion may arise as well from what was brand new at that time but is now common place and common sense. In this sense there are, in some of the essays, parts that now seem somewhat boring. However, when taking the essays seriously, and relocating them in the time and space of their origin, they reveal an important methodological aspect of what we now call critical agrarian studies: going into details is not pedantry, but reflects the capacity to understand the wider context (even at the level of details) and the willingness to reshuffle the relevant whole and the elements that compose it. Where needed I will highlight the messages that, at first sight, are lost in what might now be perceived as long-windedness.

The preface of Sasha Nikulin, Irina Trotsuk and the late Teodor Shanin offers an excellent biographical context of the 6 essays in this volume. The 'biographical aspects' of each essay (where and when was it written, for whom, and its objectives) are further specified in short notes that precede each essay. *Inter alia,* this shows an amazing feature: the capacity of Chayanov to speak different 'languages' – not in a linguistic sense but meaning that he was able to address very different audiences. *Politicians* (as personified in the fifth essay by Molotov and, indirectly, Lenin), *peasants* (to whom Chayanov was lecturing on the formation and operation of cooperatives; see the third essay), *academics* (see the fourth essay on differentiation), *agronomists* (or change agents as we would probably say in our times when referring to the 'practical work' discussed in the second essay) and *activists* involved in social movements (first essay) are among those addressed in these six essays. And they are addressed, time and again, in their own language with points of reference specific to each audience. No need to say that this also adds to the difficulty of 'digesting' the texts almost a century later, in other places, by new types of audiences with different lives and professional experiences.

For those willing to tackle such difficulties, the essays will unravel highly meaningful insights that still, or probably again, are more relevant than ever. I will not summarize here the different essays, but try to unlock some of the most outstanding points. That is: those points that appear to be most relevant at the beginning of the 2020s. I will also try to clarify the elements that may obscure understanding of these more relevant points.

The agrarian question (the first essay)

The first essay discusses an issue that has, throughout the 20th Century as well as during the first decades of the 21st, demonstrated itself to be an extremely devilish issue: the conceptualization of the agrarian question and the associated view on land reform. The remarkable feature here is that Chayanov defines the agrarian question in terms that go beyond the framework of just criticizing capitalism. Consequently, the way forward (i.e. land reform) is specified in a way that decisively goes beyond the mere redistribution of land. Land reform needs to include (1) the development of productive forces, (2) the improvement of working and living conditions in the countryside and (3) a democratization of the distribution of national income. This last point is especially noteworthy: it impinges on relations between town and countryside just as it allows for the other objectives (1 and 2). There is no need to signal here that this essay entails a fundamental critique of the Russian land reform and (implicitly of) many others that later followed elsewhere. At the same time Chayanov argues here, just as he did in other occasions, that such objectives need to go hand in hand with a strengthening of peasant agriculture, precisely because this style of farming is highly productive (brings high yields) and labour intensive: it represents, in short, "the fullest possible use of the means of production and workforce" (this book, first essay).

The explanation that is given to support this fundamental point represents one of the confusing elements of these essays. The wording used here centres on the difference between 'gross profit' and 'net profit'. The pursuit of each of these objectives renders results that differ significantly from each other. The search for 'net profit' equals profit driven agriculture that looks for the highest returns on capital invested. In that context the notion of 'gross profit' is highly confusing – and as a matter of fact Chayanov did soon (in his works after 1917) replace it with the notion of 'labour income'. This is equivalent to the surplus (the value) generated by peasant labour. The search for improvements in this labour income necessarily translates into an 'organizational plan' that seeks to simultaneously optimize productive employment and total production. As shown in current debates about agroecology, the notion of labour income has once again become highly relevant (Ploeg et al., 2019).

Social agronomy (second essay)

This essay is partly about agency, as we call it today. It is about "the will and knowledge" of the actors involved in peasant agriculture and their contribution to "sustainable rural development" as the short introduction to this essay phrases it. Social agronomy, then, specifies how "the social builders" (or: "builders of real life") can augment this "will and knowledge" in order to develop agriculture (that is: to develop the productive forces in an endogenous way). In doing so the "art of the peasant" (his or her "ability to use particulars") occupies centre stage.

The essay explains at length (it embraces 13 chapters!) the different methods and underlying concepts and puts one in mind of what is currently called communication science and/or extension studies. These are now well-developed (sub-)disciplines, but at that time did not exist at all. It can well be argued, I think, that Chayanov was, among many other things, one of the founding fathers of this particular part of social sciences (together with 'walking professors' from Italy e.g. Bizzozero). Reading now this first sketch (from 1918!) may make, at least, some readers feel a bit bored, the more so since the text goes even into the smallest possible details (such as how to write with chalk on a blackboard!). But this appearance is treacherous. Chayanov's discussion of social agronomy is like a handbook for agroecology in our times (save the chalk and blackboard may need substituting by Power Point). Full of details about transition (especially as it is a *revolutionary* transition being proposed) it shows great mastery of the many details that come with complexity, diversity and radical change. In this respect 'social agronomy' continues to stand as a highly relevant beacon.

Cooperation (third essay)

This essay was designed, and tested, as a course for peasant leaders. It is a welcome prelude to 'The Theory of Peasant Co-operatives' – the well-known scientific treatise that was published in 1927 (and recently translated and re-published in Brazil). It explains 'vertical' cooperatives (as opposed to 'horizontal' ones) as a major line of defence of peasant agriculture against a wide range of capital interests (located in trading, banking, processing, seed selection, control over machinery, etc.). At the same time the essay suggests that there is a clear line that runs from this kind of 'vertical' cooperation to the socialist organization of farming in the future. In this view the development of productive forces is again central. What is critically missing, in retrospect at least, is a discussion of how capital could again become, precisely through cooperatives, "a master [instead of] a servant" (even though the importance of peasant control over the cooperatives and their management is strongly underlined in the essay).

Differentiation (fourth essay)

The fourth essay again changes language. Whilst the previous one was oriented at peasant leaders (and consequently talked about "the death of a horse or a cow [as a] big disaster"), this one starts as a dialogue with other scientists, outlining Chayanov's own position *viz-a-viz* his colleagues. As with the other essays it contains a wealth of empirical references that are carefully embedded in a theoretical framework-under-construction. It does not stick with the relics of the past, but explores newly-emerging trends and asks new questions, moving the debate beyond a narrow focus on class relations. That is, it also links differentiation to (1) population pressure on the land, (2) the social organization of production, (3) the presence and impact of extractivist mechanisms, (4) the direction and rhythm of rural development and (5) the degree of multifunctionality (to use today's terminology) of peasant units of production. Thus different paths of differentiation are outlined (although they are not all presented in a very transparent way: they are, in places, a bit lost in the language of that time: 1927). Most importantly, though, is that Chayanov clearly shows, regardless of all his hesitations, how to proceed with theoretical and political debates of this kind: by bringing in the concrete social formation, history, main contradictions and social forces able to change society. By doing so, Chayanov shows his capacity to ask questions that are still highly relevant today: in the Chinese countryside, the settlements of the movement of the landless in Brazil (MST) and in European agriculture. It turns the reading of this essay into a breath-taking experience. This is especially the case where Chayanov hypothesizes the existence of a 'farming entrepreneur' embodying the American path of agricultural development. The same applies to his early and prescient anticipation of the demise of Soviet agriculture.

Socio-political analysis (fifth essay)

Following the method used in the previous essays (slotting in, step-by-step, the particularities of time, space and society), Chayanov proposes here a "fundamentally new path of rural development" – a path that differs from that followed in the USA and also from the one characterizing the overpopulated areas of China and India. The comparative approach clearly helps him to dive into the "essential difference[s] in current historical processes". Thus, several, mutually contrasting, development trajectories emerge – each representing a potential pathway towards the future but bringing highly different benefits and costs (to be distributed in contrasting ways). Thus, the analysis moves from the-situation-as-it-is to the situations-that-can-possibly-be-realized. Consequently, the dialectics of the real and the potential (what Karl Kosik far later refers to as the 'dialectics of the concrete') are put centre stage.

It is exciting to read how this fifth essay distinguishes between peasant agriculture and entrepreneurial agriculture (the latter characterized by "high-commodity enterprises" and an elevated dependence on financial and trading capital). Chayanov argued that Russia was, precisely at this juncture, having "a unique chance" to define and realize its own trajectory. Central to this choice were the "new peasants": a concrete peasantry that had gone beyond "grandfather's traditions". It was, instead, a peasantry trained and disciplined "in the schools of revolution and [the war] front", which gave them a far "wider outlook", and meant that they were "more mobile and open to agro-improvements". In short: a class that could put its imprint on future pathways.

Things went differently, as we all know. But the analytical tools and views elaborated by Alexander Chayanov remain valid and to the point. Maybe more so than ever.

Organizational work (sixth essay)

This validity is underlined and made explicit in the final essay. It is, in a way, the Chayanovian version of '*What is to be done*' (Lenin, 1902/1961) – as much as it is a riposte to it. This essay sets out the organizational work that Chayanove argued needed to be done at the local level. It is very clear that this work is far from the "agro-technical tale and show" that became dominant in many parts of the world later on in the 20th Century, which was focused on the large scale introduction of agro-chemicals, genetically modified seeds and all other kinds of agro-technical artefacts and the associated scripts about how to use them. Equally it is far from "the abolition of peasants" (and the subsequent introduction of kolkhozes), as the text courageously states. Instead, this organizational work is about *unfolding, developing and strengthening peasant agriculture* (about "fermenting and organization", resulting in the "rebirth of our peasant villages", as Chayanov phrased it in the language of those times).

This organizational work entailed a clear programme. It was, in the first place, about developing the productive forces within and around the peasant farm. This needed to occur through the building of proper infrastructure, local markets and the co-operative processing of food; the development of agricultural production through improved crop-rotation, irrigation systems, etc.; and an overall improvement of the quality of life in the villages. All this was, in effect, about putting 'social agronomy' into practice.

Secondly, this organizational work was to build on, and contribute to, "the peasantry [becoming] the master of the agronomic progress in the countryside after the Revolution". The peasantry and peasant agriculture figure explicitly here as major forces in the progressive construction of a new society.

Thirdly, the organizational work was to be in line with, just as it was fundamental to, the building of a social economy in the countryside (in particular) and to the construction of a planned economy in general.

This organizational work assumed and required active and knowledgeable actors. Here Chayanov is also outspoken: these actors were to be "the local agronomists, cooperators, and other rural workers" (social activists, as we say today), who were closely linked with the local peasants and thereby able to transform farming, the countryside and contribute to changing society as a whole.

Reading all this attentively is like walking together with Chayanov through the fields and villages that together make up today's peasant agriculture – wherever located. It surely is an exciting stroll.

References

Chayanov, A.V. (1925), *The Theory of Peasant Economy*, republished in 1986 by D. Thorner, B. Kerblay and R.E.F. Smith as "A.V. Chayanov on The Theory of Peasant Economy", Manchester University Press.

Chayanov, A.V. (1927/1991), *The Theory of Peasant Cooperatives*, Ohio State University Press, Columbus.

Kosik, K. (1963/1976), *Dialectics of the Concrete* (translation by J. Schmidt), Reidel, Boston.

Lenin, V.I. (1902/1961), *What Is To Be Done?* Lenin's Collected Works, Vol. 1, pp. 119–271, Foreign Languages Publishing House, Moscow.

Ploeg, J.D. van der, D. Barjolle and others (2019), 'The economic potential of agroecology: empirical evidence from Europe', *Journal of Rural Studies*, Vol. 71, pp. 46–61.

CHAPTER 1

A.V. Chayanov on the Agrarian question

Moscow: Joint-stock company 'Universal Library', 1917

This text is a translation into English of the brochure *What is the 'Agrarian Question'?* published by A. Chayanov in the summer of 1917, between the February and October Revolutions in Russia. The 29-year-old professor Chayanov took an active part in the revolutionary events of 1917, trying to justify the fine-drawn plan for agrarian reforms for the New Russia. Chayanov became one of the initiators of the creation of the League for Agrarian Reforms, which included many leading agrarians of various political trends in Russia with a view to discussing and developing a holistic strategy for agrarian reforms in Russia. The popular-science version of his views on agrarian reform, summarizing the most varied ideas of the League for Agrarian Reforms, Chayanov presented in the brochure *What is the 'Agrarian Question'?*. In the ideological basis of this work lies the realization of the revolutionary demand 'Land to the working people!', which affirmed the necessity of transferring the landlord's land into the hands of the peasantry. Chayanov considered various options for such a transition of land in the form of agrarian programmes of socialization, nationalization, municipalization of land, a single land tax, and the system of state regulation of land ownership. In reforming, Chayanov proposed to be guided by two principles: 1) the greatest productivity of peasant labour applied to the land; and 2) democratization of the distribution of national income. The extensive development of peasant cooperation was to ensure the implementation of these principles. Chayanov also stressed in every possible way the importance of taking into account regional and national peculiarities in resolving the agrarian question in such a huge country as Russia. Personally, Chayanov was inclined to the way of agrarian reforms combining state regulation of land ownership and progressive taxation.

However, the October Revolution under the leadership of the Bolsheviks and left-wing socialist revolutionaries in their 'Decree on Land' declared the implementation of the most radical version of agrarian reforms: the socialization of the land, stopping the search for the best compromise agrarian solutions that Chayanov and his colleagues tried to implement in the League for Agrarian Reforms. Chayanov's brochure *What is the 'Agrarian Question'?* is a model of theoretical and practical search for alternatives to the fine-drawn solution of the agrarian question in the interests of the peasants on the basis of a broad political coalition of democratic forces.

Introduction

The Revolution has presented Russian society with the very great task of creating a new, democratic Russia. The Russian democracy will need many years of hard, creative work for its political, civil, and economic development.

Our political and civil tasks are clear and relatively simple; they depend entirely on our will and human laws, whereas the task of economic development is much more difficult. Economic life develops according to its own spontaneous laws, which are almost independent of the will of man. Therefore, when starting to reform our economic system, we must remember that far from everything in economic life is subject to our will.

We must know the basic laws of economic development. Having learned them, we must adopt our human state laws according to them to bring the future economic development of Russia closer to our social ideals. If we choose any other way, we will inevitably doom ourselves to bitter disappointment! This is especially true of the agrarian question, which is the most important for our economic life.

In our country, three-quarters of the population work on the land. Agriculture is the basis of the entire national economy of our homeland.

By providing our agriculture with a democratic and sustainable structure, we will ensure a solid foundation for the entire national economy and our statehood. Therefore, we are to start the agrarian development with a clear awareness of our greatest responsibility, thoughtful caution, and firm determination. If we take a closer look at the leaders of our public opinion, we admit with a feeling of profound satisfaction that they all share these ideas.

Today, discussions about the agrarian question rarely take the form of intolerant party disputes. There are almost always serious debates that respect different opinions and joint work aimed at one goal with unpredictable results. The very creation of the inter-party League for Agrarian Reforms, which unites the Narodniks, Marxists, and supporters of a single tax system, testifies to the statements above.

There is no doubt that all old agrarian programmes should be revised, and the agrarian question should be addressed anew. The old programmes were created by us 10 to 12 years ago in a completely different situation than the current one.

The peasant economy of 1917 is not the peasant economy of 1905. It has changed: fields are cultivated differently, livestock is kept differently, and peasants sell more and buy more. The peasant cooperation covered our village and transformed it; our peasantry became more developed and more cultured. The Stolypin land reform confused land relations to the extreme, and the peasantry bought millions of *desiatinas*[1] of land in private ownership. The political situation has also changed radically.

But the most important thing is that the agrarian question must be solved tomorrow. Today is not the time to proclaim some common ideas, nor the time for bare principles.

We need detailed draft laws, organizational plans for land redistribution, instructions for land surveying, and financial calculations for the reform ... The agrarian question has moved from the world of abstract ideas and conflicting principles to the field of specific, organizational, economic work.

Certainly, we cannot give up our guiding ideas; our social ideals will still remain our guiding lights. However, we must remember that today's task is not only to profess certain ideas, but also to find specific forms to bring these ideas to real life. Such an implementation should not be superficial or forcibly squeezed into the very body of the national economy. It should enter economic life organically and merge with it. We cannot block the flow of the developing economic life, but we must direct it according to our social interests by all the means available to us.

To resolve the agrarian problem, we must delve into the very nature of farming. All of our activities aimed at this goal must be consistent with the basic laws of agricultural development.

In the vastness of our huge homeland, the forms and directions of agricultural development are far from the same. Different economic patterns determine different land relations. In Asiatic Russia, we still find pasture land; in the southeast, there is still farming without manure but with long-term fallows instead; and in central Russia, dairy cattle breeding and fodder crops are rapidly developing.

Under such circumstances, the agrarian question cannot be solved uniformly for the whole country. There should be a special solution for each agricultural situation. This is the new formulation of the agrarian question in all its complexity.

We will need many months of hard work to see clear and concrete ways to solve it. There will be conflicting opinions and contradictory methods for agrarian reform. However, we clearly understand the key solutions of agrarian disputes.

Everyone agrees that the peasant labour economy should be the basis of the agrarian system in Russia, and that this economy should use the land of our homeland.

This land transfer must be carried out according to the state plan of redistribution. It will take into account households and economic features of certain regions of our fatherland and will be systematically and orderly implemented without disturbing the intense production activities of the national economy.

We are all clearly aware that the land system is only a part of the solution of the agrarian problem. After providing the peasant economy with land, we must organize this economy by enriching it with culture and agronomic knowledge, by creating powerful cooperatives, strengthening its position in the market, and providing it with affordable loans. This is the path our agrarian reform will follow.

Formulation of the agrarian question

Under the current revision of agrarian programmes, as when solving any question, success depends largely on how correctly the question is posed.

If the question is asked correctly and successfully, the question will solve itself by half. However, if we make mistakes in the very formulation of it, then all our efforts will be fruitless, and the work will be fatally doomed to failure. Therefore, before we begin to solve the agrarian question, we must carefully formulate it.

We must clearly identify exactly what the question in the agrarian problem is and what requirements the answer to this question must meet. Without such clarifications, our work on the agrarian programmes will inevitably remain random and deprived of systematic planning.

The agrarian question can be approached from various starting points. Many of us tend to believe the solution to the agrarian problem is the realization of the basic social ideas in our world-view.

Some say that light, air, and land by their very nature are free elements and cannot be seized by anyone in private property. They belong equally to all and everyone. From this point of view, the agrarian question can be solved by liberating land from the shackles of private property. The agrarian reform should pursue this very goal, and once it is has been achieved, the agrarian question will be solved.

Others approach the agrarian question using the principle of state socialization of all processes of national production. They consider agriculture to be a branch of state production, which delivers the products of farming and cattle breeding. Using this point of view, the agrarian question can be solved by organizing agriculture as a branch of the state economy based on the same social principles as other industrial sectors.

We, the social builders of today, certainly do not deny the great importance of these social ideas, but we cannot accept them as a starting point to solve the agrarian question. Explanations of this denial are listed below.

Every social phenomenon consists of two principles – spontaneity and reason. Spontaneous development does not depend on someone's guiding will and follows its own laws, which people can learn but are powerless to cancel or replace. The other principle is the dictate of social consciousness.

The organized public mind presented by the state and other forms has considerable power to influence social and economic development. However, when confronted with spontaneous laws of social development, it is far from absolute.

The impact on economic life of the organized public mind is especially limited, for here the spontaneous processes are extremely powerful and poorly amenable to rationalization. That is why when we start laying the new foundations of the agrarian system of our homeland, we cannot draw a plan that relies solely on reason or our abstract ideas.

These ideas do not depend on time and place. The agrarian systems deduced from them are equally applicable to the Assyrian agriculture of Ashurbanipal and the era of Aristotle or Robespierre; to the subsistence farming in Russia at the times of Radishchev's *Journey from Moscow to Saint Petersburg*; and to the contemporary Russian village covered by cooperatives and reorganized into a monetary-commodity economy.

This is a situation with which we, the builders of real life, cannot agree. We believe that at different phases of agricultural evolution, we face different issues of agrarian policy that need different solutions.

In the Kyrgyz nomad camps of Central Asia, there are some problems of agrarian development in the Tambov three-field system – completely different problems. The agrarian system of the Estonian village outlines a different path of agrarian development from the vineyards of the southern coast of the Crimea, or *kishlaks* with irrigated rice and cotton in the Zeravshan valley.

Finally, there is very private land ownership that does not meet our ideals. Nevertheless we do not consider it a social misunderstanding accidentally determined by seizure. For us, private land ownership is a social fact generated by time and place. It has social roots not only in the seizure by those in power.

Thus, the only way to solve the agrarian question seems to be a detailed and thorough analysis of the existing organization of agricultural production and of the agrarian and labour relations determined by it. It must include a study of the origins of the systems of economy and agrarian relations together with possible ways and tendencies of their further development.

However, such research is not the end of our work. We must not only study and describe the reality and trends hidden in it, but also estimate it. We must give a social assessment of the observed facts.

Therefore, at the next stage of work, we should set theoretical criteria that allow an evaluation of both the analysed organization of production and the agrarian relations inherent in it. The criteria should include possible ways for their further development.

Then we should use these criteria to reveal shortcomings in the existing agrarian and production systems to develop such forms of an agrarian system that would lack the existing shortcomings and not contradict the spontaneous development of economics. Finally, we should use these criteria to suggest a number of necessary state and public events to realize our plans. Only this way promises us real success and protects us from heavy disappointments.

Our statistical, economic, and historical research provides us with strong weapons for doing this. The most crucial task for our entire work is to set social criteria determining the direction of it.

Usually, one of these criteria is the development of productive forces. Any changes in the economic system that increase the productive power of the national economic mechanism and multiply the country's total national income are progressive.

For us, the representatives of labour democracy, the development of productive forces in agriculture can be expressed in the improved conditions and methods of the people's work on the land. This increases the productivity of this labour. Such an interpretation considers the increase in national wealth not per unit of capital or land, but per capita. All reforms and any impact of the organized public mind on our economic life should be evaluated from this point of view.

However, we cannot use only this criterion. For us, the democrats, it is not enough to organize national production; we must also think about distribution. We do care about the fate and possessors of national wealth produced by the people's labour in our fields.

Therefore, in addition to the production criterion, we must develop a criterion that allows for an assessment in terms of the distribution of national income. This criterion is the democratization of the distribution of national income. In other words, it is the most uniform distribution among all people contributing to its creation.

When applying this principle to the organization of our life, we cannot confine ourselves to agriculture only, but must keep in mind the national economy as a whole.

In modern society, the economic life long ago carried out a complex social distribution of labour. The labour of the peasant, agronomist, worker, merchant, engineer, employee, banker, and sailor has divided our society into special production groups and classes. Our national income is the product of not any one of these groups, but of their joint work. In a piece of cloth bought from a rural merchant, you will find the labour of a farmer, a factory worker, a railwayman, an engineer-technician, and an inventor of a steam engine. It is difficult to discern in the final product which part of its value was created by whom. The same applies to all products.

Thus, when we start to organize the distribution of our national income among all the workers who created it, we cannot confine ourselves to any one branch of the national economy. Instead, we must aim at the general redistribution of national income.

When speaking of the redistribution of our national income, we hardly consider something like the black-market redistribution of available material goods. Only a young, revolutionary democracy in its youthful and naive condition could consider such an aim. It is clear to every economist that such actions do not solve the problem.

Therefore, we are talking about new production relations that will ensure that the national income will be distributed more democratically than it is now distributed.

Thus, we insist on 1) the greatest productivity of people's work on the land, and 2) the democratization of the distribution of national income. These are our two main criteria to assess the existing system of agrarian relations, their historical past, and possible ways to the future.

These criteria can be also used to evaluate conceivable systems of production relations, including the system of state socialism and anarchist communism, which can be considered ideal organizational expressions of the second criterion.

When applying these criteria to evaluate our agrarian projects and state measures, we should not forget for a moment that there are two criteria. We should evaluate each phenomenon from both a production and a distribution point of view. Such assessments can be conflicting and even opposite, for what increases productivity does not necessarily ensure democratic distribution, and vice versa – not every democratization increases production capacity. However, we cannot offer a general solution to these conflicts and should try to creatively and harmoniously combine both organizational principles in each case.

'Land to the working people!'

The main demand of all democratic agrarian programmes is the slogan 'Land to the working people!' According to this slogan, all land used by the large landlord economy must be given to the peasant labour economy.

Before accepting this demand, we should evaluate it using two criteria from the previous chapter. First, we should decide if the peasant labour economy, in which only the owner and his family work, is just as powerful and perfect an economic organization as the large, capitalist economy, in which work is done by wage workers, while the owner deals only with the control and general management of the enterprise.

In due time there were many scientific papers and heated debates about the struggle of large and small economies in agriculture. Supporters of the large form of production pointed out that in agriculture, small-scale farming was as doomed to perish as was the manufacturing industry. This was because the capitalist factory long ago killed the artisan and handicraftsman.

Advocates of small-scale agriculture objected by pointing to a number of fundamental features of agriculture, which determine different results in the struggle between large- and small-scale production in agriculture compared to industry. If we recall these old disputes and arguments of the opponents, we certainly will admit that, other things being equal, a large-scale economy almost always has an advantage over a small-scale economy. This is a basic economic law. It would be absurd to deny it.

However, when recognizing this law, we have to ponder it and then, observing even the manufacturing industry, we will have to admit that large-scale production does not overcome small-scale production equally in all branches. In some branches it completely replaced small artisans and handicraftsmen; for example, hand spinning was crushed by a mechanical spindle. According to Barykov's research, a Kostroma female spinner-peasant selling her yarn at factory prices worked for approximately 8 *kopeks* per a 14-hour working day. In such conditions, no competition is possible.

However, in weaving, we already see a somewhat different state of things. Until now, hand weaving is still common in the Moscow and Vladimir provinces.[2] Although the conditions of its existence are difficult, it still withstands competition with the factory. Actually, commercial capital captures hand weavers, but the production remains small scale. Among locksmiths, toy-makers and the like, small-scale production still prevails. Thus, even in industry itself, the advantages of large-scale production over small-scale production are not always the same: in some branches they are overwhelming, in others they are insignificant.

Therefore, when we talk about the advantages of a large form of production over a small one, it is not enough to recognize the advantages. It is necessary to ask ourselves a quantitative question about the quantitative measure of such advantages of a large economy over a small one. If this question involves agriculture, we should answer that the advantages of the quantitative measure of large-scale farming over the small one are insignificant. This is primarily because in industry, large forms of production displace small ones mainly if there is a possibility for the spatial concentration of production, i.e. if tens of thousands of horsepower can be reduced to one steam engine or if thousands of workers can be placed under one roof of a multi-storey factory building.

Such changes provided huge savings and significantly reduced the cost of the manufactured product. If there was no way for such a spatial concentration, there was no victorious procession to large-scale production. In agriculture such a concentration is unthinkable.

What is agriculture? At its core there is the human use of solar energy at the surface of the earth. One cannot collect sun rays falling on 100 *desiatinas* on one *desiatina*. One can only catch them with the green chlorophyll of his crops on the entire territory of his field. In its very essence, agriculture is inherently connected with space, and the larger the agricultural enterprise, the larger area it should occupy. No spatial concentration is possible here.

I will give a small example. A manufacturer with an engine of 100 horsepower willing to increase his production by 10 times can install an engine of 1,000 horsepower and, thus, significantly reduce the cost of production.

A rural owner ploughing his field with one horse and willing to increase its crops 10-fold, certainly, cannot get a horse 10 times larger in size. He is forced to get 10 horses of the same quality as the first one. He can slightly reduce the cost of production by transitioning from horse traction to a tractor (automotive). However, an owner of one tractor cannot increase its power according to the 10-fold increase in crops. He is forced to get 10 of the same machines working simultaneously in different spaces, which will reduce the cost of production insignificantly.

The same applies to other implements – seeds, fertilizers, cattle, etc.

A rural owner willing to increase his production in most cases should increase the number rather than the size of his implements. Therefore, the quantitative measure of the benefit of enlargement cannot be significant.

Moreover, it should be noted that the very nature of agricultural production puts a natural limit on the enlargement of the agricultural enterprise. Whereas agriculture is inevitably scattered in space, the farmer has to move a huge number of objects throughout this space – people and animals, machines, fertilizers, and products must be transported.

The larger the farm and its cultivated area, the greater number of products will be transported for a greater distance. The cost of transportation within the farm will increase per the economy as a whole and per unit of production.

The more intensive the farming, the deeper and more careful the cultivation of the land, the more fertilizers and care for crops are needed. Also, the more often the farmer travels from the farmstead to the fields, the more expensive these trips are for the cost of the product.

The extensive grain system in our Orenburg or Saratov provinces allows the farmer to make only two trips – for sowing and harvesting. However, if he begins autumn ploughing for spring crops and brings manure to the fields, the number of trips will increase accordingly, which we can observe in our central agricultural provinces.

Further intensification in the form of pre-sowing tillage for industrial crops and replacement of cereals with beets, turnips, and potatoes will increase the number of trips to such an extent that every extra *sazhen*[3] on the way from the farmstead to the field makes a difference. All the benefits of the enlargement of production are brought to naught by the rise in the cost of within-farm transportation. The more intensive the farming, the sooner this happens.

Our Orenburg and Saratov farms often consist of a manor managing a territory of two or three thousand *desiatinas*. In the Poltava Province, such an enlargement would be impossible. In the Kiev Province and cultural countries of Western Europe, the costs of within-farm transportation further limit the size of the economy – to an optimum of 200–300 *desiatinas*.

There are cases under the intensification, in which the large owners were forced to divide an estate into several separate farms (*khutors*). At the time, they were large landowners and small or medium-sized farmers. Thus, the very nature of the agricultural enterprise limits its enlargement, so the quantitative measure of the advantages of a large-scale economy over small farming can never be particularly significant.

However, for us, such an admission is not enough. Let us examine where the advantages of a large-scale economy over small farming are mainly manifested. The large farm mostly wins in the relations with the outside world. A large buyer and a large seller in the market of a large-scale economy enjoy all the benefits of the wholesale market and cheap bank loans, whereas the peasant remains in the power of buyers and usurers.

Further one can note significant advantages in the use of complex machines, such as separators and grain-cleaners, of males for breeding such as bulls and studs, and, most importantly, of agronomic science by inviting agronomists and specialists.

However, in all these spheres, cooperative practice clearly indicates the possibility of making the advantages of a large economy available to a small peasant economy. It is sufficient to separate those branches of the peasant economy, in which large forms have undoubted advantages over small ones, from individual peasant farms without destroying their individuality. It is also possible to organize them into a cooperative, i.e. to make them a large-scale production. In all cooperatives, small peasant farms reach such a large size and production capacity that they exceed the possibilities of any large, private farm.

Russian cooperative centres – Moscow People's Bank, Moscow Union of Consumer Societies, Central Partnership of Flax Growers, and the Union of Siberian Dairy *Artels* – unite hundreds of cooperatives and millions of peasant farms with a turnover of tens of millions of rubles.

Therefore, because of the features of agriculture and the potential of the peasant economy to cooperate in separate branches, a small-scale, peasant economy as an economic organization is technologically not inferior to a large, capitalist, agricultural enterprise.

However, to prefer the peasant labour economy to the landlord or capitalist economy, we need to identify not only the lack of advantages for large farms, but also their availability for peasant farms. Are there any advantages? To answer this question, we have to delve into the nature of the peasant economy.

So far, we have considered large and small farms, but, today, for the majority of economists, this opposition seems obsolete and wrong in its very formulation.

Speaking of small and large economies, we again contrasted quantity and quantity, although, in fact, this is a qualitative opposition. We have to contrast not small and large economies but rather a labour economy based on the workforce of its owner and his family and a capitalist economy based on wage labour. These are two fundamentally different types of economic organization.

A semi-subsistence peasant labour economy is nearly always closely connected in its organization to the consumer budget of the household. This determines the task of this type of economy. This task is to obtain the means of subsistence for the household with the fullest possible use of its means of production and workforce.

Such a statement in no way applies to the capitalist economy for it denies the last condition. The whole definition is eventually reduced to the following: the task of the non-labour economy is the fullest use of capital invested in the enterprise, or, briefly speaking, maximum profit on this capital. This definition, in its turn, cannot be applied to the labour economy because it admits the possibility of benefits of a smaller profit on capital (by calculating profit by assessing one's work according to wage rates), if there is an opportunity to use the family workforce much more extensively and eventually achieve a greater increase in the means of subsistence.

In other words, the task of the capitalist economy is net profit, whereas the task of the labour economy is gross profit. A high gross profit does not always coincide with a high net profit. Thus, there is no need to admit in many proofs that, from the point of view of the greatest productivity, the interests of the labour economy largely coincide with the interests of the national economy as a whole. This is a huge social advantage of the labour economy.

I will try to explain my idea with a small example. We have a flax crop and an oat crop. As a labour-consuming crop the former requires 100 working days per *desiatina* and ensures a high gross profit, whereas the latter requires only 20 working days and provides a small gross profit but a higher net profit as can be seen from the table:

Crop	*Gross profit (rubles)*	*Cost of labour (rubles)*	*Other costs (rubles)*	*Net profit (rubles)*
Oat	40	20	5	15
Flax	115	100	10	5

Limited in its land area, there is no doubt that the peasant economy will always prefer flax to oats, whereas the capitalist economy will always do the opposite and will sow oats. The flax crop increases the national income and the scale of work on the land, which is also desirable for the national economy in general.

From the point of view of production, these are the grounds that make us prefer the peasant labour economy over the capitalist landowner economy. It is hardly necessary to prove that we should also choose the peasant economy for the democratization of the national income.

What should we do with forests and special types of economy?

In the previous chapter, when we considered the peasant labour economy to be the most perfect economic organization of people's labour in agriculture, it combined some of its economic branches into a cooperative, and we meant the most common forms of agriculture, i.e. growing traditional field crops and breeding cattle.

One is tempted to ask whether our findings can be applied to all types of agriculture, or do some of them constitute an exception to the general rule?

These questions refer mainly to forests and special types of agriculture, such as livestock breeding, plant selection, horticulture, and so on. Some technical features of these types of economy make them exceptional.

A properly organized agriculture that divides forests into many dozens of plots, which are gradually cut down at the age of 60–80 years old and then artificially planted, requires huge areas. It also requires a plan of development for future decades and a single will to implement this plan with the hands of numerous workers, watchmen, foresters, sawyers, forest wardens, clerks, estate managers, forestry scientists, plant pathologists, and entomologists. The size of such an economy and its inherent complexity in the division of labour among numerous categories of workers make it impossible for a labour economy. Therefore, when forests are made public property, they cannot be divided among individual labour economies or even communities (*obshchinas*). Instead, they must be placed partly under the management of self-government bodies and partly under state management (forests of national importance).

Quite different reasons turn our attention to livestock breeding. These include selection and other types of economies, which require greater knowledge and workmanship than large capital and numerous workers.

There are very few such farms, and their organization consists of two elements. The first is a creative mind, which has mastered the whole stock of knowledge accumulated by mankind in this field; a mind that explores and often guides the economy intuitively. The second element is numerous workers performing tasks assigned by the agronomical mind.

No one can deny the great importance for the state of such economies, and the number of leaders who can manage them is negligible. The importance of their knowledge and workforces is significant for the creative will of the state. Their own hands, but also a number of other hands form a powerful working device to fully realize this will.

We do not now resolve the controversial issues of whether such economies should become state or cooperative, or what should be done under the reform with the privately owned ones. It is clear only that these economies cannot become labour economies.

After these lines I can be accused of inconsistency. One can ask that if I value cultural economies so much, why do I not stand up for the preservation of private farms, which are, on average, much more developed in terms of their culture than peasant economies. If private farms are given to the currently unenlightened labour economy, the productivity of the land will certainly and significantly decrease.

I will answer this reproach by stating that privately sown areas make up only 11 per cent of the total sown area of European Russia. A reduction of their yields by half will reduce the total national yield by only 6 per cent. Undoubtedly, the rise of agronomic technology after the land revolution will quickly cover this deficit.

It is much more dangerous that the harvest of these 11 per cent of the sown area was sold nearly totally by private owners, whereas the harvest of the peasant economy for the most part was consumed by the household. Thus, more than 40 per cent of the total amount of bread on the market was the bread of private farms. Certainly, the transfer of private lands to the peasant will weaken the commodity character of their exploitation, and the supply of grain bread to the Russian market will immediately decline, which will significantly raise prices and reduce our exports. However, the growing needs of our peasant way of life will force the peasantry to increase the monetary value of their economy and, thus, gradually increase the supply of bread.

Land question or agrarian question?

A few days after the formation of the provisional government, a large red poster, 'Land and Freedom – Ministry of Agriculture', was hung at the entrance of the ministry in Petrograd. The old Narodnik slogan that has been the banner of revolutionary demonstrations for decades, became the banner on a state building.

> What will be the government work under this banner?
>
> What is 'freedom'?
>
> What is 'land'?

For us, the builders of New Russia, freedom means not only liberation from the arbitrariness of the old authorities and police surveillance, but also the free creation of the democratic state and democratic *zemstvo*. It means the joint work of all the living and cultural forces of our homeland on the development of public education and health and the organization of the spiritual and economic life of our people.

Similarly, when we talk about land, we think not only about *desiatinas* of arable land, meadows and forests. The land itself is of little interest to us. When we talk about land, we mean work on the land. The labour of the farmer is the economic basis of our state, and it must be protected and organized by democratic Russia. We must facilitate work on the land, multiply its power, improve all its conditions, double and triple its productivity.

The first condition of the farmer's work is certainly land; therefore, the first step of our agrarian reorganization must be land reform. All the lands of our homeland should be given to free labour. However, we frankly admit that the land reform alone cannot help our village.

For half a century after the liberation of peasants, they bought about 27 million *desiatinas* of mostly arable land from private owners.

The complete nationalization of non-peasant private land will mean that the price of 20 million *desiatinas* of land permanently leased from owners will be reduced and paid not to the owners but to the state. It means also that about 10 million *desiatinas* of owners' ploughed land (a part of the income peasants have already received in the form of wages), will expand the area of the peasant economy.

If our peasant labour economy absorbs all the capitalist ploughed land and means of production, its expansion will be insignificant. Before the Revolution our agriculture was predominantly peasant.

The agricultural census of 1916 shows that in 44 provinces of European Russia, 89 *desiatinas* out of every 100 *desiatinas* of cropped land were peasant, and only 11 *desiatinas* were of the landlords. The census also shows that 93 horses out of every 100 horses in agriculture were peasant, and only 7 were of the landlords.

Nevertheless, we still consider land reform the first and most important step of our agrarian reform. This is because the quantitative value of private lands given to peasants is insignificant, but their moral value is great. For the peasant, there are so many memories of serfdom associated with private lands that the moral significance of each landlord's *desiatina* is many times greater than its economic value. Therefore, the land question is urgent, and the land reform is our primary state duty.

However, to start the reform we must clearly remember that it is only an introduction to our hard and long-term work on the organization of agriculture. Land reform is only a part of agrarian reform and, perhaps, the easiest part.

First of all, we must not only give land to the working peasantry, but give it in an organized form and, at the same time, organize the land of the peasantry.

The strip allotments of land in 1861, the endless division of land in redistribution in rural communities, the unsystematic allotments of separate farms (*khutors*) and pieces of land, the Stolypin consolidation of land – all of this determined an incredible land chaos in our village.

Correct land surveying, the rounding of borders, getting rid of strip farming and small strips in rural communities, i.e. the general organization of land, will provide our peasants with not less but more benefits than giving him private lands. If the general organization of land is combined with the latter, we will witness the greatest era in our agrarian history.

Certainly, such a land system will be complete only if supported by extensive reclamation works on drainage and the irrigation of uncomfortable lands. It must be accompanied by the resettlement of the population from land-hungry to land-rich areas.

This will be the final step in the organization of one of the conditions for the people's work on the land, which is land itself. However, agricultural labour requires not only land but also other means of production: buildings, machines, implements, and seeds.

Before the war, the supply of rural households with means of production was in the hands of private commercial capital. Only the *zemstvo*, cooperatives, and in part the Resettlement Department tried to organize the distribution of the means of production on a voluntary basis.

The supply of agriculture with means of production was guided not by the interests of production, but by the goal of maximum profit for private capital. Due to its exceptional circumstances during the war, the supply of the country with machinery and binder twine was concentrated in the hands of the association of three *zemstvo* partnerships, the People's (Cooperative) Bank, and the state represented by the Department of Agriculture. It is necessary to consolidate this achievement so that the supply of agricultural labour with the means of production will be confidently controlled by the democratic state and public institutions.

The human labour must organize the economy from land and the means of production. And, in this organization of production, we must help our peasantry. Despite huge changes of the last decade, our peasant economy is technically backward. Many arable lands are still organized in the form of our grandfathers' three-field system and hoed by plough, and the peasants' method of cattle breeding aims mainly at manure production.

Meanwhile, the future of our country, the entire strength of our democratic statehood depends on the dynamic and rapid rise of our agriculture. It depends on how successfully we will 'make two ears grow upon a spot of ground where only one grew before'.

Our Constituent Assembly can nationalize land and transfer the country's supply with the means of production to the state. However, neither the Assembly nor any other power can order and force the Kalmyk to grassland farming and the Tula peasant to intensive dairy farming with the use of skim milk to feed Berkshire pigs.

Indeed, in due time, the Empress Catherine, King Frederick the Great, and other representatives of enlightened absolutism used violence with guns and executions to introduce potatoes. However, there are grounds to believe that such methods are beyond the power of the public mind, even with all the power of the state. There are millions of economic agents with their own skills and ideas about agriculture, who will not obey any orders. They will do everything on their own and according to their understanding.

It is necessary to draw their attention with verbal and written explanations to the possibility of changes in traditional methods of work. It is necessary to convince the population of the advantages of new agriculture by examples and obvious cases, to prove its greater profitability, and, moreover, to awaken the population to activity and give people an emotional push.

These tasks have been solved for more than a decade by *zemstvo* agronomists in the very heart of our village. These tasks are as follows:

1. Introduce into the national economy the improved methods of farming and cattle breeding.
2. Change the organizational plan of the peasant economy in the direction of greater compliance with the current economic realities of the country.
3. Organize the local population into unions and groups. On the one hand, this will use the cooperative generalization of individual aspects of production to provide the small farm with all the advantages of the large one. On the other hand, it will take on consolidation and the further development of new economic principles.

Today, when the frozen agrarian forms become flexible and are ready to turn into a new agrarian system and when the people's psychology gets rid of the ossification, the social agronomy faces an exceptionally important challenge of bringing agronomic reason into the spontaneous process of creating a new agrarian system and a new agriculture.

Our young cooperative movement is no less responsible for this than the organized economic initiative of our peasantry. The task of the state is to provide all possible support to both types of creative work. By supplying the people's work on the land with the means of production, by organizing the peasant economy on new principles, and by strengthening its power with cooperation, we will facilitate the relationship of a peasant economy with the world market.

We must bring the peasant closer to the market by building new railroads; we must facilitate the use of transportation by revising our tariffs in the interests of agriculture; we must protect the products of our agriculture in foreign markets by new customs treaties and trade agreements. We must also correlate the heavy post-war tax burden with the capacities of the peasant economy.

I can continue this list of tasks for our agrarian development, but from the above, it is already obvious that our future work goes far beyond land reform.

The agrarian question we are to solve is much broader than the land question. Yet, because of its inherent social acuteness, the latter can push out of public attention all other issues related to the people's work on the land.

Forms of land socialization

Certainly, the land question will be the part of the agrarian reform that will attract the greatest public attention. We put it in first place due to its inherent social acuteness and great moral significance. However, the fact that the land question is brought to the fore does not mean that we must first carry out the land reform and then proceed with the development of other sections of the agrarian programme. It is our deep conviction that all aspects of the agrarian reform should be developed and implemented simultaneously.

The reform of land use is inconceivable without restructuring economic organizations. Therefore, the land reform will yield insignificant results if it is not accompanied by land resurveying, amelioration, agronomical reforms of production itself, and a credit system for restructuring farms.

To take land from private owners, especially large ones, seems a relatively easy task. It is much more difficult to organize this land, distribute it among labour economies, and organize the cultural labour economy that is not inferior in its productivity to the old private economy.

If we consider and imagine only the organization of the distribution of land taken from the private owner, we will face a huge and extremely difficult task, which requires efforts of all the organized forces of our state.

The simplest way to expropriate private property would be to allow neighbouring peasants to seize private estates and follow the principle of 'grab what you can'. However, such a land reform would confuse and complicate the agrarian question rather than solve it. Only the neighbours of landed estates would benefit from such seizures, whereas the majority of peasants would stay with what they had. Landed estates would be seized mainly by strong peasant economies with the greatest economic power who are capable of cultivating the seized lands. It was these strong farms and not the land-hungry ones that rented most of the landlords' land. Now, undoubtedly, they will try to secure the lands that are already in their use. Such results are unlikely to correspond to the social significance of the reform we are planning.

It seems perfectly clear to us that the organized public mind must use all the power of the state and public authority to direct the agrarian reform to the state solution of the social and economic tasks that we face.

The national economy of Russia outgrew its previous subsistence forms long ago. Our national economic organism is a single whole. The agrarian need is the need of this very national, economic whole and not of individual villages or peasants. Individual farms and areas are different parts of the same economic mechanism. They do different work but are connected by the unity of joint movement.

Therefore, our land reform, the transfer of land to the working peasants, should be carried out not by unorganized seizures, but according to the state plan of a land use system. This plan takes into account households and economic features of different regions of our country and is systematically implemented without disrupting the production cycle of our national economy.

The last circumstance is evident for all of us, who painfully survived the severe food crisis. Once again it stresses the need to conduct the agrarian reform in an organized and state form. We cannot afford a single unsown *desiatina* and a single smashed and destroyed herd.

What are the main ideas of Russian public opinion considering the state solution for the agrarian question?

The idea of land socialization to the greatest extent contradicts the basis of the existing agrarian system. According to this idea, land is a public domain. We emphasize that it is a domain and not a property. It belongs equally to everyone, like light and air. The peasant labour economy is only a user of this free element.

To organize this use, the working peasantry unites into special bodies of land self-government and land communities. The state transfers land for distribution to these bodies according to the economic and social order, in the form of communal or households' land tenure. It can also introduce a large-scale, commodity economy on the whole territory.

If land is free, if it cannot be owned, and does not have value, then every farmer should use it for free. State and local taxes are imposed on the economy, not on land.

However, the difference in soil fertility and in the position of farms should be taken into account by taxation that must put all workers in the same conditions of labour productivity. For temporarily weak and inefficient farms, the land community should organize public ploughing and harvesting. Buildings, implements, and livestock should remain in private property together with agricultural products.

The idea of land nationalization is based on quite different creative grounds. Land rent and land value are not excluded from the existing social categories claiming that land can and should be a property. But land is to have one owner – the state.

As an owner, the state gets 1) the right to all land rent, which is the main source of public finances, and 2) the right of disposal of all the country's lands in the national interests. According to the latter right, the state gives a part of land to the labour economy on terms similar to rent and makes sure that the usable land of each family does not exceed the labour standard. And the state does not interfere in the internal structure of the economy and allows the possibility of wage labour.

Forests and special types of economy can stay in state and public use or be exploited on capitalist terms if it corresponds to the national economic interests. The supreme command of land is in the hands of the state; at the local level, land is managed by local land authorities based on the principle of self-government.

One of the forms of nationalization, in which all local lands are at the autonomous disposal of the *zemstvo* self-government (its rights are limited only by the national law on land), is called land municipalization. Under municipalization, the local, self-government bodies collect land rent.

These are the basic ideas of the land system that are most common in our socialist circles. These ideas are somewhat similar to the ideas of the followers of Henry George. They recognize the right of all people to land and the right of every person to the products of his labour. They seek to establish these rights by taking away the unearned income from land (rent) in favour of all the people.

The single land tax in the amount of land rent is sufficient to solve the agrarian question, because land without rent will lose its value and, therefore, attractiveness for capital. Capitalist land tenure will lose its meaning, and we will have only a labour economy and such a capitalist economy that is intensive and rational enough to survive under the tax equal to rent. This type of capitalist economy is of great value for the national economy.

Thus, the single tax system is similar to land socialization and nationalization by giving all land rent to the state bodies. But it is different for it does not suggest to the organized public mind to dispose of land. This system claims that without state intervention, the labour economy regime will establish itself on the lands free of rent.

This idea is particularly interesting, because it implies a solution for the agrarian problem not by an active state reorganization of the existing system of land tenure, but rather by creating a land regime in which the spontaneous process of economic evolution itself would lead to the sought-for ideals.

This idea is most developed in the system of state regulation of land tenure suggested by some economists. Under this regime, private land property remains, but the free sale and purchase of land are completely destroyed. Land ceases to be a free commodity. It can be sold only to the state and be bought or received only from the state. All lands at the disposal of the state form a land fund, which the state uses in the national economic interests by giving land either for use or into possession of farmers. Moreover, the state organizes and carries out the reclamation of lands at its disposal.

To speed up the transition of private farms into labour economies, a system of land tax is introduced. It reduces taxes for the labour economy, raises taxes for small and medium-sized private farms up to the alienation of land rent, and raises taxes for large farms even above land rent. In addition to this tax pressure, the state reserves the right to compulsory alienation of any land if it is necessary for the land system of a particular region.

When comparing the above-mentioned land systems, we should first note that their main differences are determined by motivation and justification rather than by specific conditions of land use. Under all the systems, the farmer pays to the state or local self-government bodies a part of his income equal to or about the same as land rent. The difference in the names of payments or their justification does not matter from an economic point of view.

Furthermore, using various state measures, all systems seek to turn the economy into the labour type. We can arrange them in the following order of the increasing impact of the organized public mind on everyday economic life: socialization, nationalization, state regulation of land tenure, and, finally, a single tax system.

Land socialization simply prohibits wage labour in agriculture. If some types of economy cannot manage on their own with the labour efforts of the family, this system imposes on the society the organization of work on a labour partnership basis.

Land nationalization approves the labour principle by a compulsory restriction of land use by labour standards; however, it allows the use of wage labour in special types of agricultural production.

State regulation of land tenure places the capitalist economy in extremely difficult tax conditions. It forcibly directs all land resales in the interest of the labour economy.

The single tax system considers it sufficient to destroy land rent as the only source of landed property and capitalist farming.

In fact, all these systems aim at the same goal but use instruments of different power to achieve it.

The implementation and maintenance of land socialization requires the exceptional activities of all the organized forces of the public mind and an extraordinary amount of work. The implementation of the single tax system requires minimal state efforts, because it leaves all the work on the development and strengthening of the labour economy to the spontaneous process of economic evolution free of rent.

The basis of all organizational skills is the ability to correctly scale the estimated means to the sought-for goals and the means for achieving it to the possibility of their implementation.

A successful solution of the problem is the one that is based only on necessary and, at the same time, sufficient means. Therefore, to choose one or another way of approving labour economy, we should clearly answer the question of whether the planned set of measures is really necessary for the desired effect or can it be achieved with less effort and less waste of resources.

On the other hand, the opposite is also true: for example, when assessing the single tax system, we have to answer the question of whether the selected means are sufficient to introduce and maintain the labour economy. Considering quite a number of other measures, e.g. the prohibition of wage labour, we have to decide if such measures are feasible at all.

Only after evaluating the above-mentioned systems from the organizational-technical point of view, can we accept them as the guiding principle of real work.

However, we must remember that they are presented here as ideal schemes. And we have to do a lot of work to turn these schemes into reality and concretize them according to the conditions of the Russian village.

Therefore, I ask all those wishing to purposefully choose and implement any system of land use to imagine a well-known rural district (*volost*), for instance, the Shchipovatovskaya *volost* of the Volchansky district of the Kharkov Province, or the Murikovskaya *volost* of the Volokolamsky district of the Moscow Province. Then, consider the possible outcomes of the implementation of a particular system of land use for these familiar villages and farms.

The above-described schemes can be fully understood only if translated into a whole world of concepts and living representations. We can confidently say that they will be differently turned into reality by residents of Samara, the Mogilev Province, Vologda, or by the Cossacks from the Don.

Our vast fatherland has absorbed countries that are so diverse in their economic and everyday life that by enumerating them inwardly one can trace the economic history of all mankind.

The Siberian *taiga* reminds us of the period of hunting life, the steppes of Central Asia represent a nomadic economy, the Akmolinsk region and the Orenburg steppes preserve examples of a fallow economy. We know the belt in the Samara and Saratov provinces, where the three-field economy is only developing; we know all the phases of the decay of the communal three-field economy; we witness the rise of the grassland economy near Moscow, and observe the western regions of intensive farming and dairy cattle breeding in the Vologda Province and near Moscow.

According to the differences in the organization of production, there are different production relations and ideals. In the northern Siberian regions, land is as free an element as light and air, and there are no grounds to introduce any right to it.

In some regions of Siberia, there is still a grabbing right to land: the farmer who cultivated a new land will be its owner as long as he works on it. Here, the right to land is the 'right of labour' spent on its cultivation. If population density increases, the grabbing right to land leads to conflicts and determines the need for some social regulation of agrarian relations. Thus, the land community develops. Its regulating activities lead to, according to the figurative expression of K.R. Kocharovsky, the 'right to work', i.e. the right to get land to work on. The workforce becomes an allotment unit for land redistribution.

Today, in some parts of the Astrakhan Province and the south-east, we witness only the emergence of this regime and land ideology. But, in the regions where the land community is alive, the number of workers is the land redistribution unit, and the 'right to work' is still the main idea of egalitarian redistribution.

In land-hungry areas, where the available land is too small to provide work for all under the existing field crop cultivation, because the land is barely enough to feed the population, the idea of the 'right to life' spontaneously develops, and the land redistribution unit is the number of mouths to feed rather than the number of working hands. Consumer redistribution was discovered by *zemstvo* statisticians in a number of land-hungry areas.

Finally, when commercial agriculture develops and land becomes value and capital, the egalitarian community begins to disintegrate, and the ideology of private landownership begins to win the minds of farmers. Here and there we see only the start of this process, whereas the entire west and south-west of Russia have long ago switched to household land tenure.

Undoubtedly, such a diversity is not accidental; it has deep economic and everyday life roots. Therefore, it is absolutely clear that we have to coordinate the content of our plan of land reform with the features of the local economic order.

A member of the land community from Samara willing to transfer his entire agrarian ideology will probably be greeted with stakes in the Mogilev Province. Not a better fate will befall the fanatic from the Mogilev Province in the Balashovsky district. And no matter how deeply we, the leaders of democratic Russia, are convinced of our agrarian ideals, we cannot follow the path of 'enlightened absolutism' and forcefully introduce a single land regime in all areas of Russia regardless of their everyday and economic order.

Thus, our agrarian ideas are preliminary guiding schemes, and the task of local land committees and local departments of the League for Agrarian Reforms is to turn them into specific plans of the new land system.

Land reform

The ideas of land socialization, nationalization, and municipalization as the bases of the ideal land regime do not clarify the essence of land reform. They allow us to imagine a land system after the reform but say nothing about how the reform will be implemented and what the path will be from the existing land regime to the ideal one.

Meanwhile, this is exactly the question that can cause great discrepancies and even irreconcilable confrontations between us, representatives of democratic Russia. Therefore, special attention must be paid to this question.

Actually, in many party programmes, we find some indications of the path of agrarian reform. However, we can confidently say that these sections of programmes are the least developed and the strongest parts of them. Only some issues of the agrarian reform have become sufficiently clear.

First, for most of us, it is clear that the future land system should be based on the interests of the state as a whole, and in the same way, the paths to this new system should follow the interests of the state. There can be no regional or local ways to solve the agrarian question.

We must take into account household and economic features of different regions. We cannot impose on the local life recipes for those aspects of the agrarian organization that concern them and only them. However, in the course of our agrarian reform we must not for a minute forget the interests of our national economy as a whole. One example will be enough to prove the importance of what was said above.

Imagine our south-eastern provinces. Peasant and Cossack economies there still have large enough plots for extensive grain farming of almost a fallow type. There are also large private and state lands in these provinces.

Perhaps, for Samara and Orenburg peasants, the best solution will be to divide these estates among peasant farms, thus, increasing their size by 10 or 15 *desiatinas* each.

However, such a solution is unacceptable for the state, because an increase in the already large plots would strengthen for years the most extensive forms of farming and would not contribute to the growth of the productivity of our national economy. From the state's point of view, it is much more valuable to use these alienated lands to settle settlers from land-hungry provinces.

In the Kiev and Podolsk provinces, in some parts of the Poltava Province, overpopulation is so enormous that, despite exceptionally intensive farming, not even half of the people's labour can be used.

The outmigration from these provinces to the south-east will reduce their population and, undoubtedly, will intensify our south-eastern economy and, thus, significantly increase our national income. However, we are equally certain that the settlers will encounter a very hostile attitude and the serious opposition of the local population.

Here, the interests of the whole are confronted with the interests of the units. The key secret of agrarian reform is the ability to reconcile these interests, which is an extremely difficult task. Local interpretations of the state issues are the most dangerous pitfalls of the agrarian reform.

In one of the chapters I pointed out that every social phenomenon consists of an element and reason. These two manifest themselves not only in the future agrarian system, but, unfortunately, in the very implementation and discussion on the reform.

One element that does not take into account arguments of reason and does not accept the laws of logic will play an important role in our future agrarian development. Nevertheless, reason should not lay down its arms. It must exert all its power to direct the resultant force of the historical progress closer to the state course of the reform.

What does reason tell us? How does it portray the desired course of the agrarian transformation?

First, it tells us that the organized egalitarian redistribution of state and private land in the interests of the working people requires an infinite number of the most difficult statistical, land surveying, and organizational activities. Even if there are no social difficulties and social resistance to the reform, such a huge work will require many years to finish it. Therefore, whatever regime we take for an ideal, we will approach it only after a long transition period.

Only systems of the single tax and state regulation of land ownership can be introduced almost immediately, because they establish new conditions for economic life and do not create a land system. This is especially emphasized by the fact that, for example, the state regulation of land ownership as we described it in the previous chapter can be both an independent land regime and a transition stage for land socialization, nationalization, or municipalization, depending on the policy of regulation.

The state regulation of land ownership is such a powerful instrument of the organized public mind that, provided the strong pressure of the state, it can force the spontaneous process of agricultural evolution to automatically come to nationalization or municipalization in one or two decades.

It is our deep conviction that three means of the state regulation system – progressive land taxation, abolition of free land purchase and sales, and the right to expropriate any land – are necessary and sufficient for the state to get full control of land reform. However, we admit that political conditions and the understandable impatience of the broad democratic masses can force the state to speed up the reform by a violent method of implementation.

At the same time, we must clearly realize that the immediate issuance by the Constituent Assembly of a decree declaring that, from some date, all land is state property is not yet a land reform. The state should not only declare that all land constitutes its property but it must also organize this transfer of land into its hands. The very fact that the decree was issued does not really make land a public domain.

If the law on land nationalization is issued without a system of measures for the transition period, we will have only a dangerous state fiction. That is why we will have a long transition period in all cases. During this period, we have to be extremely careful in two respects.

First, with respect to those relatively few private estates, which are centres of culture. Livestock-breeding farms, plant selection farms providing the country with seeds, horticultural economies, stud farms, dairy farms, and other similar types of economy are the cultural treasures of our country and a public domain. It is our deep conviction that almost all these types of economy can become labour economies on a cooperative basis.

Today necessary cooperatives have not yet matured, and we do not have organizational forces to transfer all these types of economy into the hands of the peasantry. Therefore we should take special care to ensure that the fine thread of our cultural agronomic tradition does not tear.

Cherry orchards should not be cut down, stud farms and breed herds should not be sold and destroyed, fields of selection farms that produce new varieties of plants should not be sown with a poor grade of oats. All these cultural values are our common cultural heritage. In the name of our future we must save them from being plundered and destroyed.

The second issue that requires a particularly cautious approach is land privately owned by peasants. Over the last decade, our peasantry has bought from other classes about 27 million *desiatinas* of land.

This land is scattered among thousands of peasant farms and often bought with hard-earned money. It is not uncommon that this land exceeds the labour standard. Quite often it exceeds allotments of whole land communities and even districts (the Cossack lands). Therefore, we consider it dangerous for the state to be pedantic in the implementation of the reform and to begin immediately to alienate all peasant land above a certain labour standard. Such a measure is acceptable only after socialist ideas penetrate deeply into all minds of our village and become firm beliefs. Otherwise, violent strife among peasants and Cossacks is inevitable, which will pave the way for a counter-revolutionary strike. Thus, although logically this measure is a correct conclusion from the idea of land socialization, politically its premature implementation will be fraught with terrible dangers.

The same or nearly the same applies to the question of refundable or gratuitous alienation of private land. If one believes that landed property is an accidental social mistake, then this question can be easily solved by the gratuitous alienation of private land.

However, for us, who believe that even though it does not correspond to our social ideals, landed property is a fruit of the historical development of national economic life with sufficient social roots, the question of alienation of private land cannot be so easily solved. We cannot consider the existing landowners as invaders and usurpers. They and their property are the consequence of the existing economic system, which has developed historically and is now close to destruction by virtue of the same historical necessity.

Land reform is the reform of our economic system and not the division of wealth between different groups of the population.

When we consider agrarian reform a complex organizational-economic task, we are interested in only one question: what is the easiest way (i.e. with the fewest difficulties and costs) to socialize land and give it to the labour economy?

From this point of view, we have to oppose, on the one hand, several billions of rubles of gradually paid-off state debt resulting from the state's payment of compensation for the alienated land. On the other hand, we must oppose a severe financial crisis determined by the denial to pay mortgage debts and aggravation of social antagonism, which paves the way for counter-revolutionary movements. We solve this opposition in favour of refundable alienation.

Our private land for the most part is mortgaged to the eyeballs in state and private land banks. Therefore, the value of private land largely belongs not to landowners, but to depositors of land banks and holders of mortgage bonds. In other words, gratuitous confiscation of private land aimed against landowners, in fact, misses the aim and, for the most part, falls on our financial system and on holders of mortgage bonds scattered among diverse social strata.

As of 1 January 1916, the amount of money lent by land banks on land and real estate in cities and districts (*uyezd*) reached 5.5 bn rubles. If we subtract from this amount loans secured on city property and mortgage bonds of the Peasant Bank, we will get about 2.5 bn rubles issued to landowners as loans secured on about 50 million *desiatinas* of land.

This money was given by depositors of land banks and holders of mortgage bonds scattered among diverse social strata. Suffice it to say that the deposits of our savings banks amounting to more than 800 m rubles are placed in securities of land banks. These few figures clearly indicate the possible financial danger and social discontent that would occur with the refusal to pay land debts.

The idea of gratuitous confiscation with paying mortgage debts does not stand up to scrutiny from the point of view of elementary justice. This system implies paying debts of the squandered nobility at the expense of those cultural enterprises that managed to survive without indebtedness and had a large positive impact on our national economy.

Moreover, it is necessary to take into account the political outcome of this measure, because it will affect a huge number of small peasant landowners who have bought approximately 27 million *desiatinas* of land in private ownership since the reform of 1861. We consider it very difficult to carry out socialization of these lands in the near future, and yet their alienation without compensation will encounter extremely strong resistance and is fraught with political dangers.

When accepting the idea of refundable alienation, we involuntarily ask ourselves: in the end who will pay the landowners for their alienated lands? We suggest the following financial plan for the land reform. To our state debt, which by the end of the war will exceed 50 bn rubles, another 5 or 6 bn will be added to compensate for the alienation of private land.

The owner of the alienated land will receive government liabilities for an amount equal to the real value of land and not to its market price. The state will annually pay interest on these liabilities and gradually repay them by extending the repayment period for 50–100 years.

Payments will be made from the general state budget. Because its revenue part is democratic, i.e. based on income and rent taxes, the propertied classes will bear the main burden of land reform. Certainly, the peasantry will also participate in paying rent and income taxes, thus contributing to the financing of land reform.

However, it should be remembered that according to the basic idea of income taxation, families with income below the statutory subsistence level are not taxed at all. A large number of land-hungry and weak peasants have incomes below this level. That is why only the well-to-do strata of the village will have to pay income taxes, and will thus pay the compensation for the alienated land.

The financial plan of land reform can be developed in different ways, but we have to bring to the fore the principle stating that the need for land is not the need of individuals or classes but the need of the state as a whole. Land reform should be carried out according to the plan and at the expense of the state as a whole.

Conclusion

In the previous chapters, we considered almost all the key issues of the agrarian problem. We did not seek to offer final solutions for these issues but rather tried to correctly formulate questions and outline some directions for their possible solution. We think that, at the present moment, when these lines are being written, we cannot take on any other task. We expect many months of hard work by many hundreds of local land committees, the State Land Committee, and League for Agrarian Reforms.

By no means can such work be considered predetermined; otherwise the very existence of local land committees would lose all meaning. It is our deep conviction that they alone are capable of transferring agrarian reform from the world of abstract ideas and concepts to the real world of live representations and of making the reform a fact.

This painstaking and difficult work will gradually lead us to the solution of all the above questions. Such decisions will take into account local experience and follow the idea of social development.

The creation of local and central bodies of land reform as its efficient apparatus, which is deeply rooted in the local life, will be the main token of the success of the undertaken reform. It clearly feels the heartbeat of local life and at the same time uses the full power of Russian economic science and the state's creative thought.

However, the work of these bodies can be fruitful only if comprehensively supported by the living public opinion of the general Russian public. Agrarian reform is the long overdue need of our entire state; therefore, it is every citizen's business and a direct duty for each of us.

The basic law of citizenship ethics tells us that participation in state affairs is everyone's responsibility. The most serious reproach to our civil conscience is that we did not do what we could do in our state building. That is why we believe that we have the right to call all citizens to participate in the solution of the agrarian question and to remember that each of us is responsible for its successful solution.

CHAPTER 2

A.V. Chayanov main ideas and methods of social agronomy

Moscow: Moscow Publishing Partnership on Agricultural Economy and Policy, 1918

The book by Alexander Chayanov *Main Ideas and Methods of Social Agronomy* is one of his key interdisciplinary works written and published at the beginning of the October Revolution and the Civil War. In this work, the economist Chayanov is a social philosopher considering rural evolution as determined not only by the market and the state but mainly by the will and knowledge of rural households that can be led to sustainable rural development by the organized public mind (a kind of synonym for civil society). Its most important social institution in the rural sphere is social agronomy. Chayanov emphasizes that social agronomy is one of the youngest social institutions. It appeared in the late 19th century in Europe and North America and in three decades turned into an influential movement uniting agrarian scientists, agrarian activists and a huge number of peasants striving for agricultural knowledge for more productive and cultural development of their households. In this book, Chayanov is not only a social philosopher but also a social activist and organizer, teacher and psychologist. The book is based on his seminar, 'Social Agronomy and Agricultural Cooperation', which incorporated many years of personal communication with peasants, agronomists, and agrarian scientists about dissemination and application of agrarian knowledge by peasants. For the contemporary reader, this publication is not only of historical interest. Chayanov's ideas are still relevant for the effective interaction of professional agrarians with the rural population, peasants, and farmers in the organization of agricultural knowledge, agricultural cooperatives, and agricultural consulting. In the first chapters, Chayanov focused on the strategic and world-view aspects of social agronomy; in the second part, he analyses tactical directions of social-agronomic work: methods of oral, social-agronomic propaganda; conversations, lectures, courses, and agronomic consulting; agricultural exhibitions, demonstration plots, model farms, and peasant excursions; agricultural warehouses, rental points, and grain-cleaning stations; organizational work of the agronomist; social agronomy and cooperation; the equipment of the agronomic station; and registration and evaluation of social-agronomic activities. In all these chapters, Chayanov shows how creative the work of the social agronomist should be, how many diverse and unexpected challenges he faces when interacting with peasant communities, audiences, and households. The interaction of social agronomy with another influential institution – agricultural cooperation – is of particular interest. Chayanov analyses in detail the contradictions and distinctions in the work of agronomists and cooperators, in their common tasks of developing and improving the peasant life. Despite the fact that the book was published 100 years ago, it is not only of historical interest but presents many valuable answers and practical recommendations for the contemporary agricultural consulting and rural development activists.

Foreword

Today our homeland faces an agrarian reform exceptional in its scale and depth. According to the unanimous opinion of Russian agrarian thought, this reform cannot be limited to the new foundations of land relations in our villages and should aim instead toward the development of the productive forces of our agriculture.

Social agronomy is one of the most important ways to solve this task, which, despite great difficulties, hastens the publication of this book. It is based on the author's notes compiled for the seminar, 'Social Agronomy and Agricultural Cooperation', held at the Peter's Academy since 1913. Despite using extensive literature, the author considers it necessary to mention that he obtained most data from personal conversations with direct participants of social-agronomic work: V.A. Vladimirsky, K.A. Matseevich, A.N. Minin, A.P. Levitsky, V.I. Teitel, M.E. Shaternikov, M.N. Vonzblein, N.I. Kostrov, K.K. Dyssky, A.V. Shalin,

I.V. Matveev, E.M. Sharygin, and other fellow workers to whom he expresses his deep gratitude.

The author considers it his duty to express special thanks to his dear teacher, Aleksei Fedorovich Fortunatov, who directed his work for many years.

The publishing partnership's difficult conditions forced us to shorten the text significantly, omit the descriptive-illustrative part, and remove two chapters: 'Social Measures for Cattle Breeding' and 'Training the Agronomist'.

Gorbovo village, summer of 1917

Chapter 1. The tasks of social-agronomic work

Within economic policy, social agronomy is perhaps the youngest institution not yet fully developed. Although customs policy, land policy, transport policy, taxation, and other areas have extensive experience because of many centuries of development (which has been summarized and analysed by a number of prominent researchers), our sector of economic policy has been nearly unaffected by theoretical analysis. Only in the last decade has it begun to systematize its experience.

Social agronomy was born in the last decade of the 19th century. In a short time, it managed to become the largest social phenomenon and attracted thousands of agronomists in all countries of the cultural world. Three decades of their social-agronomic work have already created an extensive experience, which unfortunately remains scattered across local agronomic organizations. It has been collected and discussed to a very limited extent at various agronomic congresses and in articles.

In the early 20th century, there were first attempts at theoretical generalization, and the works of A.I. Chuprov, A.F. Fortunatov, D.N. Pryanishnikov, V.A. Vladimirsky, K.A. Matseevich, Paul de Wuyst, A. Bizzozzero, and some others laid the first theoretical foundations of social-agronomic work. The first attempts to generalize and systematize local experience allow the identification, at least in general terms, of the main tasks and methods of social agronomy.

First, we have to define the very term 'social agronomy' and its place within other institutions of economic policy. In the most general form, social agronomy can be defined as a system of social measures aimed at the evolution of the country's agriculture towards most rational forms (in terms of time and place).

However, this definition is too general and cannot satisfy us with regard to the measures of customs policy, land policy, taxation, and other forms of economic policy, which affect the evolution of agriculture and, thus, also correspond to this general definition. To narrow and deepen it, we need to define the very evolution of agriculture, at least in the most general terms.

We know that the agricultural production of all countries consists of many individual enterprises run by their owners' will. Peasants combine elements of production into a particular production system according to their own understanding and desire. Simple observations and numerous statistical studies show that for the areas with similar historical, natural, and economic conditions, these methods of combining production factors are quite the same and therefore present several similar types.

A deeper analysis shows that the historically evolving, average type of production system emerges and becomes sustainable because it is the most adapted to the conditions of the given place and time. However, such production systems do not remain unchanged; they undergo radical transformations and restructuring as the general conditions of their existence change.

The most powerful factor affecting production systems is the increase in population density. However, changes in market conditions and technological rationalization are of great importance too. Certainly, there is nothing in agriculture like the Industrial Revolution that was determined by the steam engine. Nevertheless, separators, chemical fertilizers, tractors, and harvesters significantly restructured agricultural production.

Unfortunately, the question of the forms and mechanisms of the agricultural evolution have not been sufficiently studied theoretically. This book aims to answer the questions about the evolutionary process, at least in the most general terms. What is the mechanism of the agricultural evolution, i.e. how does one average type of production system turn into another average type under changing conditions? To what extent is this spontaneous restructuring of agricultural production controlled by the public, and what is the quantitative effect of this impact? Both questions have been poorly studied, and we can outline only the direction of their study.

According to the typical answer to the first question, the transition from one production system to another under changing conditions is spontaneous. Let us try to define the term in this case. As we have already mentioned, agricultural production in all countries consists of individual enterprises. Their heads combine elements of production into a system, which they consider the most profitable and which, due to the same conditions, brings all economies to one organizational type.

However, this does not mean that all economies of a homogeneous region are identical in their organizational structure and stay in constant organizational rest. The personality of the peasant, his creative energy, the features of the location of individual economies, and the quality of the land make individual economies constantly move away from the average type. We can find that such massive deviations are determined by the inquisitiveness of the human mind and that all households in an organizational perspective are in a kinetic state of constant attempts, searches, and creativity.

The worst economic stagnation has not stopped such searches. This has been proven by numerous manifestations of the peasant economic creativity as collected by V.V. in his book *Progressive Trends in Peasant Economy*. The book describes the Russian village as full of sad memories and shattered hopes in the 1870s and 1880s.

Quite often, deviations are unsuccessful and make peasants return to the average historical type. However, there are lucky seekers who introduce and keep new production forms that attract followers. This is a kind of natural selection of economic forms, which only partly resembles natural selection in the animal kingdom. The most successful forms that are most suitable for the existing conditions survive, whereas the rest are carried away into oblivion.

These constant organizational revivals and quick deaths of unsuccessful forms are a spontaneous, creative principle. Without participation of the organized public mind, this principle inevitably leads the individual economy to the average organizational type as the most rational under the given conditions. A great example of this social power is the production system of migrants on virgin territories.

Sometimes in Siberia, there are new settlers from the Volyn Province, Kharkov steppes, Kostroma forests, and the black earth of the Kursk Province. The resettled families keep the production skills of their homeland and, in the first years, try to apply them in the new place. A long series of failures and creative attempts eventually brings the natives of Volyn, Kharkov, Kostroma, and Kursk to a new average type of production organization as the most appropriate for the new conditions. After one or two decades, only minor details of the former production system remind them of the abandoned homeland.

If economic conditions do not change, the average type of enterprise and farm creatively fluctuates without fundamental changes around the objectively best forms. The situation changes when some condition of economic life undergoes a major modification and the previous, average, organizational type ceases to be the best possible one. The economies that are creatively deviating towards better forms secure these forms for themselves. Their success fosters imitations and slowly but surely makes other economies give up the old organizational forms in favour of the new ones. Thus, in a few decades, masters of the country will spontaneously find a new, average, organizational type that is the most appropriate to the new conditions around which their creative searches fluctuate.

This is the most general scheme of agricultural evolution. In this process, there is no socially organized will, no public consciousness, no commander, and no plan. It is almost as spontaneous as the natural selection of species in the animal kingdom.

Now we can consider the second questions: how can the organized public mind influence the described spontaneous process of agricultural evolution, and what are the forms of this influence? The public mind has two ways to influence the spontaneous evolution of agriculture.

1. It can change the economic conditions and allow the dark, spontaneous process to adapt organizational forms of the economy to the new economic system. This mode of action has been consecrated by centuries of state practices. The state took control of agricultural evolution many times by changing the price system with customs rates, by destroying the power of space with improved means of transportation, by encouraging some production groups with tax rates, credit and tariff policies, and by authoritatively interfering in agricultural development with new land laws. Nobody doubts the power of this form of influence; it was and will always be a powerful instrument in the hands of the public mind.
2. On the other hand, it can influence agricultural evolution by affecting the will and mind of peasants, by directing their creative searches towards forms they consider rational, by preventing them from taking false paths of creative searching, by supporting successful undertakings by its authority, and by accelerating and rationalizing the process of evolution. Such an introduction of rationality into a spontaneous process is the essence of social agronomy.

Thus, the public mind faces two tasks: 1) A most in-depth analysis of the natural and economic conditions to identify technical and organizational forms that are most rationally adapted to them. Agronomic science, experimental institutions, and economic research are to solve this task. 2) Because agronomic thought can identify the required technical methods and organizational forms, it has to influence agricultural evolution and direct it towards the identified forms.

We can specify these tasks in the following three points. Social agronomy has to 1) introduce improved methods of farming and cattle breeding; 2) change the economies' organizational plan towards greater compliance with the current conditions of the country's economic reality; and 3) organize the local population into unions and groups which, on the one hand, provide the smallest economy with all the advantages of the largest economy by cooperative generalization of individual aspects, and, on the other hand, take on consolidation and further deepening of new economic principles.

Thus, having identified the tasks of social-agronomic work, we should emphasize that they are not as important for social agronomy as methods for solving them.

Chapter 2. Methods of the social-agronomic work

If we admit that the task of social agronomy is to accelerate and rationalize the spontaneous evolution of agriculture towards greater compliance with changing conditions, then representatives of social agronomy can be called organizers of the ongoing agricultural reform. However, the word 'organizer' is not quite applicable to the term 'spontaneous process' and, thus, has an unusual meaning.

Let us consider a private economy with thousands of *desiatinas* of land, which unites hundreds of agricultural workers, uses outdated methods, and needs radical reorganization and organizational reform. The agronomist-organizer assigned to implement this reform studies both the economy and local conditions to develop new rational plans for organizing the economy and the transition from the old production system to the new one according to both the economy and local conditions. Then, by force of his will, the agronomist-organizer sets in motion capital from the economy and numerous land workers without taking their desires into consideration or even asking their opinions. By the force of his will and without considering the understanding and will of the reform participants, the agronomist-organizer implements a reform plan by combining production elements of the economy into a new system. The term 'agronomist-organizer' is usually associated with the type of activities described above.

The organizational activities of social agronomy consist of this type of action. Social agronomy considers the reform participants not as dumb beasts but as independent peasants who organize and run their economies by their own will and mind. Only they can manage their economies, and nobody has the right to order them to do anything.

Therefore, we have to admit that social agronomy does not run any economies, and it cannot implement any programmes by its own will and desire. Its methods are limited to reviving the creative initiative of working people by influencing their minds and will and making this initiative the most rational one. In other words, the representative of social agronomy is more a social worker than a technical one. His activities are focused on people, their minds, will, consciousness, and relationships rather than on fields, livestock, and household equipment.

If social agronomy wants to create a new agriculture, it has to create a new human culture and a new people's consciousness, so that this new human culture will create a new agriculture. Social agronomy as an institution is aimed at social activities, and this social nature of activities is the most important and essential distinguishing feature of social agronomy.

One may ask whether such an influence on evolving economies is the only right and possible one. Perhaps the public mind would be more successful if the organizational reform of agriculture were similar to the organizational work in the private economy. There it consists of adopting special laws that foster the restructuring of farms and training special agronomic administrators with ample strong powers. The Empress Catherine, Frederick the Great, and other representatives of enlightened absolutism introduced potatoes with cannons and executions. However, we believe that such a task is beyond the powers of the public mind, even with the full power of the state.

The activities of the peasant are so local in nature and so much determined by the features of the cultivated patch of land that no external will can run this economy more or less intensively. We can say that the art of the peasant is his ability to use particulars. Only the peasant who has studied his economy for many years in practice can successfully run it and especially reform it. Therefore, the idea of replacing the creative work and intuition of the peasant with the organized public mind is hardly realizable, even by Laplace's 'universal mind'.

Even if this idea were feasible and the society had enough creative organizing forces to completely replace the will and thoughts of the peasant, such an unconsciously adopted reform would not be deep and sustainable. Moreover, wishing to take the place of all local peasants and manage production, the existing public-state bodies would not have sufficient financial means to solve this task. The reform would be too expensive compared to the usual methods of social-agronomic work.

Thus, we can argue that social agronomy should not replace national economic forces but rather should play the role of an enzyme that boosts them and directs their work. Social agronomy deals with a large number of 'managing people' who have skills and ideas about agriculture, to whom nothing can be ordered and who do everything based on their own free will and their own initiative.

We need to somehow draw the attention of peasants to the possibility of changing their usual working methods. We need to replace the old ideas of the local population with new ones, awaken this population to activity, and give it an emotional impulse by verbal and written persuasion. We need to do so by examples and visual evidence to convince them of the advantages and greater profitability of the new techniques over the previously practised ones. Without such an impulse, no evidence would be proof, all propaganda would turn into a curious story, and social agronomy would lose its meaning.

Agronomic workers have numerous means of influencing the mind and will of the population. Places for oral propaganda include conversations at peasant gatherings, in taverns, on market squares, at lectures with visual demonstrations, and short courses for the most active peasants. Wall posters vividly promoting the basic agronomic truths, popular brochures, leaflets, and local popular agricultural journals-newspapers use the power of the printed word. Agricultural exhibitions and demonstrations of the improved machinery at work, experiments on the peasants' fields, demonstrative feeding of livestock, machine rental offices, machines promoted for testing, and the whole demonstration economies provide social agronomy with the persuasiveness of good examples.

Selecting the most active and conscious peasants from the local population – 'Sidorovs and Karpovs who want to improve their economy' – organizing independent peasant groups from them, awakening local public life in the very depths of the village, and teaching peasants the universal skills of social work – this is the field for the organizational art of social agronomy. If we add to this the organization of agricultural warehouses that supply the population with agricultural machinery, seeds, and fertilizers, the opening of breeding and seed-cleaning stations, consultations for individual economies, and other similar measures that play a special role in the social-agronomic work, we will outline its scope of activities. This scope is extensive in form and possible content. Therefore, agronomic thought has developed some guiding ideas that help find one's bearing in this scope and systematically organize social-agronomic work.

Chapter 3. The programme of social-agronomic work

Social agronomy aims to influence the mass, spontaneous process of agricultural evolution. Therefore, it should use mass means, e.g. all rural population should be the object of its influence, and all its measures should affect all peasants and not only individual Sidors and Ivans.

Certainly, agronomic workers always deal with individuals, but social agronomy should consider individual economies not in their specificity but as representatives of the national economy. Therefore, when identifying the initial goals of its propaganda, social agronomy should focus on those aspects of the economy that are common to all peasants in the region. As a rule, the social-agronomic programme identifies two or three pressing economic needs that are easy to meet with a deep, visual effort to solve the problems.

Such a focus and certainty of the programme are of particular importance considering the low cultural level of the rural population in the countries with widely developed social-agricultural work. Almost everywhere, before promoting agrarian reform, social agronomy had to promote itself and often conduct general cultural work. Therefore, the social-agronomic work has to be organized in such a way that it makes the brightest, most sensible, and strongest impression possible on individual minds and has a strong, mass impact on peasant psychology.

The pioneers of social agronomy were destined to stir up the sluggish minds of the inert peasantry and inspire peasants with the very possibility of new ideas. This is why in Russia, Italy, and Belgium these pioneers started with common and clear issues that affect and interest everyone. The success of one such case in the village of Elizavetino quickly became known, interesting, and understandable in the village of Sudislovo and many other villages.

According to this intensive model, first social-agronomic programmes consisted of elementary, almost obvious, technical reforms. If the wooden plough rules in the *uyezd*, then the programme contains a paragraph about the widespread use of ploughs; if the *uyezd* suffers from insect pests, then the programme introduces measures to fight them; if in the *uyezd* there is an extremely abnormal ratio of grain and forage areas, then the focus is on grass growing. In the same way, programmes introduce bare fallow, autumn ploughing, and so on.

According to the programme, for years the pioneer agronomist destroys winter cutworm, introduces grass growing, and promotes bare fallow. His practice is limited to this; he is not interested in other details of the economy. Moreover, he cannot be interested in them in order not to disrupt the implementation of his main programme. It is hardly worth mentioning how important and responsible the proper implementation of the main programme is.

There can be neither general provisions nor standards, because in each region we must proceed from hundreds of particulars that cannot be foreseen by general considerations. Therefore, we will not be mistaken if we say that the most important task of social agronomy is the correct diagnosis of local needs and defects in the agricultural system. Certainly, methods and promoted techniques of the social-agronomic work are so elementary that their implementation does not cause great difficulties. However, it is important to direct this work correctly and to plan all measures according to the results of the scientific analysis of local conditions.

Another equally important task is to compare the forces and means of social agronomy with the tasks set in its programme. As a rule, material and human resources are so limited that we have to ensure that the work gives the maximum social effect per unit of effort and means, i.e. the work is the most socially profitable.

These are the first steps in the general scheme of the social-agronomic work. We should note that its inherent limitation – a focus on two or three paragraphs of the main programme – does not mean a refusal to reform other aspects of the peasant economy, which is a single whole. In other words, if the reform affects its foundations, the reform determined by the creative initiative will easily affect other aspects of the economy.

Because of social-agronomic work development, the elementary tasks of the main programme are gradually solved. After a few years of hard work in the thick of village life, agronomy will become a part of the peasant economy. The practice raises a number of often unpredicted questions, and the population becomes accustomed to the activities of agronomic assistance. There are new tasks, which make us deepen our agronomy, and life itself often provides us with new fields of work.

Previously the programme of social agronomy considered only those needs that were to be torn out of the context of regional economies. But today we return to this context and individualize our work so that it focuses on smaller areas and even groups of economies. According to such intensification of social-agronomic work, the very structure of social agronomy changes – the amount of work per unit of area significantly increases, the number of agronomic workers and amount of funds spent also increase, and there is a significant differentiation of work.

Russia passed this turning point in the first decade of this century, which resulted in the transition from the *uyezd* type of agronomy to the district one. In *uyezd* agronomy, one agronomist served the territory of the whole *uyezd*, whereas in district agronomy, the *uyezd* was divided into several small districts (two to three *volosts*), and their small area permitted the quite intensive use of the agronomist's efforts. Intensification of work significantly changed its character. The *uyezd*-agronomy work was not difficult and consisted of two to three usually clear and well-developed paragraphs of the programme.

This does not apply to the work of the local agronomist. When the programme increased its content, it lost its general character. When the agronomist became district and plunged into the real economic life of specific economies, for the first time he faced a production organism in all its specificity. For the first time he not only could but also had to understand a private economy position. He began to evaluate net and gross profitability and their importance for the general organizational plan of the economy; he began to consider economization, use of the labour of people and animals, and the ordering of the money economy. For the first time he carefully analysed the organizational plan of the peasant economy and began to think about its radical reorganization.

District agronomy keeps elements of the programme in the interest of regularity. However, the new district programme generalized a smaller set of economies, which made it much more complex and diverse. As the social-agronomic work deepened, it lost more and more elements of the programme's nature. A typical example of this is the Belgian social agronomy before the German invasion.

Today, as a result of 25 years of agronomic organization efforts, Belgian farmers use rational methods in their fields and stables. The whole country is covered by a network of local communities that emerged from the thick of the rural population. They aim to further improve the country's agriculture.

The agronomist's role lost its initial features described above and gradually became quite different. Today the Belgian agronomist is no longer a propagandist of new ideas who strives to gain people's trust and convince them of the need to improve technologies. Trust was gained long ago; agronomy as a science was recognized long ago; the agronomist does not need to go to the people, but the people come to him.

Thus, we see that not only was the goal of the primary period achieved, but all three tasks set in the first chapter were solved. The social agronomist has increasingly turned into a case adviser, organizer of social-agricultural life, observer, and researcher of new ways.

In general, this is the peculiar nature of the new institution of economic policy, the main features of which are its temporariness and constant changes.

To conclude, it is necessary to consider one social question that is still of concern to agronomic workers: which layers of our peasantry is social agronomy to serve? Should it advocate to the whole peasantry or should it serve only a group of peasant economies in the most conducive position for agronomic progress? In other words, the question is what is the ultimate social goal of social agronomy – to help the local economy or to help the local population?

The most extreme supporters of the former, south Russian agronomists, argue that, for the agronomist 'there is no population, there is only agriculture'. Their opponents, agronomists of the north, object that this is fair for individual members of the agronomic organization. But, as a whole, first comes the population and only then agriculture as one of the most important aspects of this population's life. This contradiction has determined differences in social-agronomic work.

In recent years, the idea of a 'differential programme' has become widespread. It claims that each group of the socially stratified peasantry has its own path to economic progress. This idea poses very difficult organizational questions about the fate of poor economies. It does not allow leaving to their own devices those economies that still do not understand the form of their economic progress.

Chapter 4. Developing an agronomic programme

No branch of the national economy is more dependent on local time-space conditions in its techniques and organizational basis than agriculture. Sometimes, a barely noticeable topography or a railway station fundamentally changes the organizational foundations of agricultural enterprises.

Therefore, general considerations and standards cannot determine the programmes for the activities of social agronomy that aim to heal the ills of this branch of the national economy and organize agricultural production on a new basis. When developing an agronomic plan for the Voronezh or Chernihiv Province, one cannot rely on the social-agronomic programme developed for the Moscow Province. Local workers need to consider local conditions creatively in their agronomic consciousness. They need to develop a programme of activities each of which is determined by a deep and detailed analysis of the local economy.

In this creative work, careful studies are the most important element for the correct diagnosis of agricultural needs and a prerequisite for success. Social agronomy can work confidently only when based on such research results. Otherwise its activities would be misguided, and its success would be random.

On which elements of local life should social-agronomic research focus to gain necessary awareness? Let us identify them in a number of points.

1. First, social agronomy should study in detail the activities of the local area, as well as the borders of this area, the location of rivers, hills, and settlements to easily navigate in the spatial dimension of any observed phenomena.
2. To localize the object of our study in space, we need to localize it in time. To do so, we need to identify the main lines of the historical development of the region and its settlements and the most important stages of its economic development. Only after creating this historical perspective will we fully understand the phenomena of current life and the temporal stages of its agricultural evolution.

3. After localizing the object of our study in space and time, we can start a more detailed analysis. We have to begin with a natural-historical study of the region: its geological past, rock outcroppings, soils, topography, and orography, climatological and geo-botanical data and, finally, pests common in the area. The natural-historical study results in a museum that consists of an herbarium of local flora, mineralogical and soil collections, summary tables, diagrams, cartograms, etc., which we will consider in more detail in the chapter on agronomic equipment.
4. After a study of the natural conditions of the region, we can proceed to a study of the local agricultural technologies. We should surely start with experimental fields and plots and different collective experiments in the area of an agronomist's activities and surrounding territories. Despite the young age of Russian experimental work, it has managed to accumulate extensive, agricultural-cultural experience. However, it exceeds all reports. Therefore, it is absolutely necessary for every worker of social agronomy to study the work of these observatories of agricultural life through personal and repeated visits.
5. Even a comprehensive study of experimental fields and their results will not provide a complete picture of the local agricultural technologies, which makes us pay special attention to the experience of local peasants. The easiest way to study this experience is to visit local, large economies – state, *zemstvo*, or private – because their agricultural experience is the most systematized and studied. However, social agronomy working in the thick of peasant economies should focus on their centuries-old experience. It is very difficult to study because it is often insufficiently considered by the population. It has the form of custom or uncritically accepted tradition, but it is very valuable for agronomy because of its local origin.

Unfortunately, our agronomists are often mesmerized by 'school' agronomy and sometimes fail to consider this peasant experience with due respect. This is a big mistake, because, for ages, technologies of the peasant economy have been selected purely spontaneously for the local conditions and have often turned out to be ideal for them. We can confidently say that any new technology can be mastered successfully only if social agronomy considers it through the local, peasant experience.

Therefore, no matter how difficult the study of the peasant agronomic experience is, it must be studied by observing individual techniques and how they are combined and by analysing their agronomic essence. It must be studied by logically linking actions that are traditionally connected in the peasant mind, so that the peasant economy provides us with a whole system of extremely valuable agronomic knowledge. The study of the evolution of peasant, technical methods and the analysis of the causal dependence of this evolution on economic and technological factors are particularly instructive.

6. Thus, we can summarize the results of natural-historical and agronomic studies of a region in a normal, agricultural calendar that would provide us with a picture of a usual agricultural year.
7. After a study of farming and cattle-breeding technologies and their natural-historical basis, we should proceed to a study of managing peasants. This requires, first of all, an analysis of the ethnographic-demographic composition of the population. A study of the people living in the region, their beliefs, customs, legal and family traditions, and folklore gradually opens the everyday environment of the agricultural production process that interests us and inevitably affects the organization of the economy. The study of the age and gender composition and migrations together with labour forces and consumer units, and, finally, the study of the sanitary conditions and cultural level of the population provide us with a general basic understanding of the object of the future agronomic impact.

8. We have to consider in much more detail the economic mode of life in the region. We have to identify the need for material goods, study the nature of the consumer budget, and explain its sources in general terms. It seems absolutely necessary to study in detail the existing types of the organization of the economy to learn the combination of production elements in all types of labour and capitalist economies, to calculate the costs of production of various goods, the composition of the economies' capitals and forms of their turnover, depreciation rates, profitability, and so on. In other words, we have to describe clearly the existing agricultural enterprises in a private-economic perspective.
9. After the study of the agricultural production in the region in a private-economic perspective, we have to consider those social-economic relations that are based on the production process. When studying land relations, we have to consider the statistics and evolution of land ownership and land use to identify the foundations of the existing forms of community and household ownership, the economic nature of land rent, types of land mobilization, strip holdings of land, etc.

   We should conduct the same detailed analysis of labour relations in the region, its seasonal and local crafts, the processes of differentiation in peasant economies or their levelling-off, capitalization, and other evolutionary processes. It is unnecessary to emphasize that the social-economic relations mentioned above should be considered in an evolutionary perspective. We have to pay special attention to the trends that the economic evolution currently implies and to its factors.
10. It is especially important to focus on a detailed analysis of market relations. We have to study the development of monetary elements in the peasant budget in the region of social-agronomic work; we must consider the local market organization and trace how agricultural products alienated by local economies get to a wider market and how local economies get the purchased products that they consume.

The study of all market conditions is absolutely necessary for organizing agricultural progress, because its opportunities and paths are determined primarily by the market.

11. Within market research, it is important to study the local cooperative movement by focusing on the organization and internal order of cooperative life. At the same time, it is necessary to pay particular attention to the importance of cooperation in the economic life of the region. This requires, on the one hand, studying the relationships of the cooperative economy with member households and, on the other hand, the role of cooperation in local commodity and monetary markets.
12. Other forms of local community work should not be ignored: public education, public sanitation, all activities of the state, and *zemstvo* and public organizations in economic life. It goes without saying that exceptional attention should be paid to social agronomy and its history.
13. Finally, we should make an inventory and study the composition of all cultural strata of the rural population in the region. Like any social work, social agronomy relies on people and can influence agriculture only through people. Therefore, social agronomy has to register and establish close ties with all those living forces in the region who can become pioneers of a new culture. Outstanding peasants, students of agricultural and cooperative courses, leaders of local cooperatives, and rural intellectuals are the first and most important actors of the agronomic influence and major allies of social agronomy. They should be registered, and their possibilities should be used fully. The organization of social ties in the area of the agronomic work is one of its most complex and crucial tasks.

This organization is an outline of the elements that have to be considered when developing the agronomic work programmes. One might say that a detailed and comprehensive study of them requires many years of hard work, numerous scientific institutions, and completely back-breaking social agronomy. Although this is true, we do not propose to put all research work on the shoulders of the agronomic organization. In many cases, it can use the work of statistical offices, soil and geo-botanical expeditions, and the reports of meteorological stations and experimental fields. However, a considerable part of the research is to be conducted only by the agronomic organization. All or nearly all social-agronomic organizations do perform all the tasks mentioned above, because otherwise social-agronomic activities are unthinkable.

Although some data can be found in literature about the above-discussed issues, the remaining data must be collected through the personal research and observations of social-agronomic workers, especially data to diagnose the local agricultural needs and find ways to meet them.

Unfortunately, our social agronomy has not yet developed a methodology of this diagnostic, and the very nature of agronomic work does not suggest any prescriptions or standards. The only thing that we can describe here is a general outline of the stages through which agronomic thought must pass to develop a programme of activities.

The first task of this analytical work is to reveal the discrepancies between the local conditions of economic life and the existing organizational forms of peasant economies. Then, by studying the existing market conditions, taking into account the available and possible productive forces of economies, and analysing the forms and trends of their development, we have been able to identify both the content and direction of the progressive evolution of the local economy.

Without such a projection, any agricultural production is unthinkable; moreover, without predicting a further course for the natural evolution of agriculture, we cannot develop its reform. This work is to provide at least a schematic definition of those organizational forms that represent a kind of economic ideal. After creating such 'ideal' organizational plans, we have to develop forms for their technical implementation in the given soil and climatic conditions.

Having set a goal, we have to develop forms very carefully for the transition from the existing system to the intended ideal. The necessary organic, gradual, and painless restructuring of economies and funding have to be thought out especially carefully and deeply.

Thus, we have fully outlined the reform that economies of the region under study should implement. Let us consider an illustrative example – one of the Moscow-region *uyezds* in a three-field, flax area. The gradually expanding density of the population has made the three-field economy expand cultivated land by ploughing forage land. At the same time, the excess labour force and budget have gradually developed a monetary and labour-intensive flax crop on spring-sown fields at the expense of oats and barley. The reduction of the forage reserve and destruction of the spring straw stocks have undermined the basis of the peasant fodder production and forced peasants to significantly reduce cattle breeding, which has harmed field crop cultivation because it lost the necessary manure fertilizer. All this resulted in economic collapse, and flax that exhausted the soil is gradually reducing its yields.

Market conditions allow the development of flax cultivation and require its economic efficiency. On the other hand, the proximity of Moscow allows the development of dairy production and other forms of productive cattle breeding unknown to the local population in its commercial form. Even the shallowest analysis of the situation proves the need for grass cultivation, which, on the one hand, would compensate for the exhausting effect of flax and strengthen its position in crop rotation. On the other hand, it would provide the necessary forage basis for productive cattle breeding, which requires an improved breed of livestock and the introduction of dairy *artels* and control unions. Dairy factories would provide the economy with skim milk just as the local production of linseed oil provides it with cake. Together, skim milk and linseed cake allow the fattening of calves or pigs.

This is how an organizational ideal is created: flax cultivation is based on proper fodder grass cultivation; grass cultivation is the basis for linseed oil production; skim milk and linseed cake determine the development of swine breeding; sales of flax and linseed oil production can be combined with some other aspects of production. It goes without saying that this 'ideal' can be achieved gradually by the peasant economy by developing grass cultivation and, on this basis, implementing the rest of the reform.

When striving to achieve what is desired, it is necessary to not be carried away by technical effects. This is quite understandable for the agronomist who is passionate about his art, because results that are technically effective often turn out to be of low profit. For instance, it would be a mistake for northern Russia to strive to increase meat-dairy breeds in order to evolve towards breeding dairy cattle.

After developing a plan of economic reform in detail, we have to begin taking those agronomic measures that support the reform, accelerate, and guide it. The first step is to develop an agronomic propaganda programme. Based on the data about the peasant economy and the directions we set for its progressive evolution, we have to identify those elements in the organizational plan of the peasant economy from which its reorganization would start and also the crucial elements for applying the power of agronomic influence.

From the previous chapters, we know that this programme has to be laconic. It has to consist of only those elements that, first, allow the meeting of the general needs of the entire region, and, second, ensure the quickest and most powerful economic-social effect.

Paragraphs of the programme are to be completely technically specified. We should not only promote grass cultivation but also set the recommended crop rotation, the composition of grass mixtures, and the methods of tillage and sowing. In the paragraph about ploughs, we have to name the promoted companies and brands according to the soil and other features of the economy and take into account the type of propulsive force. To improve the livestock production, we have to develop a detailed programme for crossbreeding or breeding depending on the local livestock and economic tasks, etc.

Having set the content of the social-agronomic programme, we have to develop forms of its educational implementation, i.e. to identify by what methods its paragraphs can be implemented. We need to determine in which cases we should use oral propaganda, in which cases we should use demonstrations and experiments, when training courses can be very useful, and where the help of cooperatives is especially needed. Such specification determines the whole set of necessary social-agronomic actions; without such specification we cannot proceed to designing a social-agronomic organization capable of solving all the tasks.

Chapter 5. Agronomic organization

In the previous chapters, we intentionally did not mention the words 'social agronomist' and used the term 'social agronomy' to emphasize that we talk not about individual agronomic workers of the *zemstvo*, state, or cooperative offices, but about the whole public-state institution formed by the unity of actions and the guiding will. This unity of social-agronomic actions is primarily determined by the unity of the organizational plan of the agricultural enterprise. Because it is impossible to consider any branch of agriculture separately from all others, measures for changing any branch of the economy should not be implemented without careful coordination with measures affecting other branches of this economy. Therefore, the whole institution of social agronomy rather than individual specialists has to diagnose local agricultural needs, develop programmes of social-agronomic work, and control their implementation.

As we already know, forms of social-agronomic work are extremely diverse. They range from oral presentations, visual presentations that vary from wall posters to demonstrations of machinery, to a model experiment or a whole model plot. They also include popular literature and agricultural periodicals, organizations of all kinds of *zemstvo* enterprises, participation in cooperatives, special technical consultations for peasants, and other forms. If we admit that social agronomy constantly needs tireless research as the only basis for its productive activities, then the scope of the social-agronomic actions becomes extremely large and diverse and requires a great variety of knowledge and practical skills. It is obvious that to implement all the above-mentioned measures, we need a large staff of different specialists who would organize their work on the principle of complex cooperation and more or less follow the principle of the division of labour. In other words, gathering staff for social agronomy is a serious and complex organizational challenge.

The art of the organizer of large-scale activities implies the successful achievement of three main goals.

1. It is necessary to divide a complex action into a series of elementary processes – simple to perform and accessible to the average performer.
2. It is necessary to coordinate the whole mass of individual elementary processes in time and space to ensure an overall result of their coordinated action.
3. When setting goals and dividing complex actions, it is necessary to rely strictly on the means at the disposal of the organizer and to pay special attention to the correct account of forces and abilities. On the one hand, it is unacceptable to put difficult and hard work on the shoulders of people who cannot cope because of personal qualities; on the other hand, it is economically and socially not profitable to involve qualified employees in the tasks that can be solved by less gifted and trained people.

A good illustration are usual statistical censuses; their technique has been perfectly developed in recent decades. According to the statistical tasks, one day the census institution is to talk with millions of the country's residents and ask them personally about the gender and age composition of their families, employment, literacy, etc. These data are to be calculated and studied in detail in different perspectives in the shortest possible time, which is an extremely difficult task.

However, a well-developed method makes it easy to solve. The country is divided into census areas and smaller regions that are divided into census divisions – small territories administered by experienced statisticians; the census division is divided into a few dozen enumeration districts to which census takers are assigned.

Before the census day, the special staff prepares lists of villages and, for cities, lists of householders based on old data and preliminary surveys. In each enumeration district, a sufficient number of questionnaires is prepared (one per resident), in which the census questions are specified and printed together with columns for answers. The questionnaires are given to every census taker.

A few days before the census, the census taker goes around his district, informs the population about the future census, collects preliminary data and sometimes distributes census forms for self-reporting. On the census day, the census taker visits all residents, collects the completed forms or fills them in himself. All this work is monitored by the head of the enumeration district and his assistant. The collected data are checked and criticized by inspectors who pass the data to the special staff preparing questionnaires for counting. Workers in the statistical office group the questionnaires according to various criteria and then count them. The results are grouped in special tables and counted by other workers. The final results are analysed by scientists who write and publish the census report.

Thus, we see how a complex task is divided into a number of elementary ones, how elementary actions aimed at solving elementary tasks are coordinated in time and space, and how coordination of elementary actions ensures a general complex result. Something similar should be done with any complex task, including the social-agronomic work.

When solving separate tasks given to him, every agronomic worker can devote all his attention and energy to only the technical aspects of solving tasks. However, the will of the entire social agronomy institution that guides him has to combine the individual actions of agronomic workers to ensure a unified impact on agriculture as a whole, taking into account its social-economic complexity.

When describing specific forms that allow solutions to organizational problems, first we have to emphasize that the existing types of agronomic organizations are determined not so much by the logical development of some organizational idea as by the historical evolution that depends on and adapts to a variety of temporal-spatial conditions. Therefore, in different countries and even different regions of the same country, we see various organizational types of social-agronomic work that are determined by differences in the structure of the state and society. They are also determined by the struggle of social groups and classes and, finally, by the structure of those organizations that were founders and developers of social agronomy.

Often, we see pathological forms and even competing agronomic organizations that are hostile to each other. Moreover, forms of agronomic organizations are never ossified. They constantly move from one phase of evolutionary development to another and change under the pressure of changes in the content of agronomic work and even under the influence of the social-political conditions of the time.

In Russia, this evolution has already completed three stages in the development of the organizational forms of social agronomy. Those stages are: 1) when there was one agronomist per *uyezd* – the extensive stage; 2) the district agronomy development – when intensification of agronomic work determined an increase in the number of agronomic workers in proportion to the territory and limited the area of each agronomist's activities to a relatively small one; and 3) the current period, which combines the work of district agronomists with the work of specialists in different sectors of the economy. This marks the further intensification of agronomic work. Each stage produced its own relevant organizational forms.

Our tasks do not include an ideographic description of the history of agronomic organizations. Therefore, we will focus on the study of the main organizational issues. To understand clearly the organizational features of any agronomic organization, we have to answer the following questions:

1. Of what people and bodies does the agronomic organization consist?
2. Which bodies set tasks and questions of the social-agronomic work?
3. Which bodies make decisions and, according to them, develop programmes of the social-agronomic actions?

4. Which departments authorize these decisions and approve the developed measures?
5. How is the executive apparatus organized?
6. How is the unity of the social-agronomic will ensured?
7. How are accounting and control over the social-agronomic work ensured?
8. How is the system of the social-agronomic measures funded?

When using these questions to consider the existing agronomic organizations of Russia, Western Europe, and America, we first have to admit that agronomic organizations are very rarely established as free enterprises of people who unite in education societies, labour *artels* of agronomists, or special consulting agronomic bureaus for ideas or earnings. In most cases, agronomic organizations are created by the rural population, represented by the state, local self-governments, or cooperatives to meet their agricultural needs.

This fact affects the nature of agronomic organizations by creating them from two elements: first, elected representatives of the local population (*zemstvo* administrations or boards of cooperatives); and second, invited specialist agronomists doing the work. This dualism in the organizational structure extremely complicates the issues of the governing will, initiative, control, and so on.

On the one hand, certainly, representatives of the most organized population have to play a guiding role, because this population will 'acquire' an agronomic organization to serve its needs. Therefore, it has to set tasks, lead in their development and solution according to local needs and conditions, control all works, and request reports. On the other hand, it is equally certain that the social agronomist should not be a soulless executor of someone's orders. Slave psychology is unacceptable in the creative work of the agronomist, where sometimes enthusiastic inspiration means much more than methodological diligence.

Because of its importance, the work of social agronomy goes beyond *uyezds* and provinces. The rise of the country's agricultural life is a common civil concern, and the agronomist who dedicates his life to this great concern is the same public figure as an elected representative of the population. He certainly serves not so much the population of a certain patch of land as the task of the general, agricultural revival of his homeland.

Therefore, because councils and boards of cooperatives represent the local population, agronomists of agronomic organizations represent social agronomy. Some social agronomists even argue that the population representatives are only to set tasks and the general direction of work and to approve reports, whereas the rest – specification of tasks, development of relevant measures, their implementation and control – should be provided only by practical workers, i.e. the third element.

We do not agree with this extreme point of view and believe instead that the whole scope of work should be performed by a board consisting of representatives of both the local population and the agronomic community. On issues of a general and fundamental nature, representatives of the local population should have some dominance, and on technical-organizational issues, representatives of the agronomic work should.

According to this rule, the Russian *zemstvo* agronomy developed two types of collegiate bodies governing the work of social agronomy: the economic council and the agronomic council. The former consists mainly of elected representatives of the population, is in charge of all fundamental issues of the region's economic life, and is responsible to the *zemstvo* assembly of heads of social-agronomic work and other economic activities. In contrast, the agronomic council consists mainly of representatives of the agronomic community, i.e. the third element. The agronomic council directs the work of agronomists within the domains set by the economic council and has to pre-develop all issues submitted to the economic council.

These are the bodies that represent the organized social-agronomic mind and will, directing and governing agronomic work under the supreme supervision and sanction of the population represented by the *zemstvo* assembly.

Let us now proceed to the analysis of the executive staff. When comparing Italian and Russian social agronomies, we can distinguish two types of executive staff: in Italy, the area served by the agronomic organization (*cattedra ambulanta*) is not divided, and all members of the organization serve it together, sometimes specializing in a particular sector of the economy; that is, the division of labour is object-oriented. In Russia, after the introduction of district agronomy, the agronomic organization is based on the principle of the territorial division of labour, and the majority of work is performed by district agronomists serving a certain small territory in all sectors of agriculture. This organizational type is based on the unity of the organizational plan of the peasant economy and on the fact that all its sectors are so closely connected that any separation is undesirable.

However, this principle does not contradict the availability of specialists who serve certain sectors of the economy: they specialize in animal husbandry, dairy husbandry, gardening and horticulture, beekeeping, flax cultivation, and cooperation. They all collaborate with district agronomists in the technical consulting of the population in different sectors of the economy and do not influence the work of district agronomists on changing the organization of economies in general. Thus, even with the assistance of technical specialists, agronomic reform and its management are entirely the duty and responsibility of district agronomists.

The object-oriented division of labour in agronomic organizations is not limited to the division of the staff into district agronomists and specialists. It goes further and introduces the position of the *uyezd* agronomist. His duties include representing the agronomic organization, bookkeeping and reports, counselling *zemstvo* administrations on agricultural issues, and supervising all-*uyezd* agronomic institutions and undertakings, such as agricultural warehouses, courses for peasants, exhibitions, etc. The duties of the district agronomist are sometimes performed in turn by all district agronomists. They are performed more often by the district agronomist of a suburban area and are significantly reduced to make his work easier. However, as a rule, the all-*uyezd* special duties are so numerous that a special person with a special assistant clerk is needed to perform them.

The special *uyezd* agronomist sometimes does not have a special position on the agronomic board. Because of his personal authority, he becomes a spiritual leader for the entire agronomic family. Sometimes he becomes the formal head of the agronomic organization and personifies its will, ensures its unity, and possesses the right to control and inspect the work of other members of the board.

Besides the already mentioned positions, the agronomic staff includes 'support personnel' who are not a part of the agronomic board and perform only executive functions. They include all kinds of agricultural headmen, master-hands, junior instructors, and so on. 'Trainees' hold an intermediate position between agronomists and support personnel. These future agronomists are mainly students who do their practical training as agronomic support staff.

This is, in short, the system of the *uyezd* social-agronomic organization practically developed by the Russian *zemstvo* agronomy [...] The *uyezd* social-agronomic organization is a complete, working organism and a part of the provincial agronomic organization. The relationships of the *uyezd* organization with the provincial organization are still to be established by agronomic practice.

Uyezd zemstvos and provincial *zemstvos* are not subordinate, and the division of their work in most branches is based on cooperation that should not limit the independence, equality, and freedom of *zemstvos'* initiatives. According to the Russian agronomic congresses, the local practical work is to be done by *uyezd* agronomic organizations, whereas the provincial *zemstvo* is to unite the activities of *uyezd zemstvos*, to develop common provincial activities initiated by provincial or *uyezd zemstvos*, and to support financially the weakest *uyezd zemstvos*. Moreover, the provincial *zemstvo* can take independent social-agronomic measures that are of general importance or impossible for individual *uyezd zemstvos*: research, courses, experiments, zootechnical measures, etc.

In its structure, the provincial agronomic organization is similar to the collegiate bodies of the *uyezd* organization. Its distinctive feature is that a significant part of the provincial agronomic council or congress and almost the entire executive staff are representatives of *uyezd*s and are not in the service of the provincial *zemstvo*. Therefore, the unity of the agronomic will and its working discipline are maintained only by the authority of the provincial organization and indirectly by the financial dependence of some *uyezd zemstvos* on the provincial *zemstvo*.

This is the scheme of the extremely complex Russian agronomic organization. Because of the introduction of the *volost zemstvo*, this scheme will change significantly, but this is a matter for the future, which we have no data to predict.

To conclude our essay, we will consider one extremely important and pressing issue of agronomic development. As we have already shown, the governing will in social-agronomic work belongs to collegiate bodies, but the practical work remains individual. It is very important to find out for what cases the collegiality of decisions is absolutely necessary and for what cases the right to decide can be granted to executors.

A lack of collegiality destroys the unity of agronomic work and weakens its unanimity and strength. On the other hand, the application of a collegial form of discussions and solutions to a very wide range of everyday agronomic issues leads to 'collegiality hypertrophy', which makes us spend more time on endless meetings than on work. There are cases in which agronomists have spent more than 100 days at meetings in a year. Certainly, this situation is undesirable. We believe that only issues of fundamental importance, guiding activities of local workers, or of a general nature are subject to collegial decisions. The unity of the agronomic will can be ensured by cooperation of *uyezd* and provincial agronomists responsible in every action to the collegiate bodies and acting on their behalf and by their authority.

Chapter 6. Methods of oral, social-agronomic propaganda

The main weapon of the social agronomist is his words. Live speech is the most important means of changing minds and the only way for extensive social work. The social agronomist spends most of his time on oral, pedagogical work – talking with groups of peasants in taverns and teahouses – sometimes at peasant gatherings, cooperative meetings, or 'meetings of the agricultural society'; giving lectures; and organizing training courses.

In his cultural, pedagogical work, the social agronomist is not alone – *zemstvo* organizers with education obtained out of school, political propagandists, and cooperative instructors work with him. Thousands of conversations and lectures, hundreds of peasant courses, people's houses, libraries, cooperative meetings, and the Russian rural theatre movement prove the pedagogical significance of the current period in the history of the Russian peasantry. Our village was never under such a powerful, educational influence. Certainly, its success will depend mainly on how well its actors are trained for their pedagogical work.

The majority of today's workers – agronomists, lawyers, natural scientists, economists, and philologists – have no theoretical training in pedagogy. Therefore, when taking up the task of mass pedagogical work, they are forced to find its methods with great difficulty, by trial and error. The lack of special training dooms them to making unacceptable mistakes, about which we constantly hear. They often take several years to discover the pedagogical Americas that were already known in the days of Jan Amos Komenský. Thus, we have to include the huge pedagogical experience of humankind in the training of future cultural workers of the village.

Someone might object that the lecturer's work is a part art, and that no science can make someone a good lecturer. We agree but still argue that if science cannot make someone a lecturer, it can help him to become a lecturer. If someone is to become an educator, knowledge of the organized experiences of humans would certainly help his work. Knowledge of the key features of the object of pedagogical work, of the methods to influence his mind, memory, and will according to his mental abilities, of the techniques of such influence – these are the necessary weapons of every agronomist, cooperative organizer, and lecturer.

The need for such training has long been known and recognized. We do not see it in real life primarily because of a lack of relevant works. Most theoretical teachers focus on teaching methods for children and youth rather than on the out-of-school methods for uncultured adults. In the Tula or Yaroslavl Provinces, the psychology of a 40-year-old peasant as an object of pedagogical influence is significantly different from a 7-year-old, American schoolboy. Therefore, pedagogical techniques successfully applied to the latter do not guarantee success when applied to the former. Thus, in addition to already collected, and systematized, pedagogical experiences, it is necessary to conduct a special study of our object and use the still unsystematized experience accumulated by the work of agronomists, cooperation instructors, and lecturers of people's universities.

Certainly, this book does not aim to fill the above-mentioned gap in pedagogical work but rather sets a more modest task – to outline in the most general terms those pedagogical issues, which every lecturer faces when speaking to people and about which the author of this book and his colleagues in the cooperative and agronomic work have repeatedly thought.

The first of these issues is the task of the lecturer in speaking to people. The assessment of the methods and results of his work is possible only if we know its goals and only in terms of their achievement. There are four groups of the numerous tasks of the people's lecturer: first, to provide the audience with new ideas and, thus, to broaden its world-view. In many of the darkest corners of our homeland, this task is the most important. For instance, the cultural workers of the Volyn Province visited villages in which the whole world of the peasants was limited to a radius of five *versts* (1.06 km). In the regions of commercial seasonal work, this radius is larger, but the peasant's world-view is still very constricted.

In such circumstances, the lecturer has to enrich the peasant's world-view not only with new representations related to his course – separators, chemical analysis, artificial fertilizers, consumer shops, secretaries, accounting books, etc. – but also with many general cultural, geographical, and natural-historical representations.

The second task of the lecturer, which is much more complex, is to explain new concepts and systematize the old ones for the peasant audience. The first part of this task – the presentation of the concepts still unknown in the village (cooperation, production credit, Raiffeisen principles, chemical processes, and elements, etc.) – is very complex. Nevertheless, it does not face the obstacles of the second part of the task, which is the rational organization of the traditional concepts.

The peasant's thinking is empirical in nature, a common example of which is folk omens, such as 'red sunset means windy tomorrow', 'on St. George's Day take your cattle to pasture', etc. The peasant's mind mechanically connects two representations or concepts as constantly related without rationalizing or explaining their relationship, and uses it as an empirically established law. In the same way, there is a historically established, empirical relationship of some concepts that make up the peasant world-view – 'women are long of hair and short of brains', 'it's a sin to plough on a Holy Day', etc. Different peasant representations and concepts are connected by the elementary empirical relationships-statements. The entire, centuries-old life of a peasant consists of everyday skills and a rigid collection of disconnected statements that lack flexibility and cannot be logically systematized.

The people's lecturers have the honorary task of rationalizing this experience, making it flexible and changeable, and transferring the peasant from the path of empirical thinking to the path of logical thinking. In other words, the lecturer is to radically change the entire organization of peasant thinking by replacing everyday experience with logical reasoning.

These two key tasks are not the most important ones. Informing the peasant audience about new ideas and concepts and systematizing the centuries-old, peasant experience allow the peasants to stay completely passive. However, if we seek the revival of the Russian village, the most valuable path for the peasant audience is the active and deedful perception of the foundations of the new culture. We have to raise a number of pressing questions and draw the attention and will of our listeners to them.

Moreover, these questions should not be rhetorical, should not be determined by the construction of our lecture, but should be clear for our listeners. These questions should interest the listener; in his soul, there should be a persistent thought – 'How can we really solve this question?' Without such a thought in the listener's soul, our lecture loses two-thirds of its meaning, because our main task is not to inform the population of as many new ideas and facts as possible, but to wake up the initiative of the population and direct it to the right path.

It would be a miserable utopia to think that the reform of the Russian economic and cultural foundations can be implemented by creating recipes and by having agronomists or cooperative instructors instruct all peasant economies individually. We play the role of the fermentation enzyme that sets in motion powerful spontaneous forces. Only the self-active peasantry can implement the economic reforms that we dream about.

This ultimate goal of our work determines the fourth task of our lecturer – to give his audience an emotional impetus, to share with his audience the social energy inherent in the powerful stream of the Russian revival. Without such an emotional impulse, our lectures are just curious stories about how the German peasant sowed clover or how profitably the Danish peasants sold eggs in cooperation, but such lectures would lack the necessary feature of the social progress engine.

Thus, the lecturer of the people's audience faces four groups of tasks: 1) to broaden the listeners' horizon of thinking and enrich it with new ideas; 2) to create a series of new concepts in the minds of listeners and organize all their empirical experience; 3) to pose a number of questions to the audience; and 4) to give listeners an emotional impulse to awaken their initiative.

When starting to achieve these tasks, the thoughtful lecturer has to think about an issue that requires very careful consideration. In addition to the concepts from the peasant world-view and experience, upon which we can build our lectures, there are many concepts and ideas that contradict contemporary science and ethics – for instance, the well-known idea of the chariot of Elijah-the-Prophet as the generator of heavenly thunder. Should we fight these false concepts and try to erase them from the peasant consciousness, or should we accept the amorphous and fragmented nature of such outlooks and ignore those false ideas when developing a scientific world-view in the peasant mind? The latter is the only acceptable path for the lecturer. If he starts a debate about the centuries-old images and concepts, he often does not have enough authority to refute them, but, in the attempt, he revives these false images and ideas in the listener's mind. Moreover, we cannot answer the straightforward question: does a drill-seeder or the chariot of Elijah-the-Prophet rumble in the thunderclouds?

It seems that the task of the Russian revival is to enrich the peasant thinking with a contemporary, scientific world-view without breaking the centuries-old epic: in the practical world, the chariot of Elijah-the-Prophet must give way to the electric charge, but outside the practical life, it should become a legend and take a place of honour in peasant everyday life.

When identifying how to solve the above-set tasks, we first have to consider the object of our influence – the peasant audience – in a pedagogical perspective, because its nature and features are the starting point for developing our training courses. People's lectures should be based on the ideas and concepts of the listener. When starting his course, every lecturer should mobilize all elements of the peasant experience that he needs and use them as a basis for new ideas and representations. If the lecturer forgets this basic rule, he risks losing firm ground and speaking incomprehensibly to his audience.

However, despite the fact that all the above has long been recognized by all representatives of out-of-school education, there is still no detailed analysis of the adult peasant audience as a pedagogical object. Nevertheless, it is obvious that this audience is fundamentally different from both children and students. In many ways, the soul of a child is a blank sheet for the teacher. It has few representations and almost no concepts or general ideas, which allows the teacher to choose the circle of representations and ideas that will become the content of this young soul and set the sequence of their perception. In other words, the teacher is free in pedagogical plans.

The situation is different when the educator meets an already grown adult. He has limited freedom, and, in his pedagogical work, he should proceed from his student's type of thinking. In one of his conversations with agronomic students, V.A. Kilchevsky compared student and peasant audiences and identified their difference. He concluded that the student audience is exceptionally full of general ideas and concepts and, to the same extent, lacks specific representations, whereas the peasant audience, on the contrary, is full of practical ideas and has almost no abstract concepts.

Such a difference determined two completely different pedagogical tasks for these one-sided world-views with different types of one-sidedness. According to one of the greatest thinkers of the 18th century, 'Thoughts *without* content are *empty*; intuitions *without* concepts are *blind*.' These words describe the difference in our pedagogical tasks: in one case, we have to help the blind to see; in the other case, we have to fill the emptiness of abstract representations with specific content.

It would be strange for the lecturer to a peasant audience to develop his course as a series of syllogisms based on some general idea absent in the minds of his listeners. Certainly, the more relevant way for argumentation would be an analysis of specific examples and a purely inductive approach to the general idea.

Besides the above-mentioned features of the peasant audience common to all its listeners, we should take into account its typical diversity. This is not a student audience made homogeneous by monotonous preparation of the secondary school and by the selection procedures of higher education; this is not a children's audience homogeneous due to the lack of life experience. This is an audience that consists of both old peasants hardened by the three-field agricultural life, foster-children of the *zemstvo* school, and experienced city industrialists, literate and illiterate, who either read newspapers every day or never read a line, etc. It is impossible to identify an 'average listener' to whom to adapt your presentation, because this audience consists of separate groups that differ by readiness to listen to your words.

The experienced lecturer takes this fact into account and acts differently depending on his goals. When the task is wide, mass propaganda, he focuses on the least prepared group and either bores the more informed and well-read listeners or carries them away with an interesting form of presentation. When the course focuses on a few trained workers, the lecturer ignores the least prepared groups. Many lecturers develop their courses for all groups – repeat each section of the programme twice or thrice with varying degrees of popularity and completeness; if the lecturer is experienced and talented, this method gives good results. However, we recommend, whenever possible, to divide listeners into groups according to their level of knowledge and training and to give lectures to each group separately.

In general terms, these are our tasks and the object of our influence. What pedagogical techniques should we use to enrich this object with ideas, concepts, and representations that make up the content of our courses? Certainly, pedagogy does not provide us with any universal method of giving lectures. The individuality of the lecturer, the nature of the data presented, the task of the lecturer, and, finally, the type of audience determines the choices and changes of pedagogical techniques.

Therefore, when studying how to present different issues, first we have to abandon the idea of finding a universal recipe and limit our task to the critical consideration of the existing methods for organizing courses. The most famous among them is Herbart's scheme – 'formal steps in teaching': 1) preparation, 2) presentation, 3) association, 4) generalization, and 5) application.

As a first step – preparation – the lecturer reminds the audience about already known facts; he mobilizes the listeners' experience, which he needs, and connects this experience with his presentation, i.e. he prepares the basis for his lecture. The preparation step should be sufficient for the listener to remember the whole set of ideas and concepts necessary for understanding the further presentation. This step should not be too long so as not to tire the listener nor waste a significant part of his attention necessary for further and more important sections of the course. The American psychologist-educator Dewey compared the audience's holding up the process for a long time at the preparation step with a jumper who takes such a long run that he can hardly jump over the hurdle.

At the second step – presentation – our task is to enrich the audience's experience with new ideas and data. We have to be extremely choosy and economical when selecting them so as not to overload our lecture with unnecessary content, which is, unfortunately, very typical for beginning lecturers. Human memory, attention, and perceptive ability are very limited, and their overload rusts and hinders the understanding of ideas and data. For instance, lecturers make a huge mistake when they press the semester course on soil science at the Petrovsky Agricultural Academy into a two-hour peasant lecture. The amount of information presented should be both necessary and sufficient; unfortunately, only the lecturer's personal experience can provide him with a sense of proportion in giving lectures.

At the third step – association – we systematize information, compare it with the previous experience and eliminate particularities of the examples considered. This gradually leads to the fourth step – generalization of the new and old experiences of the audience and recognition of some new concepts. Thus, according to Herbart, in the first part of the scheme, the lecturer first approaches the solution of two tasks set in the introduction in a purely inductive way. Having enriched the minds of his listeners with new concepts, the lecturer has to fix them and make them effective elements of peasant thinking, which is achieved by relating them to the rest of the peasant world and by describing their application in some cases. The fifth step – application – is purely deductive in nature and completes the scheme of 'formal steps in teaching'.

Thus, the full scheme of 'formal steps in teaching' is mainly inductive: the lecturer mobilizes his experience and accepts some new ideas; then he generalizes this systematized and concentrated information to identify the necessary concepts and generalized conclusions. There can be (and it is often used) a completely opposite, purely deductive type of the course. At the preparation step, the lecturer reminds the audience of some general concepts and ideas, then, by a series of reasoning, he puts them into a desired form and makes some deductive conclusions that make up the subject of his course.

Two examples will be enough to prove the difference. For instance, when developing a general course on cooperation, the inductive method of presentation allows the identification of needs and hopes of the peasant economy. Then a description of the types of cooperatives, their work, and benefits of cooperation illustrates all the above with specific examples. To compare cooperative institutions with capitalist enterprises, identify the Raiffeisen and Rochdale principles and conclude by the main cooperative ideas, tasks of cooperation, its significance for social life, and its future.

This course could be organized in a completely different way based on the deductive method of presentation. First, we have to remind the listeners about ideas of solidarity, mutual assistance, and community by appealing to their knowledge and life experience, and explain the role of these ideas in different aspects of social life and in the peasant economic life. Then we should describe the benefits of mutual assistance and joint efforts in various areas of the economy together with the specific types of cooperatives. Their organizational foundations (Rochdale and Raiffeisen principles) should be deduced from the requirements of the basic ideas of solidarity and equality. We should conclude by presenting some examples of the meaning of cooperatives for meeting the needs of the peasant economy.

Another example is teaching cooperative bookkeeping. With the deductive method, the lecturer presents the ideas of economic accounting to emphasize their importance for cooperation and to explain the basics of double accounting and its features determined by the cooperative requirements. Then, to prove all the above, the lecturer explains that it is based on the analysis of the main book of accounting and its balance. This should be followed by a description of auxiliary books and, finally, by an explanation of separate notes on the phenomena under study.

The course based on the inductive method of presentation is organized differently. First, the lecturer considers some economic operations of the cooperative, identifies their key features that require registration and describes the auxiliary books needed for it. After making sure that the listeners have learned the nature and method of preparing auxiliary books, the lecturer copies all records to the main book to check the balance and calculate profitability. When analysing the already studied data, he explains the accounting system under consideration, compares it with other systems, and concludes by emphasizing the importance of proper accounting and the very idea of accounting in economic life.

When comparing both methods as applied to the peasant audience, we give preference to the inductive method of presentation. This is because, according to the deductive method, the lecturer starts from general concepts and ideas, which are often missing in the minds of his listeners. Moreover, peasant thinking is traditionally very specific; therefore, it very slowly perceives logical reasoning and lags behind the course of deductions of the intelligent lecturer who is used to quick logical thinking gained in his profession and training.

Peasants lack a habit of logical reasoning and abstract ideas. This has been determined by the general rule that the peasant audience follows more easily the lecturer who proceeds from representations to concepts rather than from concepts to representations. Therefore, we prefer the inductive method for the peasant audience, whereas the widespread use of deductive representations for the more highly educated audience is absolutely right and saves much time.

Critics of both methods argue that they require tremendous and active listeners' attention for they do not provide any incentive for attention or interest in the subject. For the peasant audience, this critical remark is of particular importance. When the peasant not used to mental work listens to a long presentation, comparison, and generalization or deductive construction of the general ideas, he often does not understand the logic of the presentation, becomes distracted, and turns a deaf ear to many important points of the 'concentrated information'.

Once I visited a lecture organized according to Herbart's full scheme: after the practical conclusion of the lecturer ('application'), the listeners demanded that he repeat the middle part of the lecture for they had not listened to it at all and did not understand its meaning, but, at the end of the lecture, they realized how important the middle part was. The critics suggest to change the logical structure of the presentation according to its aims, i.e. to begin with a clear and accurate explanation of its practical meaning and tasks, to continue with a list of issues that will be considered, and, having drawn the attention of the audience, to proceed to the gradual solution of the tasks. Certainly, the solution of the tasks can be both inductive and deductive.

In addition to the above-mentioned logical types of the course's programme, lecturers often choose other types of presentation which are based not on the logical development of discussion but on other forms of connecting different aspects of the training programme. One of the typical examples is a very common historical presentation, i.e. the presentation of scientific knowledge as a description of the history of science. For instance, according to one basic, biological law, individual development reproduces the development of the whole species in all its phases. Proponents of the historical method apply this law to spiritual development and argue that for every person the easiest way to learn contemporary, scientific knowledge is to study it in the exact sequence of its historical development.

The detailed reconstruction of the history of science for presenting its foundations is often used in higher education for courses in philosophy, the natural sciences, and other disciplines, because this method has obvious advantages. It contributes to the understanding of concepts by analysing their origins in a specific historical period, which facilitates the further use of these concepts. On the other hand, by the logical analysis of every era of scientific data and findings, the lecturer repeatedly considers the same subjects and deepens their analysis, thus, taking full advantage of the concentric teaching method.

We can recommend this method for the peasant cooperative courses too, although its meaning for a peasant audience is somewhat different from a student audience. In peasant courses, a general course on cooperation can have the following programme: the beginnings of cooperation among people and animals; cooperative initiatives before the early 19th century; a history of Rochdale pioneers; development of cooperation in England; Raiffeisen and Schulze-Delitzsch; a history of cooperation in Germany; unions of cooperators in Western Europe; the power of the contemporary cooperative movement in Russia. Such a method of presentation broadens peasant horizons with new, historical and geographical representations, and lectures take the form of a curious and interesting story.

For the lecturer, such a programme implies a chronological sequence of presentation, and the narrative form of lectures means less stress than logical proofs and the above-mentioned types of presentation. However, the lecturer must remember that his task is still to describe the foundations of the cooperative movement with the historical method of presentation rather than to inform his listeners about the historical development of the contemporary cooperative movement. Therefore, the lecturer should not overload his course with historical details and comparisons unnecessary for understanding the basic principles of the cooperative movement. Another limitation of the historical method is its weakness in organizing the peasant experience and in teaching logical thinking to the peasant audience.

All the above-mentioned teaching methods are based on a positive presentation of the subject, i.e. on describing and assessing its inherent features. An opposite method presents the subject by identifying its differences from other important subjects. 'B is not A due to the following difference, but B is not C due to the following difference.' In a general course on cooperation, this method would determine the following programme: the differences between cooperative and forced unions (state and local government); the differences between the cooperative as a union of economically individual members and the communist community; the differences of the cooperative from other freely organized economic unions, such as partnerships on shares, joint-stock companies, etc.

This method of presentation sorts the necessary concepts by their selection and division into parts. If there is skilful practical implementation, this method ensures great clarity and understandability of the concepts presented to the listeners. However, we would not recommend this method to the beginning lecturer, because, in a boring presentation, the statement 'B is not A' can lose the part 'not', which would make it 'B is A' in the perception and memory of the listener.

I remember from my childhood a book *Demonstrative Inconsistencies* that showed a cow at the top of a spruce, a man cutting down the branch on which he is sitting, a water-carrier with two sieves on a rocker, and so on. I do not know the benefits of this book for other children, but for many years I could not get rid of false associations that unconsciously became a part of my memory. The same can happen with listeners to a course based on the negative method (denial).

These are five types of presentation designed for the conscious perception of the subject. However, the consciousness of perception cannot be considered a necessary part of teaching. Pedagogical practice has methods for the purely mechanical introduction of concepts and ideas into the mind of listeners. A direct statement made with sufficient conviction and repeated many times often achieves greater results than a complex system of arguments and evidence.

It is believed that Napoleon said, 'Repetition is the best evidence', which is fairly true, especially for an audience that is empirically minded and unable to think logically. This method is the basis of many demagogical tricks and of the power of short political slogans; thus, it would be a mistake for the lecturer not to use such a powerful pedagogical weapon for the people's audience. Such a dogmatic method of presentation is especially relevant for the first stages of cooperative propaganda. However, the principle of repetition can and should be applied within all methods of presentation, and it is the basis of the most advanced 'concentric teaching method'. Its main idea is that when the lecturer starts the presentation of the subject, he first describes it in the most general terms and then presents it again in more detail. Finally, having prepared listeners with two presentations and having introduced into their minds some very important concepts, the lecturer proceeds to the last detailed presentation.

A gradual presentation, repetition, and diversity of the analysis allow the concentric teaching method to ensure the most profound and conscious perception. At the final step, the audience is well prepared and understands the relative importance of each part of the course. In 1913, at the Old-Believers' agricultural courses at the Rogozhsky cemetery, I tried to organize my general course on cooperation on the basis of the concentric method by arranging the course in the following three stages: 1) a general presentation of the foundations of cooperation by the inductive method; 2) a more detailed presentation of the basic principles of the cooperative movement by the historical method; and 3) a detailed description of the organizational forms of various types of cooperation by the deductive method. The most important issue in organizing a course on the basis of the concentric method is a different presentation or grouping of the data at each stage, because simple repetition of the already presented information, albeit in an expanded form, would be extremely boring for the audience and would significantly reduce its attention.

These are the most important types of lecture programmes. The description of the concentric method shows that it allows a mixed type of presentation: the lecturer divides the course into sections and presents each by the most relevant method. However, regardless of the method chosen for the programme, this very choice constitutes only the first preparatory part of work: having developed a logical programme, we should still think about forms of its pedagogical implementation.

The development of the programme depends not only on lectures but also on the lecturer's knowledge and skills. He has to select data according to the programme, sort them, systematize them, arrange them in the required sequence and choose the form of their oral presentation. It is not enough to structure the lecture; it has to be staged perfectly. The latter circumstance is especially important, because the logical structure does not exhaust the possibilities of the lecturer. When he mounts the rostrum, the lecturer has to remember that his audience is not a mechanical perceiving apparatus; it is something alive and constantly changing. Moreover, the audience's attention is very fragile and quickly wanes. At the beginning of the lecture, it is completely different from at its end; therefore, the lecturer should monitor the state of attention, refresh it, and arrange his presentation according to the expected changes in the audience's attention.

Also, the lecturer should remember that the speed of his speech often exceeds the speed of the people's audience perception, and that the audience's perception ability can be accelerated and deepened by including visual illustrations or special techniques of verbal presentation in the oral lecture. If the lecturer takes into account all these psychological aspects, he can use some techniques to quadruple his pedagogical impact.

We have already mentioned the meaning of repetition – one of the most favourite and developed techniques of oratorical eloquence. In addition to the simple repetition of word-for-word or repetition of the same phrase, which are important for the lecturer, there is also another very common type of repetition: after introducing an idea, the lecturer repeats it in a slightly different combination of words, representations, and concepts. Such a masked repetition does not annoy the audience; it enhances perception and plays for time of the subject perception, which is especially important for the peasant audience; therefore, this type of repetition is one of the favourite techniques of the spiritual eloquence that prevails in the people's audience.

One of the most skilful forms of this technique is a quotation that strengthens an idea by the authority of the cited author. Another type of the technique is repetition of what was just said written in chalk on the blackboard – final conclusions, names of the authors cited, historical names, dates, or some numbers.

Analogy is also a form of this technique, and it often affects the people's audience more effectively than any logical proof. It is much easier for the peasant whose thinking is not flexible and who is not used to logical reasoning, to identify the issue under consideration as related to some other issue, with similar elements that have already been solved by ordinary everyday skills, than to develop long argumentation. In general, logical evidence plays a completely different role for the peasant audience than for higher education and literature. With peasants, one has to be extremely economical so as not to overload the lecture, because the number and exhaustive completeness of the argument are less important than its strength. Therefore, the lecturer should choose two or three most convincing arguments that would be better preserved in the peasant memory than 10 or 20 arguments of equal value but more boring for the audience.

It goes without saying that the sequence of arguments should ensure the constant increase in the power of argumentation; therefore, it is of no use to present weaker arguments after the stronger ones. Despite the desirability of saving arguments, their duration should be sufficient for the peasant audience to perceive them, i.e. being very convincing but too short in argumentation can be missed by the slowly perceiving peasant mind. Moreover, for the peasant audience, the power of evidence depends mainly on the emotional side of the lecture. Thus, the people's lecturer should appeal not only to the minds but also to the hearts of his listeners.

This is especially important for the cooperative lecturer. By calling for cooperation and emphasizing its necessity and usefulness, the lecturer has to enrich his audience with the powerful social energy inherent in the cooperative movement. In the souls of his listeners he has to light sparks of the great flame of the creative social activity that can lead to the revival of the Russian countryside.

However, we should always remember a sense of proportion to avoid excessive pathos and blatancy, for true pathos is a great movement of the soul, which cannot be falsified. If there is no great emotional uplift in the lecturer's soul or if he tries to imitate it, we will have only a loud lecture instead of the emotional stress of the entire audience.

Finally, we have to consider the visual staging of lectures, or, simply put, the use of visual aids by lecturers. There are many misconceptions about visual aids, so we have to somewhat annoyingly and constantly repeat that visualization of teaching is not only posters, pictures, and other manuals but different pedagogical means for enhancing understanding and aural perception by parallel perception by other senses. Therefore, the use of visual aids should correspond to the method of presentation chosen by the lecturer for the specific audience. For schoolchildren, we use one group of visual teaching methods; in the peasant classroom, another group; in higher education institutions, a quite different group.

Pedagogy distinguishes three forms of visualization. First, natural visualization – when the teacher considers the subject and demonstrates it to the audience: the botanist illustrates his lecture with live plants, the physicist shows experiments, the geologist makes tours with his students to study the exposed surface, etc. Second, artificial visualization – when for demonstration the teacher does not use the subject but its picture, model, scheme, etc. There are different levels of schematization: in some cases, we present all details of the subject in its picture; in other cases, we emphasize only the most important aspects and omit all insignificant details. The third type of visualization is when the lecturer illustrates his presentation not with some visual aids but by recalling from the listeners' memory their well-known images and ideas.

All three types of visualization should be used strictly according to the type of audience. The more illiterate and less prepared for abstract thinking, the closer to the naturalness the 'visual aids' should be. The level of schematization can be increased only with the development of the audience's abstract thinking to enhance the impact of what is said. The ability to choose visual aids according to the type of the audience is the essence of visual presentation.

Besides these general recommendations, visual aids should be relevant for some particular tasks. Let us set aside all other visual aids and consider in more detail the theoretical foundations of the composition and use of wall paintings or posters. This type of visual aids can be divided into four groups with special tasks and, accordingly, with special requirements. The first group consists of lecture pictures and tables, i.e. graphic images that are accompanied by verbal presentation and illustrate the lecture. This group of visual aids needs no printed text. The second group consists of traditional posters, i.e. visual aids that aim to influence the audience with a purely visual image accompanied by a concisely styled text. The third group consists of leaflets and posters that try to affect the audience by their text. Verbal presentation is partly illustrated by drawings or paintings, i.e. leaflets that are a kind of popular brochure unfolded on the wall, and there can be no illustrations. Finally, the fourth group stands somewhat apart from the ones mentioned above and consists of different wall reference tables, such as percentage tables, tables for calculating the fat content of milk, etc.

This classification proves that the tasks of each group of visual aids are extremely different; posters from one group can rarely achieve the goals of the other group, which determines different assessment criteria for each group according to its specific tasks. In the first group, the picture does not have a self-sufficient value; both in its content and image it is determined by the lecture it illustrates, and it cannot be considered separately from the lecture. Thus, the emphasis is on the living word, and we are to consider the meaning of the lecture table only together with other visual aids used by the lecturer.

Let us set aside the demonstration of objects in kind and their simplified models due only to their significant size and focus on ordinary poster images: screen, projection lamp, picture-table, and schematic drawings by the lecturer on the board. From this list, the most powerful and vivid impression would be made by the vague picture; however, it has a number of shortcomings, the most obvious of which is its extreme transience. As a rule, the lecturer familiar with his illustrations quickly recalls the image on the screen and proceeds to the next after a few explanations. However, the listener sees the picture on the screen for the first time and needs more time to consider it carefully before proceeding to its analysis. Yet, at this very moment the lecturer finishes his explanations and removes the picture from the screen; the same happens to the second, third, and fourth picture. Thus, the attention of the listener is divided between an almost impossible perception of visual images and attempts to follow the words of the lecturer, which leaves only fragmentary representations in the audience's memory.

To avoid this, the lecturer who uses vague pictures must keep each of them on the screen for at least three minutes to spend some time on a brief description of the picture. Only after making sure that the audience has perceived the picture, should he proceed to its analysis. The perception is more complete with the table-picture that the audience can see before the lecture, during it, during the break, and after the lecture, because every listener can consider the picture several times. Therefore, it is necessary to illustrate the most important ideas of the presentation with lecture pictures or, even better, to duplicate them on the screen.

The power of the light image is greater compared to the printed table, and it increases with naturalness (natural visualization), whereas its advantages are negligible for abstract schemes. Another disadvantage of the light image is the impossibility for parallel, simultaneous consideration and comparison of several images, which is possible with wall paintings. Finally, in the dark, the ordinary projection lights do not allow listeners to copy pictures, which has great pedagogical value.

Wall tables have such disadvantages as low brightness and lack of necessary materials on the market, which limits the choice and forces the lecturer to make this kind of visual aid himself. In most cases, the latter circumstance limits the variety of wall tables to schemes, diagrams, and cartograms. Here the light image is not superior to the wall lecture table, and it mainly competes with the schematic drawing of the lecturer on the blackboard.

Hand drawing in chalk (provided the lecturer is skilful) has a number of advantages: 1) it appears in a certain sequence that often corresponds to the line of reasoning, which facilitates its understanding; 2) drawing takes time and, thus, ensures the duration of perception; 3) the low speed of drawing in chalk provides enough time for copying in pencil. However, these advantages are valuable only if there are few such drawings, they are quite simple, and do not require much time; otherwise the lecturer's drawing would minimize the narrative part of the lecture and extremely tire the audience. Therefore, the experienced lecturer uses drawing only for the most important parts of the lecture and demonstrates the prepared-in-advance tables or light images for all other parts.

The same applies to the numeric content of lectures. Only those indicators for which absolute value is of great importance and a few most important numeric comparisons that should be copied by the audience should be written on the board. All the rest should be demonstrated with the prepared-in-advance tables, diagrams, and cartograms.

This combination of demonstration methods gives the best result.

To conclude our essay on the lecture visual aids, we have to warn their developers against overloading images with excessive content. If possible, they should divide their content into elementary components and provide each with a special image rather than distract or overload the listeners' attention by combining many illustrations in one drawing.

Among other types of visual aids that are not related to the methods of presentation, we will now focus on the poster, for all lecturers use it in one form or another. The theory of the poster as a complex visual aid has not yet been developed. Unlike the lecture picture based on the living word, the poster is a separate entity and independently solves a number of pedagogical tasks. First, it has to attract the attention of a person passing by. It must inform him of a number of facts (representations) in the most clear form, combine these facts into a system that constitutes a certain position, provide evidence for this position, and, finally, affect the viewer emotionally and awaken his activity related to the position. The author of the poster has to carefully select elements for the poster that would solve these very difficult tasks most successfully.

Our agronomic experience allows us to make a list of requirements for the poster. The first and main requirement is correct content ('scientific content'), which goes without saying. However, some posters, especially for a cooperative, often make us consider this requirement. Probably everyone knows the usual type of posters that shows 'the peasant economy before and after grass cultivation', etc. As a rule, such posters present the peasant economy before the reform in gloomy colours, but after the reform in exaggerated rainbow hues. We have to question the admissibility of such a technique. Certainly, it correctly presents the trend of the reform, but the emphasis is exorbitantly exaggerated and often unlikely.

Does this technique follow the first requirement? We would say no, if such an exaggerated comparison has an independent meaning and prevails on the poster; we would certainly say yes, if such an exaggerated comparison has an auxiliary meaning, illustrates and visualizes the poster, and draws attention to it. Thus, the well-known cooperative poster, 'Remember and Do not Forget' should be considered successful and correct, because its main idea is based on the tested statements that were just visualized by some vivid comparisons of 'before and after'.

The second most important condition for the poster's success is its relevant content. It is desirable that the poster vividly and clearly presents some position or idea, which the viewer remembers at first glance. The poster should not be overloaded with content, because any overload prevents understanding and deprives perception of brightness and integrity. Posters should be looked at rather than considered. Their authors make a huge mistake when, 'in the interest of completeness', they try to press the content of several book volumes into one poster. Such overloaded posters, for example, the well-known 'World of Cooperation', look like an entertaining rebus rather than a meaningful poster. On the other hand, posters with insufficient content look empty and pale. Thus, considerable pedagogical and artistic tact are needed to find the necessary content richness.

The third requirement applies to the illustration of the poster content, i.e. to its composition, which should not have unnecessary details. All pictures should be styled to some extent. The most important ones should be put forward and emphasized, because otherwise the peasant attention not guided by the living word can focus on minor details and miss the most important ones. I know some agronomic posters that are good examples of violations of this rule. For instance, on the poster, there is a village in a beautiful landscape, surrounded by gardens and rich in livestock and implements. Among other things, the viewer sees two piles of bags near a hut, one of which is slightly larger than the other. Beneath the picture, there is a surprising explanation in small letters explaining that it presents the impact of early ploughing on yields. Certainly, this example is extreme, but we can see similar mistakes on other posters, which seems inevitable for photographs. An extremely detailed and difficult to be styled, pale, and grey photographic image is necessary for books but absolutely unacceptable for posters and should give way to the artist's colourful brush.

According to the fourth requirement, the poster as a piece of art has to follow all the rules for works of art. It should ensure the unity of artistic conception and composition, and the latter should inevitably lead the viewer to the main position presented in the poster's content. If the design demands a combination of images or inscriptions, the compositional unity can be achieved by ornaments, the example of which we see on the well-known poster, 'Successes of the Peasant Economy and Cooperation'.

The fifth requirement applies to poster statements that have to be laconic, dogmatic, and with no reasoning or extensive evidence. Social agronomists should take into account the decades-long experience of commercial advertising. A laconic phrase repeated many times and accompanied by a vivid visual image affects the consciousness more strongly and deeply than a detailed and long reasoning. Statements, such as 'If shells, then only those of Katyk', or many times repeated words, such as 'Shustov's cognac', are a more powerful weapon of mass psychological influence than 100 pages of thought-out logical evidence. Residents of Moscow and other big cities felt the power of the systematic propaganda by posters that were perfectly designed to promote the war loan in 1916.

However, despite the wide experience of commercial advertising, we should not identify our tasks with those of advertisers. The designer of commercial advertising aims to introduce the name of the advertised product into the consciousness and memory of the general public regardless of the means necessary to achieve this goal. He claims that his product is the best in the world and would cure all diseases; he even promises a happy married life to those who would buy a dowry from him. However, the advertiser does not claim that people believe his words; moreover, he does not need to be taken seriously. It is enough that his advertisements attract attention, because commercial advertising aims at the semi-conscious introduction of ideas into the head of the average person.

The agronomist cannot use these tricks just as he cannot use falsification and short weights. If we use exaggerations, we inevitably make them decorated like legendary, cheap, popular prints. To attract attention and enhance impression we should not emphasize the content of the poster but use auxiliary means, such as bright colours, skilful images, and so on.

Finally, to conclude our long consideration of the poster, it is necessary to mention that its content and images should be relevant for the audience and location. For instance, posters for fences on the market square should differ in design and content from posters for the cooperative board office or peasant hut walls. Posters for peasants and cooperative members should be designed differently; posters for the initial propaganda have to differ from the fancy poster statements of the Moscow Union of Consumer Societies, with which the faithful cooperator decorates his shop like the orthodox Muslim decorates the mosque with pieces of fabric with the embroidered Surahs of the Koran.

These are a few generalizations that outline the path for the further development of a poster theory. We did not consider leaflets and reference tables, because they are not directly related to the methods of presentation. Lecturers give them to listeners after the lecture for better memorization of the material.

The issue of keeping the content of courses in the consciousness and memory of listeners is quite new and interesting for out-of-school education. Practical methods such as testing conversations, questionnaires, distribution of notes, and popular literature have a too short history to make generalizations in this field. However, the issue is important and requires a comprehensive analysis.

To conclude our essay, let us consider the preparation of the lecturer for the oral presentation of his course. All of the above describe the preparation of materials for lectures, their arrangement and systematization, i.e. the work of the lecturer before the lecture. When the lecturer mounts the rostrum, he has to creatively transform the prepared material into the living word, which is a most subtle art. As in all other areas of spiritual creativity, it is inconceivable to make generalizations here, so we present only two general positions, probably subjective in nature. First, if the lecturer selects data and visual aids according to the theoretical structure of the future lecture, it would follow only the available material, which often makes the lecturer change his plan. Second, we would recommend that skilful speakers not prepare a text but a general plan and leave the rest to one's creativity when giving the lecture.

The resulting narrative roughness would be more than covered by the freshness and brightness of direct creativity.

These are the first grains of experience in the study of presentation methods for the peasant audience.

Chapter 7. Conversations, lectures, courses, and agronomic consulting

In the previous chapter, we considered in detail the methods of oral, agronomic propaganda. The exceptional importance of this issue for every social-agronomic worker makes us also consider in detail the organizational forms of this type of agronomic activity. In the search for ways for ideas about agronomic progress to enter peasant thinking, we can identify four groups of factors that can influence the mind and will of every peasant: 1) words of the agronomist addressed to the peasant personally (all forms of oral and written influence of social agronomy on the mind, will, and imagination of the peasant); 2) words of peasant neighbours on issues of agronomic propaganda; 3) neighbours who have followed some advice of the agronomist; and 4) testing the agronomist's advice in one's own economy.

To ensure the success of agronomic propaganda, it is necessary to use all these factors and organize this propaganda in such a way that the words of the agronomist will affect as many peasants as possible and that all peasants' neighbours will talk about issues promoted by social agronomy. Also, that there will be peasant pioneers who will implement the promoted actions, and that the access to seeds, fertilizers, and implement rental will be facilitated.

The forms of oral propaganda practised by agronomists usually take into account these tasks. Agronomists try to solve them by developing specific methods for each task.

The most extensive forms of the agronomic propaganda are chance conversations at rural peasant gatherings and episodic lectures. This form of propaganda is the most widespread, affects the largest number of peasants, and, thus, should be considered a weapon of the strongest impact on the general population. However, to make conversations and lectures a mass factor, it is absolutely necessary that they involve large groups and do not consist of separate speeches in the randomly selected settlements.

We have to create a network of lecture centres so that the entire population of the region will visit them without long trips. We have to make a lecture calendar so that the days and hours of conversations are convenient for the local population. It is necessary to advertise the scheduled lectures and discussions to gather as many listeners as possible. Topics and content of lectures should be coordinated with all other social-agronomic events. Lectures on advanced agricultural machinery should be supported by the work of rental offices, exhibitions, demonstrations of machinery in operation, and agricultural warehouses. Lectures on dairy farming should be supported by the organization of tupping offices, experimental feeding, young stock exhibitions, and dairy cooperatives.

Such a series of lectures and conversations can have a significant impact on the peasant mass consciousness. However, the nature of this impact is superficial. It only prepares the ground for more intensive methods of agronomic propaganda. Moreover, lectures should be given systematically and repeatedly.

The agronomist's words first heard by the peasant audience are not perceived by its majority. Only repetitions and long discussions can ensure that the words of the agronomic propaganda will affect the peasant consciousness. One of the first Russian agronomists, M.E. Shaternikov, described the mechanism of the peasant perception as follows: 'The agronomist who came to the village for the first time to promote grass sowing is usually met with distrust and shouts of misunderstanding: "We in it, in this clover, not a bite understand." "*Barins* take care of the cattle, while we have nothing to eat", etc.' The agronomist should not be confused by such misunderstanding, for it is quite natural. Listeners simply do not want to think; they deny everything strange and unfamiliar. The agronomist should continue to talk, study his audience carefully, and try to find one or two attentive listeners with a spark of interest in their eyes. After the conversation, they usually come to the lecturer; if they do not, he has to find them to talk in more detail about grass cultivation to ensure their full understanding.

Having achieved this, the agronomist can leave and then return to the village in a week or two to meet a reborn audience – one without stupid denial, still with doubts and mistrust in the use of clover, but with more specific and practical questions: 'Where do we make the fourth field, where can we get seeds, etc.' Such questions mean that there had been numerous debates and disputes between believers and deniers. That the questions concern the technical basis means that the agronomist will find necessary decisive arguments and specific solutions.

This is the power of propaganda among peasants as believing masters who often become fanatics of the agronomic progress. Therefore, the primary task of social agronomy is the formation of a group of such peasants-pioneers. Social agronomy strives to solve this task by organizing short agricultural courses for the most educated peasants. These courses are such a powerful tool of agronomic work that we have to consider their various forms in detail.

Practical work determines the basic types of peasant courses. Their most elementary form is a series of lectures given by different lecturers in some place for several days. This series is intended for a general audience of 'everyone interested'. Despite its wider opportunities compared to separate lectures, this series is still systematic readings rather than courses.

The distinctive features of courses are the same audience, practical lessons, and a kind of individualized teaching. Courses vary in content, duration, and composition of listeners. There are general agricultural courses as an elementary encyclopedia of agriculture and special courses on different branches of agriculture; five-day, two-week and monthly courses – depending on the volume and detailing of the subject and content; courses for peasants in general, for bookkeepers, cooperative partnerships, people's teachers, etc. Each type of course has its peculiarities in both goals and organization, which are described in special literature.

If we want to turn listeners of the peasant courses into future pioneers of agricultural progress, we have to pay special attention to their selection. Some agronomic workers believe that the very desire to attend courses is a sufficient indicator of peasant development and culture. They use restrictions only if the number of applicants exceeds the possible number of listeners. Other agronomic workers consider this method of automatic selection too random and unable to guarantee the social effect of the course. They suggest that local agronomists choose and recruit listeners, or that local cooperatives make up the audience by sending listeners.

Pedagogy requires a homogeneous audience for it is extremely difficult to have classes in which some students can barely read, but others have graduated from a four-year, specialized school. We need a preliminary testing conversation to sort listeners. We also know of attempts to prepare untrained listeners for the courses by group classes or by distributing brochures. The total number of listeners is determined by the ability to organize practical classes for each of them. The number of 30–50 listeners is optimal.

Great skill and pedagogical instinct are required to develop the course programme. As a rule, general peasant courses are too multidisciplinary and overloaded with content. Pedagogically inexperienced agronomists try to press the four-year programme of the Petrovsky Agricultural Academy into a one-month peasant course.

In the previous chapter, we considered in detail the reasons for not overloading the presentation with content. We will not repeat those considerations and note only that we do not deny the value of general agricultural courses but believe that special courses are preferable in terms of social profitability. In any event, multidisciplinary courses, in which sciences and lecturers change with kaleidoscopic speed before the perplexed audience, are unacceptable. Courses for the special peasant type of thinking should be practical. They combine general ideas that teach the peasant audience about logical thinking with such data and advice that every listener can use in his economy when he returns home. The presentation should be based on local data, i.e. the lecturer should use facts about the local reality in his evidence, examples, illustrations, and statements, but this technique should not be overused. Certainly, facts from abroad and about both agricultural and cooperative life make the presentation more interesting and broaden the mental horizons of the audience. Still, the programmes of lecturers should be coordinated to avoid repetitions and omissions in the hope that some other lecturer will fill the gap.

Practical classes are an indispensable part of the course. However, they should not aim to teach someone to do something or develop some professional skills. Their goal is more modest – to strengthen the perception, because the action can be perceived in two ways: by either imagining or implementing it. The latter is more vivid and, thus, preferable for a specifically thinking audience.

Let us consider the organization of lecture staff. Despite the great advantages of relying on the local pedagogical staff, mainly the local agronomist as someone who knows the local conditions, a significant part of the lectures is given by outsiders, for no man is a prophet in his own land. New faces, even agronomists from the neighbouring areas, give the course a touch of novelty and festivity, which greatly refreshes the impressions of the audience.

The internal organization of the course is not well developed. According to the educators, the classes should last no more than six hours and leave some time for reading tutorials, individual reflection, and conversations with other listeners. Only these conditions ensure the normal perception of the new information – without overloading the consciousness and with remembering all the perceived information. A part of the free time can be used for general cultural development – concerts, reading books, excursions to local churches or estates, if they have historical or artistic value, etc. This form of recreation is often as beneficial for listeners as lectures.

The course should end with an evaluation procedure, a kind of examination. Some lecturers consider it unnecessary and even harmful, because after the exam the listener expects a certificate, a kind of diploma, and after getting it seeks a better place. Such an outflow of educated people from the peasant economy is the main scourge of the courses, primarily special and long courses that really provide some kind of professional training. Thus, the main goal of courses – to educate pioneers about agricultural progress in the very thick of the peasant population – is destroyed by this outflow, and social agronomy has to resist it by a very careful selection of listeners.

The most important issue is not so much testing the listeners' knowledge as consolidating it, because the content of lectures and practical classes is often learned superficially and is lost when peasants return to their everyday life. The lecturers try to prevent this by providing the graduates with lecture notes and small collections of books. However, the main form of consolidating knowledge is a constant relationship of the agronomic organization with the graduates – lecturers' visits to their households, their involvement in cooperative work, sending agricultural journals to them, etc. Only when this active connection with the local agronomic staff is provided, can the graduates play the role of the second and third factors mentioned at the beginning of this chapter.

Individual consulting is also desirable, especially when the graduates try to implement the advice of social agronomy. In general, individual consultation at the request of individual peasants is a feature of the developed stage of the agronomic work. This not when the agronomist comes to the peasant and tries to gain his confidence, but when the peasant comes to the agronomist on his own initiative. Agronomists of Belgium and some other European countries with old agronomic organizations pay particular attention to this form of work, which is usually stationary. Many come and often wait in line to get advice and instructions on specific issues of their economies. The agronomist waits for visitors in his specially designed office or on appointed days and hours in some other place, such as the premises of the local cooperative or a cafe.

Written consulting is usually more widespread. In some periods of agronomic work, the demand for consulting is so great and so valued by the population that in some western regions even private social agronomists appear.

In addition to the already mentioned forms of oral propaganda, there are also various local agricultural meetings and congresses. By involving local cooperative figures and members of small, regional agricultural societies, by asking them questions about the local agricultural life and encouraging them to consider such issues, social agronomy creates a local, public, agricultural opinion and involves wide peasant circles in the social life. Certainly, this gives a strong impetus to local self-organized activity, and the agronomic word falls into the most fertile soil at the local peasant agricultural meetings, the general meetings of local cooperatives, and the economic councils of the democratic *zemstvo*.

These are forms of the social-agronomic work, in which the agronomic 'tale' plays a leading role. In the following chapters we will consider forms of agronomic 'presentation'.

Chapter 8. Agricultural exhibitions, demonstration events, model farms, and peasant excursions

The impression made by our words and thoughts depends on the psychological state of people and on the importance for them of the issue. Quite often, useful and practical advice of the agronomist pronounced unconvincingly, boringly, and in an everyday situation does not affect the peasant's thinking because he is still not used to assessing the benefits of the agronomic knowledge. Therefore, the workers of social agronomy decided to organize presentations in forms that would inevitably attract the attention of broad peasant masses, affect their imagination, and make an extremely significant impression.

One of such forms is a mobile agricultural exhibition, which is always a significant event for the village, a kind of a holiday that attracts all the population. The active centre of the mobile agricultural exhibition is the living word supported by many visual aids. Usually, this exhibition consists of some agricultural machines promoted by social agronomy, which are shown to visitors in operation. They also include collections of fertilizers, weeds, seeds, models, and all kinds of agronomic and cooperative posters and pictures.

Because the main feature of such exhibitions is mobility, the set of its elements should be transportable and equipped with transportation means. If the exhibition moves by rail and makes stops at stations, it should have special carriages. However, usually such exhibitions move by dirt roads and transport their exhibits by ordinary cars. Practical experience has shown that such exhibitions need their own or at least permanent horses that will be used not only for transportation but also for demonstrating machinery. This is difficult to organize with horses hired by chance. We also know of attempts to make a special wagon-rostrum for the exhibition, but they were not successful.

After the material part of the exhibition has been organized and the programme of lectures prepared, it is necessary to plan the route of the exhibition, provide it with premises, and advertise it widely. When planning the route, one has to take into account: 1) villages that have suitable lecture rooms and at the same time are the centre of gravity for surrounding settlements and 2) duration of trips and road conditions. All other things being equal, if there is no agronomic work in the area, the exhibition should visit those settlements in which agronomic stations will be opened. If there is some social-agronomic work in the area, the exhibition should visit those settlements that, for some reason, are poorly served by agronomists.

The population is informed about the exhibition by wall posters, leaflets given to schoolchildren for their parents, and other notification methods. In the village, the exhibition is located either on school premises or in people's houses, where it hangs posters and arranges its collections. Machines and implements are usually shown outdoors or under a canopy, if there is one. The exhibition house and all its premises are decorated with flags, flowers, and colourful fabrics, which makes the exhibition look festive and affects the imagination of visitors.

The exhibition usually spends four to five days in one village: one day to arrange the exhibits, two or three days for visitors, and one day to pack up.

Lecturers at the exhibition give two or three lectures or talks a day, and the rest of the time they spend at the exhibition by giving explanations to visitors and trying to meet people. The topics of lectures are usually very general – 'needs of agriculture', 'grass seeding', 'dairy cattle', 'machinery', etc.

The lecturers and the agronomist – the head of the exhibition – are local agronomists and invited persons. In addition to the lecture staff, the practice determined that it was necessary to include the special manager of the economic section and permanent workers.

Lectures and exhibits usually make a very strong impression on the peasants. The task of the permanent agronomic organization is to ensure that this impression remains along with the social ties with the local population established by the exhibition. The exhibition tries to deepen and consolidate the knowledge provided by distributing lecture notes and popular agronomic and cooperative literature.

It is interesting to add some local exhibits to the mobile exhibition: the results of local agronomic experiments, crop samples, livestock, etc. By strengthening the local part of the exhibition, we gradually move from mobile exhibitions to small, regional agricultural exhibitions, which add to the exhibits presented by social agronomy for pedagogical purposes. These include a series of contests of local producers presenting their livestock, crop products, fruits and vegetables, handicraft products, etc. At small, regional agricultural exhibitions, the exhibits of social agronomy can be presented more fully and in more detail than at mobile exhibitions, because the former do not face transportation obstacles.

Besides sets of machinery, seed collections, fertilizers, and posters and graphs explaining the results of regional experimental fields, some exhibitions demonstrate different models of fireproof roofs and even ways to harden ravines. Items exhibited at the contest have the owner's address and the explanatory notes of agronomists. The special export commission examines all exhibits and identifies the best, awards their owners with honorary diplomas, valuable gifts, and often cash. The results of this examination with explanations are announced and hung out for public display.

Competitions of bulls with their young stock and competitions of dairy cows require particularly careful organization to be successful.

Besides lectures, exhibitions should have group managers who explain the significance of exhibits to the visitors.

Small regional exhibitions have a fourfold meaning. 1) As a part of lectures and explanations, they play the role of a huge visual aid that stimulates visitors' thinking. 2) They make the local population compare exhibits with each other and with the products of their economy; instructions of the export commission develop the population's ability to evaluate the results of farming. 3) Competitions at the exhibition lead to the economies' contests, thus, encouraging economic initiative and creativity. 4) Exhibitions allow the estimation of economic assets of the region, i.e. they are a very important educational tool of social agronomy.

The main task of small regional exhibitions is to serve as the most convincing material proof of the advantages of new agricultural implements over the old ones. This meaning of small regional exhibitions is very important, although it is quite superficial and not always convincing. When the visitor sees huge pumpkins and cabbages, gorgeous bulls and calves, large and full-grain wheat, he does not know the economic conditions that made such results possible. Perhaps a bag of wheat was filled by selecting the best grain in the barn by hand, or a bull was brought from abroad, and other products cost the household a fortune.

Therefore, to increase the power of our argument and to make the advantages of improved methods of farming and cattle breeding obvious and convincing, we have to show not only the results achieved but also the process of their achievement, and not only on the experimental field but also in the peasant economy. This task can be solved by special demonstration plots on peasant fields and by demonstrations of feeding cattle in peasant stalls. Agronomists agree with some peasants on using a strip of land to demonstrate the use of chemical fertilizers, early ploughing, etc. The allotted land is divided into plots with different conditions of cultivation or fertilizers. The demonstration of feeding of cattle includes selection of two animals of approximately the same weight and productivity, which are fed in different ways – in the ordinary peasant way and according to the requirements of rational agronomy. The results make the advantages of the improved technology obvious.

Some agronomists have tried to organize entire model economies, but they usually required large funding, which weakened their authority in the eyes of the peasants. Moreover, their small number had less mass impact than numerous demonstration plots easily organized and scattered across the region.

The demonstration plot mainly affects the peasant on whose field it is located. When the peasant is convinced of the superiority of the improved technology, he becomes a pioneer of the agronomic progress.

Agronomists often try to make such plots experimental rather than used for demonstration, which is why a set of them is called a collective experiment. Such an experimental approach is necessary for regions with no old experimental institutions. However, the practice proved that the collective experiment on peasant fields cannot substitute for special experimental institutions; collective experiments are a good addition to the experimental field and can transfer results to the peasant economy. Therefore, the collective experiment should be conducted and studied by experimental workers rather than social agronomists in the narrow sense of the word.

Among demonstration activities, we should also mention rental points that provide peasants with trial agricultural machinery and implements for a small fee. We will consider such rental points in one of the following chapters.

These are forms of the social-agronomic demonstration that prove the advantages of new agricultural methods. These forms also include peasant excursions to experimental fields and other agronomic institutions, to the regions of rational agriculture, and even abroad. These excursions broaden the horizons of peasant thinking and strongly affect the peasant mind, feelings, and will with unforgettable experiences. Provided there is a good organization, they become the most powerful means of agronomic influence. Certainly, these excursions are very expensive, but their value for the agricultural culture of peasants more than covers their costs.

Chapter 9. The agricultural warehouse, rental points, and grain-cleaning stations

The distribution of improved agricultural implements and machinery is one of the most important issues in the programmes of social-agronomic work. Because the promotion required the provision to peasants of a reliable source of agricultural implements, social agronomy suggested the organization of the public trade of agricultural machinery and implements and to use it as an agronomic propaganda tool.

When implementing this idea, agronomists set the following four tasks for the agricultural warehouse: 1) to provide the local economy with good implements of those types and brands that are the most suitable for local agricultural production; 2) to provide such supplies at the lowest possible prices, thus, decreasing the prices of private traders; 3) to inform the population of the new types of improved implements by supplying their economies on beneficial terms; 4) to use the warehouse and its customers as an audience for agronomic conversations and a place to meet with peasants and establish strong social ties between the agronomist with the population of the region.

Because these tasks are precisely set, comparatively simple, and ensure quick and obvious results, it is no wonder that there were *zemstvo* agricultural warehouses already in the 1860s. They became widespread in the early 20th century and replaced purchasing partnerships. Their decline has begun recently, when the strong and fully developed agricultural cooperation decided to supply the peasant economy with a means of production. However, such warehouses still function, and we have to consider the basic principles of warehousing, because there is a complex, organizational problem determined by the duality of its tasks. On the one hand, the agricultural warehouse is a commercial enterprise; if it does not make a profit, at least it has to pay for itself. On the other hand, the agricultural warehouse is a tool of social-agronomic work that is aimed primarily at peasant education. This duality determines internal contradictions in the selection of goods, methods for setting prices, and other economic decisions.

Let us first consider hundreds of goods sold in the warehouse – sowing seeds, fertilizers, and agricultural implements which are the most difficult in terms of supplies. From the commercial point of view, it is necessary primarily to have implements and machinery, which are well known to the population and are in great and steady demand regardless of their agronomic estimates. From the social-agronomic point of view, it is necessary to have only those machinery and implements that are promoted by agronomists as the best for local production and those that should replace all others.

These two tasks often do not match. Peasants demand the machines they know, even if they do not meet the contemporary technological requirements, whereas the improved ploughs, sorting machines, etc., do not interest customers for years and become commercially unacceptable, shop-soiled goods. As the agronomic work succeeds, this contradiction is resolved; however, we still look for some organizational compromise. For instance, quite often the task of distributing and demonstrating brand new machines is commercially separated from the warehouse and assigned to rental points that are very desirable for every agricultural warehouse.

Another acute issue in the selection of goods is the number of types and varieties sold. Social-agronomic tasks require only the sale of basic peasant implements, which makes all other goods unnecessary. However, the peasant buyer demands that he can buy everything he needs in one shop – not only a plough, but also nails, wheel grease, files, and other small household items. Therefore, only organizational instinct and skill can help to find a necessary and sufficient compromise between trade and agronomic work.

Another difficult issue is setting prices, especially because prices in the agronomic warehouse usually determine prices on the free market. Commercial practice demands the highest charges on the costs of goods with slow capital turnover, the smallest shop-soiled share, and the highest demand. Social agronomy promotes the beneficial terms of purchasing new machines and implements, i.e. the goods in lowest demand and with the largest shop-soiled share. The lack of profit and direct losses from such goods could be covered by the most popular goods, especially if the warehouse were managed culturally and pursued social-agronomic goals.

Antagonism reaches a tragic level on credit issues. The poverty of the peasantry that is accustomed to usurious private consumer credit requires both beneficial and long-term credit for the wide use of the promoted machinery. However, the warehouse does not have sufficient working capital to provide such credit, is unable to assess the creditworthiness of the buyer, whom the agronomist first saw, and lacks sufficient staff to collect debts from debtors scattered across tens of *versts*. Social agronomy made warehouses open wide and long-term credit, but warehousing was gradually undermined by huge arrears and the share of long-term loans in the working capital.

These drastic consequences of the credit trade gradually determined that credit was to be separated from trade and transferred from the warehouse to the *zemstvo* small-credit funds supported by credit cooperatives. In this form of crediting, the customer receives a credit order from the local cooperative or *zemstvo* small-credit fund proving that he got a loan for a specific purchase. The warehouse accepts this order for payment and receives money from the credit partnership or *zemstvo* small-credit fund, thus making a cash turnover and transferring the liquidation of credit relations to the special credit institution, which has all the means for the proper organization of crediting.

Under such organizational conditions, a very important question is who should manage the warehouse. The use of the warehouse as a tool of the social-agronomic work presupposes that it should be managed by the local agronomist. However, the warehousing development requires so much work that it cannot be managed as a side business; moreover, the best agronomists are often worthless merchants. Therefore, the warehouse should be managed by a special person familiar with trading, but the general regulations of warehousing should be set in the instructions and supervised by the agronomic board.

Some practitioners believe that in the interests of the warehouse, its manager should get both a salary and a share of turnover. In any case, the warehouse manager should not become an ordinary clerk. He must be a member of the agronomic board and is a part of the common cause as a warehousing specialist just as the grassland farmer is a meadow specialist and the zoo technician is a livestock specialist.

In other organizational aspects, the warehouse is partly similar to traditional trading companies and partly different from them. The most important issue is the method of purchasing goods. Only unions of *zemstvos* with warehouses, which can conduct multimillion operations, can strengthen public warehouses on the wholesale market, which is proved by the history of the Russian *zemstvo* purchasing partnerships uniting dozens of *zemstvos*.

The organization of credit for the warehouse is also very important. The better and easier the credit, the less working capital is needed.

Unlike the private merchant, the public warehouse monitors the situation with the machinery sold to the peasant economy. By checking the general situation of implements in its region, social agronomy seeks to establish strong ties with its customers – the owners of the implements – to study in detail their economy, the condition of the implements, and life of the machinery. The best warehouses often keep detailed customer records and sometimes conduct complex studies.

To conclude our brief description of the warehouse organization, let us consider a very pressing issue – the possibility of the warehouse's understanding of the population needs. One agricultural warehouse working in a *uyezd* town cannot create a large client base or ensure a mass impact on the peasant economy. Many practitioners insist on the development of a network of warehouse departments with a simple assortment of goods in the very thick of the peasant population. These departments can be managed by either a local *zemstvo* employee or a local cooperative. Certainly, the latter is preferable if the local cooperative institutions are sufficiently strong and sustainable. Cooperatives are people's organizations; their management of warehousing ensures the best understanding of the peasant needs. In general, trade functions are not a feature of the *zemstvo* self-government bodies, and if sometimes circumstances force our *zemstvos* to perform them, this should be only temporary.

With the sufficient development of the cooperative movement in the *uyezd* and province, when *uyezd* and provincial unions of rural cooperatives start broad intermediary operations, the warehousing work of the *zemstvo* loses its meaning and should be transferred to cooperation. However, social agronomy should make every effort to preserve its agronomic influence on the agricultural warehouse. The cooperative supply of the population with implements and other means of production should preserve its cultural meaning and should not turn into an ordinary commercial operation.

It is necessary to say a few words about the organization of rental points and grain-cleaning stations. We believe that both should be organized on the cooperative basis, but if cooperation in the area of social agronomy is not sufficient for the broad cultural work, rental points and grain-cleaning stations should be managed by the agronomic organization.

Rental points can have a double meaning: 1) they introduce new agricultural machines to the peasant economy by providing them in temporary use; and 2) they ensure the access of the small, peasant economy to such complex machines that can be fully used only on large fields and are not profitable for the small economy where they would stand idle for most of the season (harvesting and sorting machines, root pullers, meadow ploughs, etc.). Social-agronomic rental points can solve only the first task. They cannot set and solve the second task, which can only be solved by a dense network of the cooperative machine partnerships. This difference of tasks between *zemstvo* rental points and machine partnerships determines differences in selection of implements and machines and in systems of payment. Whereas the machine partnership prefers complex machines inaccessible to small economies, the *zemstvo* rental point can have all kinds of machines promoted by social agronomy and accessible to small economies.

Whereas the profitability of machine use and the break-even balance of the rental point are decisive for the machine partnership and determine a complex and flexible system of rental rates, these issues are of almost no importance for the social-agronomic rental point that focuses on the first task. Certainly, when there are insufficient agronomic funds, rental rates should cover a part of the rental point costs; however, it is equally certain that these rates should be beneficial. The only exception when social agronomy takes up the second task are grain-cleaning stations, because their goal is not the promotion of grain graders or cockle separators but the supply of economies with cleaned grain. In other words, grain-cleaning stations provide the peasant economy with a technology inaccessible to small economies. This exception is determined by the importance of good seed for social agronomy and by the comparative simplicity of the technical organization of grain-cleaning.

Chapter 10. Organizational work of the agronomist

Among the tasks of social agronomy, we mentioned not only the promotion of improved methods of farming and livestock breeding but also the change in the organizational plan of the peasant economy towards greater compliance with the current conditions of the economic life. It is necessary to focus on the latter, because this field of the social-agronomic work is full of disagreements and misinterpretations. The task of this chapter is extremely important and perhaps prevails over other tasks of social agronomy.

According to the basic law of agronomy, if the agronomist wants to increase soil fertility, he has to analyse the fertility factors and strengthen the factor that remains at a minimum level. When studying the structure and life of our peasant economy, we can see that many provinces suffer from the lack of an organizational plan of the peasant economy rather than from the lack of water, phosphorus, or nitrogen. Therefore, the first task of the social agronomist is to develop the organization of the peasant economy. However, this seems to contradict the above-mentioned position that the social agronomist as a public figure cannot and should not deal with the organization of specific economies. The Russian agronomic practice rarely succeeds in reconciling these two positions.

Sometimes when the agronomist is convinced of the necessity of organizational work, he simply and unpretentiously spends all his efforts on organizing the individual economies of Sidors Karpovs, Vasiliys Mosyagins, and two or three other agreeable peasants, thus not achieving any mass effect. In most cases, despite all his efforts, the local agronomist, who recognizes the need for organizational work but wants to stay within social work, cannot find specific forms of the organizational work, which makes us carefully consider the organizational activities of social agronomy.

First, we should note that almost any major technical reform, especially the introduction of new economic methods, has organizational consequences that are sometimes quite major. The early introduction of fallow on the arable land in the south of Russia deprives peasant herds of pastures and raises an acute question of foraging, which makes us think about stable keeping or artificial pastures. The introduction of grass rotation provides the economy with a forage base that often exceeds the needs of the livestock, which determines the development of industrial cattle breeding. The use of the separator provides the economy with surplus skim milk, which gives an impetus to the fattening of pigs.

Thus, technical reforms and organizational consequences inevitably change all other aspects of the organizational plan, just like a small leakage destroys the whole dam. Therefore, a system of promoted techniques, balanced and supportive of the reform of the organizational plan, is itself an organizational activity. Social agronomy examines the economic system, develops a plan for the necessary organizational changes, describes their technical elements, and puts them into practice, which inevitably restructures the organizational plan of economies.

The organizational work consists not so much of the local activities of the local social agronomist but rather of diagnostics and planning. A typical example is the work of Moscow agronomists promoting grass cultivation in the Moscow Province. Their study of the economic structure of the Moscow village proved an urgent need for fodder grass, which determined the enslaving conditions for renting meadows, and dairy cattle breeding as a path for progressive development. The last achievement would be impossible without fodder supplies. Therefore, after the organizational analysis and identification of the desired path for organizational reform, the local agronomic workers developed and promoted a number of technical methods for fodder grass cultivation. Twenty years of work led to the serious reorganization of the entire organizational structure of economies affected by social-agronomic propaganda. In this case, as in many similar cases, the head of the peasant economy was a reformer and organizer of the specific economy, but social agronomy gave him only the idea of reform and helped him with the organizational work.

As all kinds of organizational reforms finally determine the transition from one combination of technical elements to another, the organizational work of social agronomy will always consist of both economic and organizational development of the promoted system of technical measures. Besides the above-mentioned assistance to the head of the peasant economy, social agronomy can help him by introducing scientific methods of accounting and calculation into his economic routine.

The knowledge of measures and weights is a powerful factor of economic life, which is, unfortunately, far from being fully used by our peasant economy. Therefore, among numerous courses and lectures for peasants, courses on organizing the economy should take the main place. With the numbers that describe the economies of the peasant listeners the lecturer can easily explain to them the most important economic calculations. What are the costs of producing a *pood* of oats or a bucket of milk? Is a mowing machine profitable for the economy of 10 *desiatinas*? What is more profitable: flax or oats? These are questions of agricultural arithmetic that can lead to the most difficult issues in organizing the peasant economy.

Due to the fundamental differences between the labour economy and the capitalist economy and to the poor development of the theory of the labour economy, contemporary economics does not provide objective methods for organizing the peasant economy. If we cannot provide the small producer with objective methods for organizing his economy, we have to give him the above-mentioned techniques of economic calculations, developed economic arithmetic, and basic economic concepts that would help him in the economic activity.

Given the specific peasant thinking, such a course should begin with accounting tasks for the listeners, which would help them learn basic concepts of the agricultural economy. After the listeners have learned the organizational foundations of their economies and the most important concepts of the agricultural economy, the lecturer should present a critical assessment of the current agricultural situation and identify the economic significance of the *zemstvo* agronomic reform.

A suggested programme for a course on organizing the peasant economy can be as follows:

1. Family composition and its consumer budget (in kind and cash).
2. What products and how much of them should be produced for the peasant family in kind?

3. Analysis of the organization of field cultivation. Farming systems, crop rotation, and various methods for restoring soil fertility.
4. Analysis of the organization of cattle breeding.
5. Analysis of the organization of fertilization. Fertilizing methods and norms.
6. Analysis of the organization of productive cattle breeding. Possible types of cattle breeding.
7. Organization of fodder production. Criticism of the existing system. Methods for calculating feed reserves.
8. Analysis of organization and methods of accounting for dead stock. The concept of depreciation. The value of machinery in agriculture. The advantages of small and large economies. The importance of cooperation for smallholders.
9. Analysis of organization and methods of accounting for outbuildings. Long-term loans, fixed capital, and short-term loans. Productive and non-productive loans.
10. Calculating the cost value of a horse's working day. Estimates of manure and other nonmarket products.
11. Accounting for field cultivation. Profitability of crops. The cost value of one's working day. The price of a *pood* of grain. Organization of sales. Market doctrine and pricing.
12. Accounting for the meadow, garden, and so on.
13. Accounting for productive livestock – an assessment of straw, payment for fodder in kind. Principles of livestock selection. Unions in cattle breeding.
14. Consolidated balance of the economy. General organization of labour and monetary budget. Machinery. Short-term loans. Calculations of profitability per *desiatina*. The concept of rent and the origin of land prices.

Our peasants rarely keep economic records, and in most cases, the available peasant account books have only records of cash receipts and payments, which does not allow the evaluation of the profitability of the economy. We know the very sad experience of the more cultured Western European peasantry and have little hope that in the near future peasant bookkeeping will become mass in Russia. However, exact numbers describing the elements of the organizational plan of the peasant economy are so important for both the agronomist and the peasant reforming his economy that the organization of peasant bookkeeping and scientific analysis of its data are the key tasks of social agronomy.

Besides bookkeeping for the entire economic turnover, there are much more successful attempts at accurate accounting for separate economic transactions, especially if accounting is of particular importance for them. For instance, the so-called 'control partnerships' aim to calculate the cost of milk, the cost of a *pood* of feed in milk, and of other organizational elements in dairy husbandry. Peasant economies unite as a control partnership and invite a 'control assistant' who collects weekly data on the composition and amount of feed per cow, milk yields, and fat content. Then the control assistant calculates the cost value of a bucket of milk and a *pood* of fat and also the share of a *pood* of feed in the price of milk, which allows peasants, on the one hand, to get rid of bad cows with a high share of feed in the price of milk. On the other hand, it allows them to introduce the most profitable and rational feed rations. The well-known Danish feed standards are based on the mass data of Danish control partnerships.

The organization of peasant bookkeeping is accompanied by another method of the organizational work with completely different tasks. Contests of economies are very common in Western Europe and quite regular in the south of Russia. The winner is awarded an honorary challenge cup, an honorary diploma, some valuable or household item, and sometimes a sum of money.

The competing farms are periodically inspected by a special commission – the jury – to be described in detail for further accounting. They maintain detailed bookkeeping and are compared at the end of the financial year. The evaluation criteria depend on the goals set by the contest organizers. Sometimes the jury considers technical advantages, sometimes the gross yield per *desiatina*, or the price of a unit of labour and capital invested. In most cases, the jury's decision is based not on the objective indicators but on the general subjective impression of how the competing economies 'made use of the labour forces and material means of production'. At the same time, such contests provide considerable accounting data.

The main goals of the economies' contests are as follows: 1) to revitalize the creative initiative of participants, to expand their organizational experience by comparing their economy with other competing economies and by communicating with the jury members; 2) to point the rural population's attention to organizational issues and to use the results of such contests for pedagogical purposes; and 3) to use the competing economies as model economies. In the following chapters, we will consider in detail the importance of model economies in social agronomy, which still have a very modest place among other methods of its work.

Thus, we considered those sections of the organizational work of the social agronomist, in which he observes, keeps account, and analyses the organization of peasant economies and uses these data to develop a system of agronomic activities and for pedagogical purposes.

In what cases does the social agronomist become a direct organizer of economic activity? As we have already mentioned, the organization and management of individual peasant economies diffuses the agronomist's efforts and cannot have a mass effect. However, there are some cases in which the direct organizational work of the social agronomist is not a waste of effort and is of great mass importance. These include: 1) the organization of auxiliary social-agronomic institutions – rental points, grain-cleaning stations, breeding-coupling stations, experimental plots, agricultural warehouses, etc.; 2) organizational assistance to public and cooperative economies and undertakings, e.g. the organization of a dairy farm, a calf-breeding station, a cooperative seed farming; organization of the intermediary operations of local cooperatives in the sales of flax, eggs, etc.; organization of land improvement and public land management (like other organizational work, they can be done by specialized staff, but, as a part of the social-agronomic work, they should be directed by the local agronomist in full accordance with other aspects of agronomic work, especially under the reform of land relations, such as getting rid of strip farming, straightening and rounding of plot borders, etc.); and 3) the most controversial and difficult type of social-agronomic work – the organization of model or experimental economies, in which the social agronomist aims not to increase the wealth of the individual peasant economy but to use it as a means of agronomic work and a kind of visual aid in agronomic propaganda.

Supporters of the third type of the social-agronomic work believe that the model and experimental economies scattered in the thick of the peasantry should be a living example that puts all their neighbours on the path of agronomic progress. There was a time when model economies were very popular, received a lot of funding, were generously subsidized, supplied with implements, and provided with soft loans and other benefits. Such enhanced support put model economies in an exceptional position and deprived their success of any significance from an organizational perspective. Moreover, attempts to organize model economies without such support and only with advisory assistance were not successful. Given the passivity of our population, they attracted very few visitors and, given the limited number of such economies, they had no mass impact.

For these purposes, the economies' contests are much more effective: they require fewer efforts from social agronomy, but, due to the large number of participants and public attention, they have a greater social impact. The demonstration fields, experiments, and sowing, which many peasant economies introduced to show different techniques for small payments, were even more successful and ensured both mass scale and mass impact. However, demonstration events have nothing to do with the organization of economies. The organization of individual economies is not of great demonstration importance but is very useful as an experimental event.

Even if the programme of social agronomy is based on a detailed, organizational analysis of the existing and emerging economic systems, in the organizational perspective it still has an abstract character. Therefore, it is extremely important to make its economic ideal more specific to assess its economic realizability and possible practical forms. Such a practical specification of the theoretical economic ideal enriches the agricultural experience of the agronomist and makes him revise the programme more than once to eliminate elements that are difficult to implement and to add elements revealed during the practical organizational work.

Thus, to lead the peasant economy to a new economic ideal, the agronomist should know the degree and forms of this ideal realizability. And just as there is usually not an experiment or model near the agronomic station but rather a test plot for sowing new crops and testing a new plough or sowing machine, there is always a neighbour or a whole village to willingly become involved in all economic undertakings, even if unpredictable in terms of success. In the agronomic progress perspective, this test economy or village is many years ahead of the whole district, because it develops specific forms of the new economic structure and serves as the best school for social agronomy. We use the word 'school' because the agronomist has teachers. His theoretical knowledge and skills of cultural management are supplemented by the peasant's practical norms and centuries-old skills. Only their synthesis can create a sustainable form of the peasant progressive economy.

Chapter 11. Social agronomy and cooperation

In social agronomy, there is no more important, difficult, and even painful task than 'to organize the local population in unions and groups that, on the one hand, would use cooperation to provide the small economy with all the advantages of the large one; and, on the other hand, would take on consolidation and strengthening of the new economic principles' (see Chapter 1). It goes without saying that the cooperative movement is of great economic importance, and that the contemporary progressive peasant economy is unthinkable without cooperative associations just as modern industry is unthinkable without capitalist forms. Moreover, cooperation is essentially important for the social development of the village. Not so long ago, centuries-old silence reigned on our rural plains, while metropolises lived an interesting and intensive cultural life full of developing and failing systems of social reforms and stubborn struggles of various directions in the name and on behalf of the broad masses of the Russian plain. However, this life rarely affected the peasant masses, who had no voice, no creative will, and no social thought because they were scattered. The Russian people was only a *demos*, a backwoods mass, but it had to be a democracy, a self-aware people. The Russian people could not turn from a *demos* into a democracy because of a lack of organization, social skills, and organized social thought.

These basic elements of the democratic culture cannot be created by binding decrees or appear all of a sudden from nowhere. This culture is based on the long and invisible work of social forces, on the unnoticeable but deep rebirth of the nation. The Russian Revolution revealed this truth with amazing clarity and showed that we still do not have a nation and that even the decree of the Constituent Assembly cannot turn the Russian *demos* into a democracy.

However, the researchers of Russian life discovered in the Russian village the smallest processes preparing a future democracy, and the most important such process is rural cooperation. The everyday routine work of boards, supervisory councils, and general meetings, union building, and endless debates about building a mill or selling flax created new people who would take on responsibility for the future of our country. This social meaning of cooperation is especially important for social agronomy.

We constantly emphasize that agronomic work can be successful only on the basis of people's initiative, and cooperation is such an initiative in the most organized forms. Cooperatives are centres of social relations, and, by influencing them, we can affect very broad masses. By focusing our agronomic propaganda on cooperative groups consisting of the most active and conscious rural strata, we reinforce our propaganda by the authority of the cooperative initiative. Because our propaganda affects the conscious cooperative circles that provide it with conscious support of the living word, personal examples and material assistance, our agronomic influence becomes exceptionally massive and powerful. Therefore, it is true that cooperatives are a resonator of agronomic propaganda.

Agronomic lectures at the general meetings of cooperatives, the distribution of agricultural literature through cooperatives, the organization of cooperative libraries, experimental fields, breeding-coupling and grain-cleaning cooperative stations, the cooperative purchase of seeds, implements, and fertilizers, loans for agricultural improvements, the pedagogical significance of the cooperative sorting out the joint sales of flax, eggs and milk, etc. – all of this is an invaluable help of local cooperatives to social agronomy. Without cooperatives the social agronomist can establish no organized ties with the population, without which his voice would be lonely and lost among thousands of economies. That is why almost everywhere agronomists start their work by promoting and directing the cooperative movement.

However, exaggerated forms of this work are harmful for both social agronomy and cooperation. Some agronomists develop a whole network of cooperative institutions in a region that has no prerequisites for cooperation. Thus, they acquire cooperation without cooperators, i.e. agronomists are forced to manage cooperatives almost single-handedly. By neglecting the self-sufficiency of the cooperative movement, they tend to consider cooperatives as a tool and means of agronomic assistance similar to warehouses, breeding-coupling stations, and other institutions of social agronomy. Other agronomists, in contrast, forget about their *zemstvo* service and become figures of the cooperative movement, members of cooperative boards and other cooperative bodies, and often differ from other cooperative members only by sources of income.

Certainly, both extremes are pathological and often lead to painful conflicts under the development and strengthening of the cooperative movement. The lack of a proper fundamental demarcation between the tasks of cooperatives and self-government bodies has repeatedly led to struggles, especially in the field of cultural-educational and commercial-intermediary work. Previously, many such conflicts were determined by the distrust of democratic cooperation with the qualified *zemstvo.* Today, after the Revolution and the introduction of the *volost zemstvo,* the task of the proper demarcation between these two democratic institutions in agronomy and other areas of the local work causes us to consider this issue in more detail.

Unfortunately, this general issue was rarely considered in our cooperative and agricultural press, and its solutions were often absurd. For instance, I have met some ardent cooperators who believed that the broad development of the cooperative movement would eventually abolish all *zemstvo* institutions. At the same time, until very recently, many members of the *zemstvo* believed that the development of small *zemstvo* units would eliminate the need to organize cooperatives.

It is obvious that both positions are wrong. There is a fundamental distinction between the work of *zemstvos* and the work of cooperatives determined by the nature of these institutions in economic life. Thus, under both – the developed, small *zemstvo* unit and the ideally developed and strengthened cooperative movement – *zemstvos* and cooperation would continue to exist. The question is how to prevent their competition in economic life and rationally separate them on the basis of their essential features.

Zemstvo is a forced union of all people living in the area; any assistance to the *zemstvo* in its economic activities consists of events and measures that would be beneficial not to Peter, Sidor, Ivan or Fedor, but to the entire population included in this forced union. Such assistance is possible only when the *zemstvo* improves and organizes, not its economic activity but its conditions. If the economic conditions are improved, every economic agent will feel the beneficial influence of the *zemstvo* work proportional to his economic activity. Therefore, the *zemstvo* aims to improve roads, organize local trade, develop public medical and veterinary care, a public network of school, out-of-school, and vocational education, organize local mail, telephone communication, and small credit offices that open the way for the wide financial market, etc. All these *zemstvo* activities are necessary conditions for the development of the local and national economy.

Cooperation is a combination of some aspects of economic activity. In its organizational plan, the small economy identifies those economic processes in which a large economy has undoubted advantages over a small one, and unites with other interested economies into a cooperative to achieve the economic scale of the large economy. The cooperative combines credit, sales, and purchase; processes potatoes, flax, vegetables, milk, resin, etc.; sorts flax, breeds pedigree cattle – in other words, rationalizes all economic activities.

Thus, although the *zemstvo*'s task is to create the best conditions for economic life, the cooperative's task is the best organization of economic activity. This is a schematic distinction of the economic tasks that is not always achievable. First, all economic enterprises including cooperatives are one of the conditions of economic life for all other enterprises. However, they are a condition by the very fact of their existence, but they do not set a task 'to be a condition' and do not work according to this task. On the contrary, many *zemstvo* activities – road construction, insurance, agricultural warehousing, small crediting – are conditions of the economic activities of all economies in the *zemstvo* area and grand economic projects. Such projects aim not to ensure the greatest profit on the capital invested but rather to create the best conditions for individual economies in the area served by the *zemstvo*. Profitability of the new roadway or *zemstvo* insurance system is measured not by income (fares or insurance premiums) but by the growth of the general regional welfare determined by the use of the roadway or insurance system as conditions of economic activity.

This is the difference in incomes from organizing an economic activity in cooperative form or in the form of the *zemstvo* institution. Cooperation provides the population with incomes from those economic operations that are combined in the cooperative. *Zemstvo* economic undertakings, however, often bring greater incomes due not to a *zemstvo* enterprise turnover but to an increase in profitability in various branches of individual economies, which is determined by the conditions created by the *zemstvo* institution. For instance, the roadway increases incomes not by collecting fares but by saving transportation costs.

Certainly, the *zemstvo* often takes on cooperative functions, especially if cooperation is not developed, and vice versa – the cooperative aims to improve general economic conditions. However, the identified fundamental distinction allows an understanding of the complicated circumstances and helps answer the question of whether the agronomist should work in cooperatives.

We have already mentioned that cooperation is an economic action, because cooperatives are an essential condition of economic life. Without cooperatives, all agronomists' educational activities will be reduced to nothing. To buy the promoted implements and seeds, the peasant needs credit; to use the feed reserves of the introduced grass-sowing project, the peasant needs industrial dairy farming, which is unthinkable without cooperation. That is why, if the *zemstvo* does not want to reduce its educational work to nothing, it should strive to create this necessary 'condition' by promoting the cooperative idea and organizing a network of cooperatives, which is absolutely essential for the successful educational work of the agronomist.

This is not the only task of *zemstvo* cooperative work. A network of cooperatives can become the best economic condition, only under normal and flawless cooperative work. Therefore, if cooperation is not developed, the *zemstvo* should support it with the advice and instructions of the agronomist or special instructor. The *zemstvo* should also provide good credit terms for young organizations. However, neither the *zemstvo* nor *zemstvo* agronomists should do the cooperative work; the agronomist cannot and should not replace the cooperator, board member, or accountant. Such a replacement would make the agronomist's work economic, which contradicts the basic tasks of the *zemstvo*. If the cooperative does not have members capable of bookkeeping and organizational work, the *zemstvo* should teach them the cooperative work by organizing special cooperative bookkeeping courses or by instructing. But, in no case should the *zemstvo* make its representative a cooperator, because this contradicts both cooperative and *zemstvo* principles.

Chapter 12. The equipment of the agronomic station

Almost every aspect of social-agronomic activities needs specific implements. Successful, and at the same time economical, equipment for social-agronomic work is a difficult task. Often the success or failure of social-agronomic work depends to a large extent on its material means. It goes without saying that the main condition of success is the agronomic staff, and, if it is poorly trained, then no implements will help. However, a good agronomist without good implements could do little, and most of his efforts would be wasted. When following the path of social agronomy and spending large funds to recruit agronomists, self-governing bodies, cooperatives, and other public organizations should recognize that the success of their work requires no less funding for material means.

The issue of the composition of these means is poorly developed theoretically and, by its very nature, does not allow the provision of recipes. Moreover, social-agronomic work varies at its different stages. Its content changes and differs at the initial propaganda stage; after several years, at the stage of intensification in relation to the cooperative movement; and a few years later, at the stage of deep differentiation and functional specialization of the social-agronomic staff.

The differences in social-agronomic work are also determined by the economic, natural, and everyday features of its area. Thus, the implements of social agronomy in the Champagne vineyards and on the slopes of Vesuvius would differ from the implements of the *zemstvo* agronomic area in the Vologda Province or Western Siberia. However, the same general idea would determine the selection of implements for any agronomic area regardless of its longitude and latitude. Every material means of social-agronomic work should correspond to its nature, its content, and the specific local economic conditions.

That is why it is impossible to write any recipes for equipping an agronomic station or the wholesale production of implements. Commercial companies easily equip beet-sugar and other factories or select items for equipping chemical laboratories, because they know that all those processes are the same for all these factories and laboratories wherever they are located. The peculiarity and variety of agronomic work exclude such a possibility. Even if there were a possibility for the wholesale equipment of an agronomic station, a large share of funds would be spent in vain, because the agronomist would never use many of the implements and would suffer from the lack of many others.

It is unacceptable to equip an agronomic station before or at the very beginning of its work. Nobody knows in advance the content of local agronomic work. Therefore, every implement should be purchased at the very moment it is needed, so that it will be used on the next day of purchase. Thus, equipment for an agronomic station should be determined by social-agronomic work. The collection of implements is never complete, because the social-agronomic work never stops at one stage but always develops and updates its content.

Although we cannot give any general recipes, we should identify those basic principles that social agronomy worked out for the agronomist. The first step in equipping an agronomic station is to choose its location. It should be an economically and historically homogeneous area that usually consists of individual economies that concentrate around one market centre. The system of the village market is an economically and socially isolated group of villages whose borders often do not coincide with the administrative regions. In most cases, the personal ties and economic and social relations of the population are limited to this little world, and our economic plans should consider it an indivisible national economic unit. Our agronomic station should be located in the natural centre of this little world near the market that every peasant would certainly visit several times a year.

Having chosen the location of the agronomic station, we have to answer the question of the facilities that are necessary for social-agronomic work, which actually consists of two parts: 1) an apartment for the agronomist and his family; and 2) facilities for the social-agronomic work. The first question is beyond the scope of our book; we merely emphasize the necessity of its satisfactory solution. The necessary conditions for the successful work of the local agronomist are the guaranteed minimum conditions of everyday life. In our Russian village, it is almost impossible to find a suitable apartment for rent, so we often have to build a house for the agronomist and his family. Unfortunately, this seemingly insignificant question sometimes becomes extremely pressing, and we know many cases in which the agronomist left his station because of the unbearable living conditions.

The facilities for social-agronomic work consist of a reception room, an agronomist's office, an agricultural museum, and auxiliary outbuildings such as rental, breeding, and grain-cleaning stations. Finally, rooms are needed for lectures and exhibitions, which are important not only for social agronomy but also for out-of-school education, cooperatives, and other sectors of the local public work. For reasons of economy and convenience, they cooperate to develop a network of lecture and theatre facilities in people's houses and schools and also to build special halls if there are no suitable facilities. When developing this network, it is necessary to identify the social-agronomic area as an optimal radius from the market centre. Buildings that constitute the agronomic station should ideally form an estate near the market square as the centre of local life.

For the agronomist, the issue of moving around the agronomic area is no less pressing than the issue of an apartment and facilities. Unlike the medical work station, by nature, agronomic work is mainly travelling, especially in its first years. The social significance of the agronomist deprived of the ability to travel around his area is close to zero. Therefore, organizers of social agronomy have to guarantee their employees the complete independence of travelling. Cutting travel expenses brings all agronomists' work to nothing. Total travel expenses are usually so high that it is better to purchase a means of transportation.

Besides an apartment, facilities, and travelling, the agronomist needs some items for research and organizational work. One of the previous chapters, which described methods for developing an agronomic programme, allows one to imagine the whole set of items necessary for the agronomist in his office. Its central part is the library with the most important books on natural sciences, agriculture, agricultural economy, law, all kinds of reference books, major agronomic and cooperative journals. The library should pay special attention to all kinds of materials concerning the area of the agronomist's activity. Historical and ethnographic studies of the province, works of geological, botanical, soil, entomological, and other expeditions in the agronomic area and surrounding regions, works of the nearby experimental institutions, descriptions of individual economies and areas of the region, reports of all local institutions, collections of statistical information on the agronomic area, albums of newspaper and magazine cuttings that describe local life – these are sources absolutely necessary for the library of the local agronomist.

In addition to the library, the agronomist's office should have devices and tools necessary for research. These include instruments for soil and seed analysis, chemical reagents, barometer, scales, a plant press, geodesic measuring tools, and all sorts of other items necessary for agronomic work according to the local conditions and the stage of social-agronomic development.

Finally, the third group of items in the agronomist's office consists of the research results of the agronomic staff. It is a kind of museum of the surrounding area and holds herbariums of local flora, collections of weeds, cultivated plants, pests, soil monoliths, examples of soil, results of seed and other types of analysis, results of experiments of the agronomist, neighbouring experimental fields and local collective experiments. There are also graphs and cartograms of the main economic elements of the region, which also reflect social-agronomic work.

The agronomist's office is not limited to the indoor premises and includes some meteorological instruments necessary for simple observations and a small plot for test planting and testing new machines, etc.

In addition to implements to serve the agronomist as a researcher, the agronomic station should be equipped with some aids necessary for the agronomist as a propagandist and lecturer. We have already described such visual aids, so let us make a few comments. First, the agronomic station should have lecture equipment – a projection lamp and cinematograph, collections of slides and tapes, lecture tables, pictures, and posters, a portable blackboard, tools for presenting physical, chemical, and physiological experiments, implements for the simplest analysis, models of flowers, grain ears, livestock, and so on. It should have all sorts of items for conversations and practical demonstrations, a portable set of butter-making machines, models of agricultural machines, and implements promoted by the agronomist; wall posters, leaflets, and brochures to be distributed or sold to listeners after lectures. Sometimes these items are combined into special collections to decorate the agronomist's reception room or to serve as a portable lecture set or a special mobile agricultural exhibition. Some agronomists designed special mobile vans for agricultural exhibitions, but this form of visual aid has not become widespread.

It is necessary to emphasize that the visual aids should correspond to the tasks and needs of the local social-agronomic work and, if possible, be based on the local material. This rule, recognized by all practitioners, is the reason the local workers are disappointed by visual aids bought in the market that sells wholesale goods but cannot offer visual aids that reflect the local regional features. Therefore, a significant part of posters and tables is made by local agronomic workers.

To conclude our brief description of the agronomic station equipment, it is necessary to mention a regional network of small libraries of popular and reference literature on the agricultural issues, which should be organized on the basis of small agricultural societies, cooperatives, and people's houses. Agronomic libraries are closely related to the organization of library services in the village in general. Therefore, the network of agronomic libraries should be developed by agronomists in cooperation with the figures of out-of-school education.

The agronomic station often includes grain-cleaning stations, rental points, breeding-coupling stations, and agricultural warehouses. We have already discussed the organization of these in the previous chapters.

Thus, social-agronomic work requires diverse and numerous equipment and, thus, considerable funding. At the beginning of the chapter we mentioned that these costs are inevitable. In many cases, the needs would certainly exceed the financial opportunities, which would reduce the agronomic budget. It would make the agronomist choose between its positions and compare agronomic expenses with other branches of the economy. It is impossible to give recipes or general rules for such reductions, because it depends on the case and local conditions. However, it is better not to begin social-agronomic work at all if there is no way to provide the invited agronomic staff with all necessary material means.

Chapter 13. Registration and evaluation of social-agronomic work

We have described all basic forms of social-agronomic work and can finally proceed to its economic and social results. Unfortunately, the methodology for evaluating social-agronomic work and its results has not yet been developed. If we consider hundreds of reports of numerous social-agronomic organizations to find out the methods their authors used to evaluate their work, we would discover very diverse methods and measures of success. Some authors measure the success of social-agronomic work by the development of a regional agronomic network, by the number of rental points, breeding and grain-cleaning stations, or simply by an increase in the *zemstvo* funding of social agronomy. Other authors rely on the number of the agronomist's visits to the area and the number of conversations and lectures given. Still other authors mention the attendance of agronomic interviews, customer expansion of rental points and other stations, and an increase in the demand for agronomic consulting. Some American reports compare the costs of agronomic measures with an increase in the profitability of the regional economy due to the growth in yields determined by the promoted improvements.

All methods of evaluation have different tasks and are based on different indicators. By comparing them we can distinguish four objects of evaluation: 1) scientific research of social agronomy that allows the identification of the local agricultural needs and development of a programme of social-agronomic work; 2) activities of social agronomy, agronomic bodies, personnel and auxiliary institutions; 3) the social effect of these activities – the number of heads of peasant economies affected by social agronomy, their impression of agronomic propaganda, their economic activity, and the social ties between the population and bodies of social agronomy; and 4) the economic consequences of the population's response to agronomic propaganda. Thus, we have to consider, on the one hand, the organizational and technological changes that the local population makes in their economies under the influence of agronomic propaganda, and, on the other hand, the economic results of innovations.

According to these four objects of evaluation, agronomic reports should have the same theoretical structure as academic research reports. However, the authors of agronomic reports usually do not analyse their work and its results and merely present short protocols of their actions. Such a limitation of the tasks of the agronomic report is extremely harmful. Without the agronomist's careful analysis of his observations, activities, and their results, social agronomy would work blindly, its success would be accidental, and its failures incomprehensible and inexplicable.

When the agronomist is overloaded with all kinds of urgent work, writing a report is often his only time for undisturbed reflection on his activities and his only opportunity to break loose from the everyday agronomic routine, to look at himself and his work from the outside, and to see a general picture and compare tasks and achievements. Thus, the agronomic report is of great importance as a collection of indicators for evaluating the whole social-agronomic work.

It might seem that we contradict ourselves and set tasks for the local workers that obviously exceed their means. Often a great agricultural practitioner, who is very skilful and has a deserved, huge impact on the local population, has neither sufficient literary talent nor interest in paperwork. In other words, he is not able to write even a satisfactory protocol report. We understand this and set the task not for individual agronomic workers but for the agronomic organization as a single collective will that organizes and directs the activities of individual workers. Moreover, our requirements are for *uyezd* and mainly provincial reports, whereas reports of local workers must follow the same principles but can be limited to a good protocol as a source material for the report of the whole agronomic organization.

Concerning the methodology of social-agronomic work, its results, and reports, let us consider first the tasks of the local agronomist and then the general report of the whole organization.

Every description should begin with an accurate registration of the phenomenon. Some agronomic institutions – warehouses of agricultural implements and machinery, breeding-coupling, rental and grain-cleaning stations – have their own accounts, but the agronomist needs a diary or relies on his memory for other branches of work. Using only memory to register numerous phenomena is an unreliable path, especially in social agronomy, because our agronomists often change their locations. Because of this staff turnover, the whole work experience and knowledge of local features, sometimes very extensive, leave the agronomic station together with the agronomist, and his successor has to start all over again. He often repeats the mistakes of his predecessor and spends great efforts to collect information that was already collected. That is why social-agronomic activities and all agronomists' observations should be registered in detail and, if possible, written every day.

Besides the most accurate protocol of all social-agronomic actions, the diary should include all the agronomist's observations of the local agricultural and everyday life, his thoughts, considerations, the results of the analysis, and other facts of agronomic life. This can be a simple diary or records can be analysed, for instance, grouped into categories. The latter allows some further analysis, for example, making a cartogram of the current agronomic work by putting on a big schematic map of the agronomic area the numbers indicating agronomic measures near the names of villages in which such measures were taken. Some agronomists even have a 'file' for each village – a kind of current report on the work in the village.

A diary and simple methods of its analysis constitute the basis of the local agronomist's report. If he wants to make an independent, detailed report, he relies on his registered observations, memory, statistical, and other local data to proceed to the monographic description of his social-agronomic work. If, for some reason, the local agronomist cannot make a detailed report, he can write a brief protocol, which is necessary for *uyezd* and provincial reports.

For the general report of the agronomic organization, the reports and protocols of local agronomists are used as source material; the main requirement is their comparability. As a rule, agronomic organizations design special questionnaires for making protocols. They are necessary even for agronomists who prepared their detailed reports, because, despite their advantages in terms of content and structure, often such reports are so different from the general questionnaire that they cannot be compared. One such questionnaire was developed by the Moscow provincial *zemstvo* agronomic organization. The Moscow questionnaire-report is somewhat cumbersome, but many of its questions are general and do not need to be asked annually. In other words, such questionnaire-reports can be 1) annual reports in the form of a protocol and 2) more complex and complete reports prepared periodically, for instance, every five years.

Questionnaire-reports, individual reports of local agronomists, reports of experimental fields and other auxiliary agronomic organizations, statistical, meteorological and other data serve as source material for the general report of a social-agronomic organization. This general report should be based on the analysis of all four sections mentioned at the beginning of the chapter. It should present the research work of the agronomist, explain tasks of the agronomic organization, describe in detail and critically analyse actions of the agronomic organization for achieving the goals of its programme, and, finally, carefully assess the social and economic consequences of the social-agronomic work.

A critical analysis of all four sections serves as a starting point for revising the programme and developing directions for future work, which can form a special part of the report. However, these four sections do not represent a plan of the report – they are only four elements that should be taken into account in any report plan. There is still no form for the general agronomic report, and its development is certainly a matter of practice rather than of theoretical analysis. Therefore, the general report should differ significantly from the agronomist's report by describing the work of many dozens of agronomic workers, by interpreting mass material, and by appropriate techniques, including those of comparison.

The dependence of the agronomic programme and the work of agronomists on the duration of the social-agronomic work in the area, the dependence of the agronomic service on the villages' distance from the agronomist's house, a comparison of agronomic programmes with the organizational plans of the peasant economies, the dependence of the peasant responsiveness on literacy, prosperity, and commercialization, a critical comparison of the success of various branches of agronomic propaganda, the mass economic effects of social-agronomic work, etc. – they all should be measured in the report with special coefficients and methods for assessing the intensity of agronomic work, its susceptibility, and social and economic success.

The most difficult part of this undeveloped method for assessing social-agronomic work is the evaluation of the economic effect. For instance, if yields grow in some province, pig breeding develops, and the export of agricultural products abroad increases rapidly, how is this agricultural progress related to the local social-agronomic work and to what extent can social agronomy regard an increase in national income as its own merit? How many rubles did the national economy receive for each ruble spent on social agronomy? Perhaps the development of the Volokolamsk grass-sowing or Kherson black earth fallow farming would be just as cooperative and fast without any agronomic work. Perhaps social agronomy provided only a few thousand out of a million rubles increase in the value of the Poltava crop, when only 7 kopeks per each ruble were spent on it. How to answer all these questions? Where to find the necessary evaluation criteria?

The increasing profitability of agriculture is an extremely complex phenomenon determined by a huge number of reasons, and social agronomy is only one of them. It is almost impossible to distinguish its separate effect in the general result. Moreover, social agronomy aims not to create new forms of production but to accelerate the economic evolution and introduce a new economic system earlier than it would develop without the social-agronomic influence. Such an impact of the social-agronomic work complicates its accurate evaluation even more.

American agronomists tried to compare the costs of experimental fields with their benefits for the national economy. They decided to consider one of their most sustainable and obvious agronomic achievements (a new, selected variety of corn, a special technique of ploughing the fallow or a combination of fertilizers), they calculated the effect of this innovation compared to the old methods in dollars per hectare, and multiplied it by the number of hectares on which the innovation was applied. This is a very rough approach, but it is quite illustrative.

Certainly, there are more subtle methods of analysis such as a comparison of increasing yields in different villages with the level of agronomic propaganda influence, etc. However, they all prove only the trend but do not provide a quantitative estimate of the effect of agronomic propaganda.

In the most general terms, this is the essence of social-agronomic reports: if they meet our requirements, they turn into voluminous works that are not convenient for reading at *zemstvo* or cooperative meetings and are incomprehensible for peasants. Therefore, the social-agronomic organization should add to the extensive academic report both a short summary of its activities to be read at the *zemstvo* meeting and a popular brochure to present the social-agronomic work to the general public. The latter is certainly of great importance for popularizing not only social agronomy but also the agronomic innovations it promotes.

CHAPTER 3

A.V. Chayanov *A short course on cooperation*

Moscow: Central Partnership 'Cooperative Publishing House', 1925

The peasant cooperative movement was one of the most important topics in Alexander Chayanov's scientific, organizational, and pedagogical work. He wrote many articles and books on agricultural cooperation, and had hundreds of classes with students at universities and with peasants to explain and discuss various cooperative issues. Finally, Chayanov presented his conception of the ways to develop agricultural cooperation in his famous book *Basic Ideas and Forms of Peasant Cooperation*. At the same time, Chayanov was a talented and passionate popularizer and propagandist of cooperative knowledge among the wider population. Thus, on the basis of his lectures for the Old Believers' Agricultural Courses 'Friend of Land' in Moscow in 1915, he published a booklet *A Short Course on Cooperation*, and in the next 10 years it was reprinted four times and became a desk book on cooperation for many Russian peasants, agronomists, and activists of rural development. This short course presents clear and unambiguous definitions of cooperation and its aims; each chapter is illustrated with popular historical and contemporary examples of the cooperative movement and of the interaction between peasant farms and specific types of cooperatives. This booklet reminds us of two great genres of world literature. On the one hand, it is a propaedeutic *ABC of Cooperation*, like Leo Tolstoy's *ABC for Children*. On the other hand, it is a political-economic Cooperative Manifesto, similar to Karl Marx and Friedrich Engels Communist Manifesto, in which Chayanov describes a fascinating struggle of the Russian and international cooperative movement for the new, just social world. Under the current rural development, Chayanov's *Short Course on Cooperation* is not only of historical interest; it is an outstanding example of the unity of cooperative thoughts and deeds aimed at improving the lives of the broad strata of rural workers all over the world. This work by Chayanov was translated into English from its fourth and last lifetime edition of 1925.

Chapter 1. What is cooperation?

When people talk about the future of the village, they usually pin their hopes on cooperation. The very term 'cooperation' has become one of the most popular words in our everyday language. In any newspaper one finds it dozens of times; the pages of books are full of it; it is heard at meetings, conferences, and congresses. After V. Lenin's last two articles on cooperation, it has become one of the foundations of our economic policy.

V. Lenin declared the exceptional significance of cooperation in the political and economic conditions of Soviet Russia and emphasized with particular insistence: 'Now we must accept, realize, and provide extraordinary support for the only social order, which is cooperative order.'

However, despite all of this and the fact that there are several and not just one cooperative in every one of our *volost* [small rural municipality], not everyone – even those who are practically familiar with cooperative work – clearly understands its essence and is fully aware of its key ideas and organizational principles.

Thus, we have to pay special attention to clarifying the very nature of cooperation in the agriculture of the Soviet republics. We have to consider in detail its possible role in our villages and what it can do for the future of our agriculture.

We know that the most characteristic feature of the economic life of our time, which distinguishes it from the old times of our grandfathers, is the improvement of production machinery and a new, scientifically based organization of industrial and commercial enterprises. Huge steam and electric engines of thousands of horsepower, giant retorts of chemical plants, multi-tonne steam hammers stamping metal products with tremendous speed, automatic scales weighing hundreds of samples per hour with apothecary accuracy, and thousands of other instruments and machines that affirm the power of human genius – those are the features of our time.

And this technical equipment is supplemented by the skilful organization of enterprises. The contemporary factory assembles hundreds and sometimes thousands of workers; it coordinates and unites their efforts in such a way that enables five workers to do the work that would require 15 workers under bad organization. No less than the contemporary production technology, workshops, factories, and enterprises of various kinds form production groups, trusts, and syndicates, thus, winning in the coordination of production and overhead and reducing costs. The entire strength of the industrial, capitalist countries of Western Europe and North America and all their economic power over the rest of the world depend on the skilful use of these two great principles of our time – advanced technology and the proper organization of enterprises.

However, until now, both principles have been applied primarily in urban manufacturing, mining, and transport. Agriculture remains somehow unaffected by these achievements of human culture. Almost everywhere, farming followed the old path of thousands and millions of individual small farms scattered, unrelated to each other, and, in general, not using much advanced machinery.

Certainly, such 'backwardness' in agriculture is not because of accidental reasons but is because the production in farming depends primarily on land, crops, and livestock. Therefore, in many respects it differs from purely mechanical industrial production. Thus, the advantages provided by large size farms and improved machinery in farming are not as great as in industry. Small, technically weak farms in agriculture can show significant resistance to their larger competitors, which is absolutely impossible in industry. The recent scientific studies (of V. Lenin, P. Lyashchenko, and other economists) of American and Russian farming prove that capitalism develops even in agriculture, mainly in the form of the exploitation of the small producer of agricultural products by all kinds of trading companies and enterprises that provide him with credit at high interest rates. The peasant wishes to preserve his economic independence but is, in fact, entirely at the mercy of financial and commercial capital, because he owes this capital a lot of money and cannot ignore it either to sell the products of his labour or to buy the necessary means of production.

All this makes the organization of agriculture on a new basis a most difficult and complex task.

When considering the millions of small, peasant economies – unorganized, dispersed, developing on their own accord like the course of a large river – any organizer of agricultural production can sometimes give up in despair. He can ask himself: Is it possible to organize agriculture like industry on new principles of modern technology and scientific organization? Are there any paths and ways to accomplish this?

We know that we have a large number of improved methods of agricultural technology: improved livestock breeds; improved machinery, fertilizer, and tillage techniques, livestock feeding, and primary processing of agricultural products. The question is how to implement these techniques in the very heart of the village; how to organize the peasantry so that all scientific and practical achievements usually accessible for only large-scale production would become available for the peasantry too.

This question is the most important one for agriculture! And the answer can be given by the application of cooperative principles to the organization of the village.

The basic idea of agricultural cooperation is extremely simple. If we carefully consider the structure of the peasant economy, which is quite complex, we will easily see that, for a number of industries, its larger form will immediately ensure a greater direct benefit. Moreover, it is almost always possible to quite easily identify huge works and combine them into one common, big activity of neighbours without disrupting the work of other parts of the economy and without destroying the labour of the family economy.

A few examples will explain the essence of this statement. For instance, everyone knows the advantages of separators and mechanical churns over home butter-making. However, separators and mechanical churns are inaccessible to a small peasant economy that has only one or two cows. For the separator to pay for itself, it is necessary to start processing as much milk as can be collected from 20 or 30 cows.

It is obvious that no single peasant economy possesses such a herd and, consequently, no single peasant economy can afford the use of a separator. However, it is equally clear that nothing prevents 20 or 40 farms from uniting into a union and building a small dairy factory together after refusing to make butter at home. Nothing prevents them from bringing their milk to the cooperative factory entrusted not only to make butter but also to sell it.

This simple idea has long been recognized by the peasant masses; in different regions of the USSR and Western Europe, dairy partnerships were established many decades ago. Today there are more than 4,000 of them in Western Siberia, the Vyatka, Vologda, and other provinces of the north and in the Kuban. We see that they have united into local unions, which, in the summer of 1924, formed the All-Russian Butter Union entrusted to sell their butter in the domestic markets of the USSR and also in England and other foreign markets. This Union combines the production of butter from the milk of 2 million cows and is one the largest global companies on the butter market. Thus, it is natural that the Union can use all the technical achievements and all the organizational improvements available today.

The cooperative basis of processing and marketing of butter nearly always determines cooperative work in improving livestock and the conditions of animal housing, the development of partnerships for the joint use of breeding bulls, and for livestock insurance against mortality. In other words, soon after a dairy cooperation starts, all the foundations of peasant dairy production turn out to follow the principles of the largest production and most perfect organization.

The same cooperative principles can be used by the peasant to organize other branches of his economy. For example, if peasants in the potato areas are not able to sell their raw potatoes, they may cooperate to create a network of potato-processing factories that produce starch and finally a syrup. This allows them to make full use of all the advantages of this profitable crop and of factory machinery to process it. At the same time, by creating fields for producing improved varieties of potatoes and by supplying the production through potato cooperatives with the improved means of production, peasants organize the whole potato business at the highest technical level without destroying the peasant economies that form the basis of it.

The potato cooperation established the All-Russian Union, abbreviated as *SoyuzKartofel* [Soviet Potato], which unites many thousands of peasant economies.

An even more powerful organization was created by the flax-growing peasants who united the peasant cooperatives of 15 provinces in a union called *L'noCenter* [Flax Centre], which was recognized in the world market as a company selling fibre of immaculate quality and sorting.

It is especially important that, despite the most difficult economic conditions of life in our Soviet country, despite crop failures, and lack of funds and credit, wherever we look – even in the most remote districts of the USSR – there are the same organizational processes in the production of many agricultural goods: bread, sugar beets, poultry, cotton, viticulture and horticulture, agricultural machinery, fertilizers, seeds, and different items of peasant everyday life and consumption.

Certainly, almost everywhere there are only the first and often timid and uncertain steps, but they convince us that the cooperative path is the only one and the right one for our peasantry. These steps show us that agricultural cooperation really allows the organization of the previously scattered peasant masses by connecting them directly to the centres of the economic and cultural life of the Soviet state and enabling them to use all the advantages of the large economy and improved machinery. Moreover, it is especially important that these large and organizationally perfect enterprises are forms of the social economy, i.e. in the social perspective, they are the highest form of organization.

However, let us consider what is necessary for peasant economies to form a cooperative, so that the joint venture will be really cooperative; what distinguishes cooperatives from private, commercial, and industrial enterprises with which they are often unfortunately confused.

We have already mentioned that the cooperative is primarily a union of farms and that the economies forming such a union are not destroyed but are still small labour economies.[4]

However, in cooperatives, only a part of production forms a union, i.e. the part in which the large farm has an advantage over the small one, the agricultural cooperative is a supplement to the independent peasant economy, serves it, and makes no sense without such an economy.

In its further development, cooperation will increasingly turn different branches of the peasant economy into a public cooperative economy. Such elements of the social economy create in the peasant economy the foundations of the future, socialist organization of farming.

To more clearly understand the very essence of cooperation, let us compare two dairy factories – a cooperative one created for their own needs by peasant cattle-breeders, and a private one owned by a capitalist entrepreneur who rented it from *GubSovNarKhoz* [Provincial Council of National Economy]. Let us ask ourselves whose interests guide and manage the work of both factories.

A brief observation is enough to understand that the private factory will pursue the benefits of the capital invested in its turnover. Its main aim will be to organize the whole business in such a way as to obtain the most money, the highest net profit on the capital.

We see a different situation at the cooperative factory. Peasants invested the same capital in its organization and turnover as the private entrepreneur, but the interests of this capital and the task of obtaining the greatest net profit are secondary. The heart and the soul of the whole enterprise is the benefit of the peasants who deliver milk to the factory and who jointly created it in the interests of their economies. The cooperative factory can ensure a zero penny of profit on the capital spent on its construction, but it will still be profitable for peasants if it allows them to get more revenue for their milk than if they sell it into the wrong hands.

Let us further consider the structure of a consumer cooperation in which peasants unite for the joint purchase of products necessary for the household. Here we find the same differences from a private shop as we saw in the dairy *artel*.

The entrepreneur-shopkeeper puts the interests of his capital first. He tries to get the biggest profit from his trade by any means, to the detriment and at the expense of his customers, but, in the consumer cooperative shop, the net profit on the capital invested in the goods is a secondary task. Certainly, capital is necessary for the consumer community, and economic turnover is impossible without capital. However, it is not the interests of capital that manage the business but rather the interests of consumers, of those peasant households that joined efforts to create a consumer shop for their own needs.

For an ordinary shopkeeper, it is beneficial to sell bad products at high prices and to get the highest net profit. For a cooperative shop, profits can be very insignificant, but the products must be good and cheap. No cooperator would like to increase the profitability of his shop by adding sand to his bread and water to the milk for his children.

The most important part of cooperation is such a transfer of attention from the interests of capital to the interests of the peasants who united and created the cooperative enterprise for themselves. Cooperation will always use capital and very large capital, because economic life is impossible without it. However, the interest from this capital does not come first in cooperation but rather the interests of the economies it serves. In cooperation, capital is a servant and not a master.

Therefore, management of the cooperative is arranged in such a way that it is controlled not by representatives of capital and not by those who gave a lot of money for the cooperative trade or production, but by the labour economies by which the cooperative was created and which it exists to serve. Thus, it is clear that the activities of rural cooperation are guided by peasant interests, and all its work is determined by them.

According to V. Lenin's letters on cooperation, in the capitalist society, the peasant cooperative movement was powerless to solve these tasks. Only after the transfer of power to the working people does cooperation with the support of state power acquire a completely different meaning and become the basis of a new social system of the village.

Therefore, cooperation cannot be limited to trade or industry. Interests of the peasantry are broader. Peasants are interested not only in buying cheaper and selling higher but also in many issues of spiritual life, issues of the mind and heart. Cooperation is not only to help the peasant to get greater benefits in his economy but also to help him in enlightenment, in the organization of his spiritual life. Cooperation can give a lot here, perhaps even much more than in other aspects of the village life.

We know that besides the opportunity to purchase a good agricultural machine inexpensively, one should be aware of the existence of such machines and be able to use them. To provide the peasantry with this knowledge, cooperation supplements trade with cultural-educational work in the village.

These are the differences between cooperative production and private entrepreneurship and trade.

After describing them we should also consider the differences between cooperatives and state enterprises, and we should find out why recently the government agencies have transferred and continue to turn a significant number of state agricultural enterprises into cooperatives.

The village is supplied with seeds and agricultural machinery, rental points, breeding bulls, and local potato-processing factories. Last year all dairy enterprises of *GosMoloko* [State Milk] were transferred to the hands of agricultural cooperatives. After the 13th Congress of the Communist Party declared a state policy of agricultural cooperation, we believe that such a transfer of economic activities from the state to the cooperative's shoulders will become more widespread.

Why is this so? Why is a cooperative system considered more perfect for the needs of the village than state enterprises?

In a republic of working people, both the state and cooperative are the governing bodies of the same working masses and serve the same needs of the working people. Therefore, the decision about which of these bodies to entrust with economic work is made every time, depending on which of these bodies is technically most effective.

The elected representatives of the working people manage the cooperative in its smallest structures under the daily vigilant control of the members of the cooperative who elected them. It is not governed by administrative orders of the centre. It is flexible in economic activities and allows the fastest and most free manifestations of the beneficial local initiative. Therefore, cooperation is the best decision if organized, local, self-activity is required, if every individual case demands a flexible adaptation to the local conditions, and if one should take into account the smallest features of every place and every month of work.

All of these requirements – the necessary initiative of the masses, flexibility in organization and activities, ability to adapt quickly, and exceptional sensitivity to the needs of the working masses – are necessary for work in the village. That is why in our Soviet state, whenever cooperation becomes strong enough, it captures – one after another – the different branches of economic work in the village, which was previously dominated by state enterprises consisting of specialists and employees appointed by the centre.

Readers can express concerns that after transferring the economic work to cooperatives, it will no longer be controlled by the governing bodies of the Soviet state. Thus, such a transfer will destroy all planned considerations that are absolutely necessary under the current, difficult conditions of our national economy. However, this fear is completely unfounded, because agricultural cooperation represented by its financial and trade centres and local unions is so deeply integrated into the general system of the government agencies of the USSR and works in such close connection and coordination with them that there can be no contradictions in their work. On the contrary, it is due to the transfer of all economic work in the village to a cooperative that the whole village is being drawn into the mainstream of the planned economy, which became possible only thanks to cooperation.

Cooperation reorganizes the scattered, individual peasant economies into higher forms of social economy, which is the main task of creating a new village.

What we have already said is quite sufficient to understand what the development of cooperation can mean for the village and what a great future cooperation has. All this makes every village worker pay special attention to the study of this new phenomenon of rural life.

In the following chapters, we will consider the history of cooperative ideas and will examine in detail the organizational forms of these ideas in every branch of cooperative work.

Chapter 2. A history of the cooperative movement

The history of cooperation can be traced from the mid-19th century. In the early 19th century in England, there was a man named Robert Owen, who was an industrial figure and, while observing the life of the working people, often thought about how to improve their hard fate.

Robert Owen believed that the human world was not arranged in the right way and too many things in people's lives did not correspond to reasonable grounds. He said that people should help each other to live with friendly joint efforts and should establish special communities to jointly organize their economic life.

His lofty doctrine on new life foundations very soon attracted many supporters in England, but the attempts to implement the ideas he preached in real life failed. Robert Owen based his doctrine on the spiritual unity of people, but he paid little attention to the development of a form for the practical implementation of his ideas and to how they corresponded to the development of the economic life of his time.

However, despite the small success of their practical implementation, the ideas of Robert Owen became widespread in England. A few decades later, in the 1840s, in a small English industrial town, Rochdale, a group of weavers, who considered themselves Owen's followers, founded the first cooperative, which became a model for others and started the practical implementation of the great teacher's covenants.

1. Foundations of consumer cooperation established by the Rochdale weavers

The cooperative founded by the Rochdale weavers in the small Toad Lane of the provincial town was not the first consumer community. In history, there were many attempts to arrange the public sale of essential goods for the benefit of people. However, all such undertakings very soon failed and perished due to the unsuccessful arrangement. And only simple Rochdale weavers, who had long thought about how to improve the life of the working people, managed to find the grounds that allowed their cooperation to develop instead of failing. Therefore, the Rochdale weavers are rightly called the founders of consumer cooperation and of the great cooperative movement.

What were the main principles implemented by the Rochdale weavers? Everyone understands that if you buy any goods from a wholesaler in a retail store not in small quantities but in large quantities, the purchase will cost less and the quality will be better. Therefore, every buyer who wants to get good products at a cheap price should buy them not in *arshins* [0.71 metres] or pounds[5] but in big pieces, wagons or *poods* [16.3 kg], and not in a small shop but directly at a factory or in a large wholesale store.

However, no matter how beneficial this advice is, the question unwittingly arises: can our peasant, worker, or simple townsman store up for the future use butter in barrels, flour in wagons, and textile in bales? It goes without saying that any consumer cannot do that individually. First of all, he never has enough money to pay for these large purchases, and the needs of his household are not measured by wagons or barrels but by pounds of bread and a few pieces of herring, by *arshins* of chintz and not by bales of it.

However, if tens, hundreds, and thousands of buyers unite to buy the goods they need together, they will immediately get the opportunity to buy goods in the largest quantities and will turn into one very large, wholesale buyer. Then the goods purchased will be cheap and of good quality.

This simple idea is the basis of consumer cooperation, and it is clear to any person who has ever thought about his economy. Certainly, this idea was known long before the Rochdale consumer shop in Toad Lane. However, despite numerous attempts, the idea failed previously to be put into practice. Obviously, it is not always easy to realize even a clear and simple plan. We will try to find out the reasons for it. Why did only the Rochdale weavers manage for the first time to establish consumer cooperation?

The simplest way for a joint purchase is when several families knowing each other decide to buy, for instance, some fabric for the summer, raise money together and make a joint purchase, let us say, at the factory of the Bogorodsky Trust, and then divide the purchased bale of chintz or *sarpinka* [printed calico] according to their orders. However, such a joint purchase is not yet consumer cooperation.

It goes without saying that if you buy all the products you need for the household in this way, you will have to gather every day, collect money for the joint purchases, take turns to go shopping. There will be no time for anything else, and the trouble will be extremely burdensome for everyone.

Therefore, people have long sought a good method for the joint purchase of all necessary goods – collecting money, establishing a small working capital, and electing a trusted person to open a small shop from which they can get the jointly purchased goods. Such a community that opens a shop of goods it needs for joint money was named a consumer cooperative.

Such shops were opened long before the enterprise of the Rochdale weavers, but only they managed to find the right principles for consumer cooperation. What were they?

In the first unsuccessful attempts at joint purchases, the public shop bought goods at wholesale prices, added the overhead costs of transportation and maintenance of the shop and warehouse, then calculated the price of goods by weight, and sold them at this price to the members of the cooperation. The goals of the community were achieved. The goods were of good quality and much cheaper than in private trade. However, such communities very quickly weakened and perished.

The cheap public sales irritated the neighbouring shopkeepers who drew such a weak and fragile community into fierce competition by dropping their prices much lower than the cost prices. They suffered some losses but achieved their goal of using the irresponsibility of buyers and turned them away from the public shop and, thus, destroyed the cooperative. There were even cases when traders bought up the goods of the public shop at cheap prices with the help of unscrupulous members of the cooperative and then sold these goods in their shops at a good profit.

However, the huge disadvantage of selling goods at cost prices was that the cooperative could not increase its capital. Its current assets, composed of meagre share contributions, had always been insignificant, and the economic strength of the cooperative was negligible. The cooperative did not have profits from the sale, could not increase its current assets, and often did not have money when there was an opportunity to buy a cheap and good product. Even with the smallest losses, its capital and the cooperative itself were destroyed.

To avoid these adverse consequences, the Rochdale weavers decided to sell goods in their public shop not at cost prices but at the same market prices as the neighbouring traders.

When trading at market prices, the still weak cooperative was not involved in a struggle with rich traders, which was unbearable for the cooperative in the beginning. The profits from market prices significantly increased its economic power, replenished its meagre working capital, and strengthened the viability of the cooperative union. That is why the principle of selling goods to members of the community at market prices, which was established by the Rochdale weavers, is considered one of the most important foundations of consumer cooperation.

However, one can ask what the benefits are for the consumer from bustling about and opening a cooperative shop, if it sells goods at the same prices as private shopkeepers?

The answer to this question can be given by another rule introduced by the Rochdale weavers: in the cooperative, the profits from the consumer, determined by the market prices and forming the income of the shopkeeper in private trade, are returned to the consumer at the end of the year.

Suppose that this year, our consumer shop sold goods for 10,000 rubles and received 800 rubles of profit. This profit is received from members-consumers and must be returned to them. For every ruble taken by the shop, 8 kopeks were the profit and 92 kopeks were the cost price of goods with all the overhead. Thus, if I bought goods in our shop for 100 rubles, then the shop received 8 rubles from me as a profit, which will be returned to me at the end of the year. For instance, if you bought goods for 800 rubles this year, then the shop received 64 rubles of profit from you, which will be returned. If your neighbour bought goods for 125 rubles, then at the end of the year he will receive 10 rubles back.

Thus, when trading at our shop not at cost prices but at market prices, we, the consumers, do not lose anything, because all the profits of the shop will be returned to us at the end of the year. Moreover, we benefit greatly from the profits of the shop. If our shop traded at cost prices, then every day we would buy small things and would get a small profit of 15 or 20 kopeks per day or even less. Such a benefit would be little appreciated and completely lost in our everyday life.

The situation changes completely if our shop takes these kopeks and 10-kopek coins as its profit. This will strengthen the shop and, at the same time, our 10-kopek coins of one day will be added to the 10-kopek coins of other days. The shop will turn into our caring piggy bank and a savings bank that will accumulate for us and give us a few dozen rubles at the end of the year. And this amount of money means a lot to the peasant, worker, or employee with a modest income. In any case, such an amount received in a lump will immediately bring much more benefit than penny savings made during the year.

That is why the return of profits to consumers according to their purchase of goods is considered the second great foundation of consumer cooperation.

However, if we study the life of our Russian consumer cooperation, we will see that even the best consumer communities usually do not distribute all their profits among customers. First of all, big money is spent to expand and strengthen trade, i.e. this money is added to the fixed or reserve capital.

We already know that without a lot of capital the public shop can be weakened, things in the shop will go badly, there will be few goods and few choices, the members-consumers will not be satisfied with their shop and will go shopping in private trade. Therefore, it is in the interest of the consumer himself to ensure the most extensive development of public trade possible and to accumulate such capital that the shop will never lack working capital. Collecting such money by share contributions is very burdensome for members-consumers, and it is much easier to get money from trade, i.e. by allotting a part of the profits.

Cooperatives also allot considerable funds for so-called 'cultural-educational purposes'.

Cooperation gets stronger when it attracts more members and when they hold on more firmly to their cooperative. Therefore, the more widespread the right knowledge about cooperation, the stronger the cooperation.

Moreover, cooperation should not forget that 'man shall not live by bread alone'. When selling cheap bread, sugar, nails, and textiles, cooperators should not ignore the spiritual life of a person. Together and under the guidance of the local departments of public education, cooperatives strive to provide their members with good, entertaining, and useful books, to establish folk theatres, libraries, folk houses, and tea houses, and to organize public readings to teach their members about the ways to farm to make two ears grow where currently the labour of the peasant makes only one grow. All this requires large expenditures and consumers-cooperators who willingly allot them from their profits.

Thus, the profits of cooperative trade are partly returned to the consumer, whereas the rest of them are spent to expand trade and for cultural-educational purposes, e.g. forming public and socially useful capital. Such an accumulation of public capital by allotting a part of the profits is considered one of the most important foundations of not only consumer but also all other types of cooperation.

However, the above-mentioned rules do not exhaust the covenants of the Rochdale weavers for us.

According to the next rule, which is often forgotten by Russian cooperators, the cooperative shop should sell goods for cash only. Taking goods on credit is not allowed in the cooperative, according to the founders of consumer cooperation. This requirement is perplexing and seems especially difficult to fulfil for the working people who support cooperatives. It may seem that the very public shop should come to the aid of the worker when he does not have enough money for daily bread. However, the Rochdale weavers strongly insisted that this rule should be strictly followed.

Why is that? Why can a shopkeeper sell his goods on credit, whereas a consumer community cannot? We will consider this issue in detail and very carefully.

Certainly, a shopkeeper selling goods on credit does not do that from a kind heart but rather for his own benefits. But what kinds of benefits?

It has long been said not to look a gift horse in the mouth! Similarly, one should not be picky and demanding of goods taken on credit. Therefore, when selling goods on credit, without money, the shopkeeper gets rid of all the shelf warmers and products of poor quality, and, at the same time, increases

Cooperative store 'Goznak', Soviet Union, 1925
Photo by J. Steinberg (https://ru.pinterest.com/pin/j-steinberg-cooperative-store-goznak-soviet-union-1925--295971006739356691)

their prices compared to the sales for cash. Thus, the losses of the shopkeeper from the delay in money return and failure to pay debts are covered by the profits from high prices and from the expensive sale of bad goods.

Public trade cannot do this; it cannot slip a buyer a bad product instead of a good one, cannot give short weight or inflate prices by selling goods to the poor buyer on credit. Therefore, public trade cannot cover the losses inevitably determined by the failure to pay debts, which can lead to other significant losses and destroy the whole consumer cooperation.

It should also be noted that when selling on credit, the public shop will always be short of cash and forced to take goods on credit, i.e. the shop will receive goods less regularly, they will be of worse quality, and the shop will repeatedly miss good chances to buy cheap goods of the best quality. Therefore, no matter how hard it is for the labour cooperator, if he values his consumer community and does not want to bring it to ruin, he should completely refuse to sell goods on credit. If there is a very great need for sales on credit, then it is possible to accumulate special capital by allotting a part of the profits, which will be used for loans to poor consumers, while the main trading capital of the cooperative must make its turnover only for cash.

Thus, there are three main foundations of consumer cooperation.

1. The selling prices of the consumer cooperative should be the prices of the usual retail trade and not the wholesale prices, because this is the only way to get a sizeable profit. Small allocations from it will allow an increase in the working capital of the cooperative and will provide the consumer community with free cash that will significantly strengthen its economic power.
2. All profits of the consumer shop should be distributed among individual buyers, not according to the money contributions made at the opening of the shop, but based on how many rubles they spent on purchases during the year.
3. To preserve the integrity of public cooperation and ensure its sustainable organization, we must refuse to sell on credit, because, without usurious interest, sales on credit are too unprofitable.

It is also necessary that every consumer makes a labour contribution to the organization of the shop, that consumers-members work as cashiers and even as countermen, i.e. that they participate in the cooperative with their own labour.

These are the foundations of the great undertaking of consumer cooperation which were laid in 1844.

A lot of water has flowed under the bridge of history since then. The structure of economic life has changed in many ways. Capitalism has developed its new forms, and the social revolution in Russia has put forward a number of new ideas of economic organization. And, certainly, the principles of the Rochdale weavers, while remaining the same in essence, have been partly modified and partly supplemented according to the 80 years of changes in the conditions of economic life and especially under the new forms of its organization in our Soviet state.

The necessity to revise and supplement the Rochdale principles was recognized long ago. Recently this question has been put forward by the conference of cooperators-communists. It should be assumed that in the coming years the theoretical cooperative idea will manage to establish the basic principles of consumer cooperation relevant for the new forms of our economic life.

It is said that Moscow was burnt down by a penny candle. Similarly, from a small shop in the basement of a small house in Toad Lane, a huge social movement began and developed so quickly that after a few decades it had spread to all countries of cultural humanity. The development of this movement did not always go smoothly. Many cooperatives perished, and, in most cases, not because the Rochdale rules were bad, but because they did not follow them.

Today, a few decades after the modest attempt of the weavers, consumer cooperation has managed to remove from its path a shopkeeper, a trader, and other intermediaries, to unite tens of millions of people, to build huge warehouses, its own factories and plants, ocean steamers and railroads, hotels, hospitals, libraries and schools... Great seeds planted by Robert Owen have begun to bear fruits.

2. Raiffeisen principles

A quarter of a century after the first consumer cooperative was established in England, in a small German village, a local *volost* foreman proposed the creation of the first credit partnership – the most important type of village cooperation.

Raiffeisen, the founder of credit cooperation – its 'father' as German cooperators like to say – was born in 1810 and died in 1888.

He devoted all his long life to selfless service to the peasantry. As the *volost* foreman, he knew the village's needs very well and often thought about how to free the German village from the hands of usurers. In those times, usury was exceptionally widespread in the German village. Just like greedy leeches, the usurers sucked all the power out of the working peasantry. At first Raiffeisen tried to solve the problem by creating special unions that bought cattle for their poorest members. However, these unions were based on charity; they existed for a while but were gradually weakened, the flow of donations ceased, and the unions perished. By the end of his life, Raiffeisen realized that charity could not help poor peasants and began to think about helping peasants not by charity but by principles of mutual help for the working peasantry. Raiffeisen knew very well the main causes of rural poverty, and, after long years of reflection, he found a way to fight against them and described this in 1866 in the book, *Credit Partnerships as a Means of Eliminating Poverty*. On 25 April 1869, in the small village of Geddesdorf near the town of Neuwied, he managed to establish the first credit partnership.

What were the foundations of this first credit partnership laid by the 'father' of credit cooperation?

Raiffeisen knew very well that every peasant often needed money for his economic turnover, especially if he had extended or improved his economy. However, it was often impossible for him to get money. The peasant tried different ways and, in the end, he still had to turn to his village's *kulak*-usurer, who willingly lent money at a monstrous interest rate. He would lend 20 rubles, and a month later demand 30 rubles. Under such loan conditions, one could never make any improvements in the economy, because the monstrous interest paid to the *kulak* would negate any profit that a new cow, thresher, or a seed drill would bring.

At the same time, quite a lot of free money accumulated in cities is put into banks and very willingly lent at small interest rates based on reliable ideas and on good securities.

It would be very good for every peasant to go to the city to a bank and borrow the money needed. However, this is hardly possible. One cannot go to a distant city to get 20, 30, or even 50 rubles, because one must pay for the train ticket and will have spent much more than he will get from the borrowed money.

Moreover, the bank will never lend money to an unknown person. And even if the peasant offered to secure the loan with his livestock, buildings, and the entire harvest, the bank cannot check his capital. This is because the money borrowed is so insignificant that no interest will cover the expenses of the bank's inquiries about the peasant's property and especially the expenses of sending a special person to collect non-payment. Therefore, there is no point in banks lending money to peasants in small quantities. The bank will not even consider loans of 50, 150, or 200 rubles.

Raiffeisen had long thought about everything mentioned above. Finally, he suggested that the peasants of his *volost* establish a union that would borrow money in large amounts secured by the mutual responsibility of its members and by all their property.

Five or six hundred peasant families united usually need a few tens of thousands of rubles for their economic turnover. This amount of money is so large that even a very small interest will pay for special trips to the city and correspondence with the bank. And, for the bank, such a large loan is sufficient to cover with interest the costs of inquiries and possible collection of non-payment. The property of 500 peasant households is more than sufficient to secure a loan.

Therefore, the first principle of Raiffeisen – a joint money loan of many peasants united, which is secured by mutual responsibility and by all the property of members – ensured the inflow of capital into Raiffeisen communities and became the basis for the development of credit cooperation.

However, this rule cannot be considered the most important one for credit cooperation. It was introduced by Raiffeisen not so much as the basis of cooperative credit but rather as a well-known security for banks and other institutions and individuals that loaned money to the cooperative. The mutual property liability of cooperative members was understandable and inspired the respect of all capitalist and financial figures of the time.

However, Raiffeisen considered the true basis of cooperative loan not how it would be secured but who would get the borrowed money and on what it would be spent. Therefore, according to the most important Raiffeisen rule, if a partnership gets money secured by mutual responsibility, this money should be given to its members only for productive needs.

Money cannot be taken from the cooperative for a dress or food but only for such expenses that affect economic turnover and, at the end of this turnover, return to the owner with a big profit. That is, money may be taken for such expenses that justify themselves and allow the owner not only to repay the loan but also to get a good profit. This is the most important Raiffeisen principle that determines all others.

If the basis of cooperative credit is the loan for productive purposes, it is obvious that the credit partnership must keep a watchful eye on the borrowed money to ensure that it is not wasted but is spent exactly for the productive purposes for which it was taken. To make such an observation possible, it is necessary to know the borrower very well and to not lose sight of his economy. First of all, it means the requirement to lend money only to the members of the partnership, i.e. to the people well known to share mutual property liability.

In order for the board of the partnership to watch its borrowers, it is also necessary that their economies are under the constant supervision of board members. This is possible only when all the economies of partnership members are located near each other, i.e. when the municipality in which the partnership works is small, the number of its members is small, and its turnover is not big.

In fact, if we unite a whole *gubernia* or *uyezd* [district] into one partnership, there will be no way to control its members' economies, its economic turnover, and the purposes for which the borrowed money is spent. Many believe that even a *volost* is too large for activities of the partnership; it is better for every five or six villages to establish their own credit partnerships. However, with such a small size, the turnover of the partnership cannot be big; therefore, all kinds of expenses – travel, bookkeeping, and record-keeping costs – become burdensome overhead expenses for every ruble lent by the partnership.

Suppose that the management costs are 1,000 rubles. If the partnership loaned 100,000 rubles this year, then, for every ruble loaned (without the interest paid by the partnership) it will have to take 1 kopek from its borrowers. If the partnership lends only 10,000 rubles per year, then it will need 10 kopeks for every ruble lent to repay its overhead expenses.

Raiffeisen believed that it was not possible to expand the area of activities and the number of members in order to increase the turnover of the partnership. He recognized the need to reduce overheads and interest on loans; that is why he tried to somehow reduce the costs of maintaining the partnership. His most important suggestion was to consider the work of members of the board, the treasurer, and secretary-accountant as public duties and honorary positions, i.e. not compensated. Such a definition of the work of the board as honorary and unpaid workers significantly reduced the overhead expenses and the interest on loans, which made the credit more affordable.

These are the main rules introduced by Raiffeisen, the 'father' of credit cooperation. We know five of them: 1) mutual property liability of all members of the partnership for its debts; 2) loans for productive purposes only; 3) loans to members of the partnership only; 4) small area of activities of the partnership; 5) declaring the work of the partnership board honorary and, therefore, unpaid.

Raiffeisen fervently preached these principles. That is why he not only founded the Geddesdorf partnership but also took a trip to the villages of his neighbourhood, where he managed to establish 12 more credit partnerships.

Their exceptional success and the incessant preaching of the 'father' of credit cooperatives contributed to the wide dissemination of new ideas. When he was dying in 1888, Raiffeisen was left with a feeling of deep satisfaction and could count up to 400 German partnerships based on his rules.

This is how the two most important cooperative ideas emerged and developed, showing the working peasantry the ways of revival.

Subsequently, as the cooperative movement spread, rural cooperation expanded far beyond its initial tasks. In addition

Dairy *artel*

Source: https://uprarchives.midural.ru/special/news/show/id/498/category/61

to credit and joint purchases, cooperation began to organize joint sales of the products of peasant labour and often combined them with the processing of agricultural products. Cooperation was also responsible for some special undertakings in cattle breeding, machine use, land improvement, etc.

In its basic idea, each of these new types of cooperation in one way or another followed the principles described in this chapter. However, the new forms of cooperation, its unprecedentedly wide scale, and especially its new tasks that came to the fore, such as some tasks of the state-planned economy, have put forward new ideas for cooperation, which we will present in the final chapters of the book.

Chapter 3. The rural consumer community

We will begin our narrative about different types of cooperative organizations with the rural consumer community.

Among all other types of cooperation, consumer cooperation is the most well-known, due in part to the fact that this kind of cooperation is also practically known to all townspeople. It is also known even more so because, until 1921, in the economic life of Soviet Russia, almost all cooperative work consisted of consumer cooperation, and *E.P.O.* [UCC – United Consumer Community] was almost the only cooperative cell in local cooperative work. Other kinds of cooperative movement began to evolve only with the development of a new economic policy and new forms of our economic life. Today the organizers of rural life focus primarily on the following production forms of cooperative work: dairy, flax, credit, and other types of agricultural cooperation. This focus is quite understandable, because these are the sectors that can increase the income of the peasant economy and well-being of the village and ensure the reorganization of farming and animal husbandry on new principles.

However, when focusing on these issues, the organizer of rural life should not forget the consumer cooperative work, because the properly organized cooperation leads to savings from cooperative purchases of consumer goods and provides the peasant with huge savings for improving his economy.

This is especially true now, when in many provinces and districts, even close to Moscow, our lack of cooperative skills and organization allows the private shopkeeper to dominate again. Therefore, the funds, which could be used to increase production and strengthen the peasant economy under a strong cooperative organization, again today increase the profits of private capital.

The figures for the drop in village prices in the very rural hinterland in the years before the war, when consumer cooperatives first appeared there, show how large these profits can be, provided the weakening of consumer cooperation. For instance, in the Stavropol district of the Kursk Province, in the years when consumer shops first opened, prices of tea and caramel fell by 10 per cent; of sugar – by 13; of matches and buckwheat – by 20; of biscuits and rice – by 15; of lemons and other snacks for tea – by 25; of vinegar and herring – by 25; and of yeast and soda – by 50, i.e. by half. And this happened at such a brisk place in the Kursk Province where it is not difficult to get to the city. We see a quite different situation on the outskirts. What was done by cooperation in the Cherdynsky district of the Perm Province can be called fabulous. [Dmitry] Bobylev, who studied the Perm cooperation, pointed out that with the development of cooperation, the prices changed in the following way: the price of sugar fell by 60 per cent; of kerosene – by half; metal scissors, the price of which is 50–60 kopeks, cost up to 1 ruble 20 kopeks; velvet, which costs up to 3 rubles, was sold at 7 rubles. However, the prices for different little things, especially of nails, increased the most. As soon as consumer shops opened in the district, everyone began to buy goods on average at half price. Bobylev calculated for the Cherdynsky district that, thanks to cooperation, an 800,000-rubles purchase of peasant economies would save them 400,000 rubles, i.e. an amount that exceeds all local and state taxes and leaves a huge sum of money for the improvement of the peasant economy. In recent years, there have been many equally good examples, when consumer cooperation supported by the state has repeatedly prevented the frenzied speculations of private traders by fixed moderate prices.

These are the results of cooperative work in the districts where consumer cooperation confidently stands on its feet.

As the above example shows, consumer cooperation provides the population with large savings and, thus, has a great industrial significance, because it allows the conversion of these savings into agricultural machinery, livestock and improved seeds. This is the consumer cooperation's deep 'production significance'.

However, it should be noted that there are no other cooperatives that are so much in danger of perishing as consumer shops. They are the weakest cooperatives. They are weak not by their foundations established by the Rochdale weavers, but by the fact that members of the consumer shop often forget their cooperative interests and break cooperative rules.

Moreover, consumer shops more than any other have to withstand a heavy rural struggle with shopkeepers and small traders. When opening a credit partnership or a dairy cooperative in a rural municipality, we add to the local economy new sources of income, which were not previously available and can now be used to varying degrees by all local people. And by ensuring incomes for many people, we do not make enemies.

The situation is different in consumer cooperation. The consumer shop immediately makes enemies among local shopkeepers. Its struggle is for life and death, and cooperation triumphs only if it manages to completely oust shopkeepers completely. Therefore, it is no wonder that the latter use all their influence and money to undermine cooperation and turn local peasants from it. Often cooperation fails, because its members do not buy goods in their own shop and prefer other shops.

However, no matter how many consumer shops fail, if we consider the reasons for failure, we will see that they are not the rules of cooperation but the cooperator himself who is irresponsible and does not follow these rules.

In Russia, already in the 1860s, after the peasant liberation, there were first attempts to spread consumer cooperatives, but they were established in cities among workers and petty officials. For instance, in 1878 in Kharkov, there was a large consumer shop that even had relations with cooperatives of Western Europe and sold English cooperative cloth. When time passed and the wave of broad social interest had subsided, consumer cooperation was forgotten, and, only in 1897 with the first normal charter of consumer cooperation, did its new development start. However, before the war, consumer cooperation was growing slowly, and only during the Revolution did it quickly develop and acquire exceptional power.

What rules do we have for cooperatives, and how do we establish a cooperative shop? We need a few peasants who clearly understand the benefits of consumer cooperation and wish to establish a consumer community for themselves and their fellow villagers. The founders should draft and adopt the charter of the consumer community. A standard charter can be found in any cooperative union. The signed charter is sent for registration according to an established order, and the consumer community can start its activities.

In the previous chapters, we have already mentioned the main differences between a consumer shop and a commercial enterprise. Let us consider how these differences are presented in the charter.

For greater clarity, let us compare the organization of a consumer cooperative community with the organization of a private joint-stock company that sells the same goods. Suppose that some people have agreed to contribute their shares, formed the capital, and begun to trade. The number of shares was fixed and limited, and our partners, while trading and receiving profits, have no longer accepted anyone into their company, because any increase in the number of shareholders would reduce their profits.

In the consumer shop, the number of members and shares is unlimited: every worker has the right to demand to be included in the consumer union, and the more members, the stronger the consumer community. This is the first difference.

Furthermore, in all private enterprises, the right to vote and the right to influence the course of the enterprise always correspond to the share contributions: if one partner contributes a large number of shares and another partner contributes a small number of shares, then the former has more influence over the activities of the trading company than the latter, according to the capital contributed. The situation is completely different in a cooperation, because every member, regardless of the amount of money contributed – 10 or 100 rubles – has one vote.

The biggest shares in the consumer community are small, usually no more than 10 rubles. Therefore, everyone can become a member of the community, especially because shares can be paid by instalment. However, it is highly desirable that the wealthy members contribute not one but two or more shares, which will significantly strengthen the consumer community. Nevertheless, as we have already learned, the profit is distributed not by shares but by purchases.

Thus, in a trading company, the capital is the owner, and it makes profit on the consumer, whereas in the cooperative shop, the consumer is the owner. He unites with other members of cooperation and, thus, makes the capital to serve his consumer needs.

Let us now consider the structure of the consumer community. According to the recent decrees about consumer cooperation, its membership is completely voluntary and accessible to all.

The activities of the consumer community are managed by a general meeting of all members. If there are too many members, then they are managed by a meeting of authorized representatives. The meeting solves all key tasks and elects the board that manages all activities of the shop. To control the work of the board, the general meeting elects a special audit commission, which monitors the correctness of the board's work. It is the responsibility of the board to develop a budget, obtain working capital, purchase all goods, set sales prices for goods, and, finally, to carefully keep records and books.

To sell the goods at prices set by the board, every consumer community hires a responsible clerk with whom it signs a detailed contract on how the goods should be stored and sold.

As practice has shown, to be successful, the consumer community needs at least 100 members. With a smaller number of members, the consumer shop cannot pay off: usually a shop of 200 members has approximately 8,000–10,000 rubles of turnover, and its capital has time to turn over approximately 10 times per year.

Therefore, such a store, with a 10,000-ruble turnover, needs at least 1,000 rubles of capital. In other words, if the peasants who established the consumer community do not want it to constantly suffer from lack of money and owe suppliers, they should collect 1,000 rubles as its share capital. Every consumer should contribute shares in the amount necessary to supply the consumer community with goods. If I buy products for 200 rubles at the consumer shop, of which half is bought by the consumer community for cash, then under the nine-fold turnover of capital per year, I have to contribute 10 rubles to the consumer community capital share.

When the necessary capital has been accumulated and the responsible clerk has been hired, the board should take care of purchasing goods. The consumer community entrusts purchases to one of the members of the board, the 'purchaser'.

He acquires most of the goods from the city Cooperative Union (textiles, flour, tea, sugar, etc.), but finds it much more profitable to buy good local products at home (sauerkraut, dried mushrooms, meat, handicrafts, etc.).

What goods and how many of them should be bought? The answer to these questions is given by buyers. Obviously, the consumer shop must have the goods that the consumer who created it needs – the goods that he needs for everyday use in his household. Therefore, the range of goods in the city consumer shop will be different from the village shop, because the needs of townspeople are different from the needs of peasants. The city shop in workers' quarters will sell one range of goods, whereas the city consumer shop organized by wealthy townspeople will sell another range of goods. A village shop in the Poltava Province is unlikely to sell bread and cereals, because its peasant members have a lot of them. But, in the villages of the Moscow Province and Vladimir Province, bread and flour are very important products because peasants do not have enough bread for the winter.

The board should have in the shop all the basic products for which there is a constant demand among its members. Certainly, it is desirable to simplify the situation and to not have too many varieties of goods. At the same time, it should be remembered that, unfortunately, our peasants' cooperative consciousness is still not strong enough, and the private shopkeeper can ensnare the peasant from the cooperative with goods that are more to his taste. Therefore, the cooperative shop should have a more or less diverse range and such goods that, despite being to some degree luxuries, are sometimes used in a peasant's everyday life – artfully painted cups, scented soaps, expensive sweets, etc.

How many goods should be bought? The amount of goods should correspond to the demand, so that they are always necessary goods. At the same time, one should not create stocks that are too large, because the cooperative needs capital that is taken out of turnover, which determines considerable losses for the community, i.e. constrains its already meagre funds.

If the product can always be bought at a cheap price, it should be stocked in the smallest amounts. If it is difficult to find some goods or you need to go far to buy them, then, like it or not, you should acquire large stocks of such goods.

Large stocks should also be made for goods the prices of which fluctuate during the year (hay, oats, etc.). Their stocks should be made at the lowest price, and the stocks should be stored in the shop and warehouse.

The shop should be well equipped. There should be a basement with ventilation, a cellar for perishable food products, and all sorts of other warehouses; there should be scales, a counter, cash register, and cabinets with shelves for goods. The goods should be put on shelves not randomly but reasonably: the most saleable articles often demanded in small quantities should always be at the clerk's hand so that he does not need to rush from corner to corner to get them. The goods should be presented neatly and beautifully to make a good impression on the buyer. The shop should be clean; its walls should be decorated with cooperative posters. The price of goods in the shop should be set before they go on sale.

The price is set in the following way: first, the goods are weighed and counted, and their future shrinkage taken into account; the weight and losses determine the purchase price of the pound, *arshin*, or piece. Then different overhead expenses are calculated – for keeping the shop and its staff, the interest on capital if the goods are bought on credit, and the profit wanted from these goods.

If the goods are saleable, the capital turns over quickly: the goods were bought today and are sold tomorrow or the day after tomorrow, so the charge should be small. For instance, if we charge 2 kopeks per ruble for bread with a daily turnover of the capital, then for the year of 250 trading days, the gross profit will be 50 per cent.

If the goods are unmarketable and turn over only twice a year (perfume, paper, etc.), then the overhead charges should be significantly increased. For instance, if the capital turnover is twice a year, and we add at least 10 kopeks per ruble, we will get only 20 per cent of the gross profit from which, to calculate the net profit, we will deduct the overhead expenses for keeping the shop and its staff.

Moreover, charges are high for the goods that are perishable or luxuries. The charge increases if, due to a profitable purchase, the calculated price turns out to be much lower than the regular retail price.

The goods with set prices go on sale. However, it is often necessary to change the prices. The prices grow when there is a shortage of goods and the product increases in price in the market. The prices fall if, for some reason, the goods are not saleable and threaten to form large stocks, thus, burdening the warehouses of the consumer community. In general, large stocks in the consumer shop harm trade, so, if there are large stocks, it is better to sell them at a cheap price, even at a loss, than to let the current assets rot in the goods stuck in the warehouse.

For good trading, it is of great importance to ensure the right order, convenient hours for the consumer, and other seemingly insignificant terms of sale. If the board ignores them, it can disperse its members, who will find it more convenient to buy goods in a neighbouring private shop.

We have already talked a lot about the distribution of profits from cooperative trade. Now we stress that when distributing profits between members of the consumer cooperative, the board should carefully calculate the cost of the purchases of all its members. The need for such records complicates the calculation and gives the countermen a lot of work.

The cooperative practice shows three ways to calculate the purchases of cooperative members. The first and the most troublesome is to record all purchases in the special clerk's book and on the membership card of every consumer. The second way is much simpler: at the time of payment the shop cashier gives each buyer special stamps for the amount of purchase. The total purchase of all members is calculated by the number of stamps given, and, at the end of the year, every member presents all his stamps received for individual purchases so as to calculate his purchase contribution. The third way is very beneficial for cooperatives and is called 'advance payment'. Every buyer pays some amount of money to the shop in advance and receives a chequebook with tickets-cheques for different amounts. When shopping, the buyer pays not with money but with these cheques. Thus, the number of advances paid is the total cost of purchases minus the unspent cheques.

When the annual profit is calculated, a part of it is used to pay off the shop itself and its equipment. Another part is divided among the members of the consumer community, as we have already learned, according not to share contributions but to purchases in the shop. Suppose the calculations show that the profit for every 10 rubles of purchases is 2 rubles; during the year you took goods for 50 rubles, so you get 10 rubles; if you took goods for 100 rubles then you get 20 rubles. Thus, you use profit not as a representative of the capital invested in shares but as a consumer.

When dividing profits, there is often an interesting question. In most consumer shops, the goods are sold to everyone interested. Therefore, the buyers of the consumer shop are not only its members but also outsiders. The goods sold to them bring a profit. The question is how to distribute this profit. Certainly, non-members will not receive profits on their purchases; so the profit from a free sale goes to the benefit of the community.

However, can we say that in such a way the community profits at the expense of outside consumers? We think that this cannot be said. According to the charter, everyone can join the consumer community, and its task is to ensure that the residents of all neighbourhoods become its members. To attract them, it is necessary to ensure that each person joining the community clearly understands its benefits.

If non-members of the community could make a profit too, then what would be the point of becoming a member of the partnership: why pay fees, why buy shares, why watch and enter the board or revision commission, if you can profit from cooperation without being its member? The fact that no free buyer can profit from cooperation is determined mainly by the intention to make all free buyers become the members of a consumer community.

The profit collected from outside buyers is often used for cultural-educational purposes and to popularize and promote cooperative ideas, i.e. to attract new members to cooperation. It is this desire to make everyone a real participant of the common cooperative business that is one of the most important features of cooperation.

If the capitalist buys stock of some trading company, it is important for him to get the highest return on his shares, although he can have absolutely no interest in the business itself. Despite receiving a return on shares, he can never visit the joint-stock company in which he has shares, and he cannot even know where it is located.

In cooperation, the situation is completely different: it is a common business, and it needs to be monitored by the public; thus, every member of the consumer shop is morally obliged to participate in this public control. A member who is not interested in the work of the shop is a bad member: every disruption should interest him; he must watch everything; and often the consumer shop arranges the shift duty of its members. Such constant monitoring is necessary to ensure that the common business really pursues common benefits.

The cooperation's attitude to various fakes, falsifications, admixtures to, and spoilage of products is also quite different from the private trade. Many shopkeepers benefit from spoiling their products by adding sand to flour, water to milk, etc., because they get profit from such admixtures. However, they cannot be beneficial to the members of the consumer shop, because the profit here is distributed not by the number of shares you have but by the amount of goods you buy per year. If by admixtures you get a higher profit, then you will also eat more sand and more water added to your food.

If you want to eat sand and water for the sake of greater profits, you will falsify products, but every consumer will probably refuse such profit. Thus, the very essence of cooperative work makes falsification impossible, because it will immediately affect the interests of all consumers as the owners of the common business.

Moreover, every trader, if he correctly understands his interests and wants to make a big profit, should keep secret the prices at which he buys products, the places and companies from which he gets the goods profitably, and the layout and combinations of goods that increase their profitability. This is because, for his own profit, it is necessary to deprive his competitors – neighbouring shopkeepers – of all the benefits that he enjoys.

The cooperative shop does not need to keep secrets because it has no competitors. Its members-buyers, if they correctly understand the common business, cannot go to a private shopkeeper after being lured by some bait. If the cooperative shop is bad, if its work does not get better, its members should rather reorganize it than run to neighbouring shopkeepers to buy goods from them.

Therefore, in a private shop, traders strive to keep useful information only for themselves, but in cooperation, all good ideas realized in one shop become known to all other shops, and, thus, everything useful and indeed good becomes widespread.

Recently, when cooperators-consumers want to achieve a larger turnover and to save more on overhead costs, they quite often do not organize small rural shops serving one or two villages. Instead they unite the population of dozens of villages in the consumer partnership, and, to serve these villages, they open not one but a whole network of shops of the same consumer community. Such large consumer associations, unlike petty ones, are called multi-shops.

Although the above-described small consumer community, not to mention the multi-shop, has a many times larger turnover than the peasant family, after eliminating a small trader it cannot buy all goods first-hand in large lots. In other words, a small shop does not achieve the main goal of consumer cooperation by eliminating intermediaries between the consumer and the producer. Therefore, to enlarge their turnover, small, rural, consumer shops create unions to make joint purchases for many tens and hundreds of thousands of rubles.

In the USSR, such unions of cooperatives now exist in every district. They also unite in provincial and regional unions, which unite all the Russian consumer cooperations in the Central All-Russian Union of Consumer Communities located in Moscow and having a huge turnover.

This union with a turnover of hundreds of millions of rubles not only manages to buy all goods first-hand but also has many of its own factories, procurement stations, and other commercial enterprises.

Centrosoyuz [Central Union], as it is abbreviated, helps its members, local unions, and cooperatives not only to make purchases but also to manage the local cooperative work. There is a special instructor department in *Centrosoyuz* whose members study cooperative issues, visit local cooperative unions, help them to keep records, and reveal their mistakes. In contrast, one of the tasks of the non-trading department of *Centrosoyuz* is promotion of the ideas of consumer cooperation. *Centrosoyuz* publishes books, calendars, and booklets on cooperation, and constantly publishes magazines and newspapers.

This is the everyday work of consumer cooperation. However, when doing this seemingly unenviable small work, our rural cooperators should not forget that they are at the forefront of the village struggle against commercial capitalism. The success of their daily work determines the victory on this front. This victory should and can be achieved not by prohibitions or administrative persecution of the private shopkeeper, but by the power of cooperative organization and the ability to organize the rural commodity turnover better than the private entrepreneur.

Chapter 4. Agricultural and credit partnerships

Agricultural cooperatives are much more important for our village than the above-described consumer partnerships, because they organize agricultural production and help to ensure that in the near future two ears will grow on a spot of ground where only one is growing now. This is the agricultural cooperation's exceptional national and state significance, and it was precisely this cooperation that we meant when we considered the reorganization of our agriculture on the basis of scientific knowledge and large-scale production. This significance of agricultural cooperation makes us pay particular attention in describing it.

The basic unit of agricultural cooperation in the USSR is an agricultural partnership acting on territory that usually does not exceed one *volost*. The agricultural partnership aims to help the peasant economy primarily in its cooperative reorganization. That includes helping in 1) the cooperative purchase of agricultural machinery and implements, mineral fertilizers, seeds, and other means of production; 2) sales of those products of the economy that are produced for sale as commodities; and (3) cheap loans for production purposes.

Besides the above-mentioned main cooperative operations, the agricultural partnership usually organizes repair shops, rental points and grain-cleaning stations, seed plots and breeding grounds, experimental and demonstration fields. In general, it seeks to cooperatively satisfy all the needs of the peasant economy, which technically do not require special organizations with a smaller area of activity.

Let us consider each type of the agricultural partnership's work separately.

We will begin with the description of the work to supply the peasant economy with means of production. In its simplest form, this operation is reduced to the peasants' joint purchase of needed supplies and implements. When the time for flax sowing approaches, peasants know from experience that the homegrown seeds' yield is always much worse than of the purebred Pskov seeds. Therefore, they collect the necessary money by banding together, send their authorized representative to the Pskov village to buy a wagon of good, selected flax seed of high germination and purity and, when sharing a purchase, also share its overhead costs.

In exactly the same way, when preparing for mowing, a group of peasants can band together to buy some scythes directly from the factory that produces them.

Sometimes the partnership agrees to band together in advance, but takes from its members the spot cash and gets a loan for a few months from the seller of the goods. It settles accounts with its members only after providing them with the ordered tools and supplies.

When the operations of the partnership expand to ensure a sufficient turnover, and, after collecting share fees and making deductions from its purchases, the partnership acquires a more or less substantial public capital, it ceases to work only on orders. It then establishes a permanent warehouse of agricultural implements and machinery, fertilizers, seeds, and fodder and keeps for sale all the supplies that the peasant economy usually needs.

The organization of such an agricultural warehouse on a cooperative basis should follow the same principles of the Rochdale pioneers that we described for the consumer cooperation. In other words, the purchasing cooperative should trade at average market prices. At the end of the year, it should deduct profits per ruble given by its members and use a part of the profit to create public cooperative capital or for public agricultural needs. Finally, it should not sell its goods to its members on credit.

We have already described the work of the consumer community in such detail that there is no need to repeat the same about the purchasing cooperation. An agricultural warehouse is organized in the same way as a consumer shop but with the obvious differences determined by the nature of goods that require other storage rooms and equipment.

However, in supplying the peasant economy with means of production, the agricultural cooperation cannot be limited to the purchase of implements and supplies. Cooperation should not be limited to replacing the shopkeeper or trader; the nature of its social-economic tasks makes cooperation enter deeply into the organization of the peasant economy's means of production.

First of all, after providing the peasant with agricultural machinery, cooperation should ensure the future replacement of spare parts and repair. A repair shop or even a network of workshops scattered around the area of the partnership's activities is a necessary part of the machinery supplies. The spring repair campaigns of recent years prove the full possibility not only of using one's own facilities for seasonal repairs but also of making special agreements with all mechanical workshops of the district (at factories, railway stations, and so on) to ensure the quick repair of the implements.

Besides the repair of implements in individual use, the agricultural partnership can also organize the joint use of large agricultural machinery: threshing sets, soil-tillers, multi-hull ploughs, Randall harrows, seeders, and tractors. Such joint use can be organized in three forms: 1) by creating on the basis of the partnership a network of rental points scattered around the cooperative's area of activity; 2) by propagating and organizing small machine partnerships that unite one to two dozen householders and have a small set of machines, which the individual peasant economy cannot afford; 3) by organizing joint tillage and harvesting by mechanical means, i.e. by tractors and complex agricultural machines.

The rental points of the partnership should pursue a twofold goal: on the one hand, to promote among its members by practical experience the improved machinery and implements; on the other hand, to allow small economies to use the machines that can be repaid only by large economies. With the development of the cooperative movement, the latter task should be transferred to small partnerships scattered around the villages, because all machines should stay near the fields on which they work. For these small machine cooperatives, the agricultural partnership should play the role of a union and a supplier for its rental points of such rarely used machines that cannot be used in small cooperatives: sward-removers, soil-tillers, meadow harrows, up-rooters, and sets for land improvement.

Finally, the cooperative organization of means of production can assume an even more complete character by turning the joint use of implements into joint tillage, i.e. by combining all arable lands of the partnership's members and their joint tillage with complex machines and tractors.

We believe that in the areas of land surplus and extensive grain economy, this method of farming has a great future and will become widespread.

We do not focus on another and even more complete socialization of means of production in agricultural communes and *artels*. There are special courses and books on this important issue of the agrarian policy of the USSR, which is broader than our topic and beyond it.

The partnership should do exactly the same work in the organization of seed improvement as with the implements. The agricultural cooperation in seed improvement aims to solve three tasks: 1) the elimination of weediness, 2) the provision and constant renewal of excellent seeds to households, and 3) the improvement of old varieties and the introduction of new ones. Moreover, all three tasks should be solved on a mass scale, because their very nature allows their solution only in this way.

The struggle against the weediness of fields should be waged not only by supplying peasants with purchased seeds but also by putting all peasant seeds through special grain-cleaning stations established by the partnership. Made aware of the benefits of sowing clean seeds, peasants will willingly bring their seeds to the grain-cleaning stations equipped with different kinds of sorting facilities, triers, cockle separators, etc.

Peasant seeds, especially flax, often reach 15–20 per cent weediness, which makes their cleaning exceptionally profitable for the economy. However, it is necessary at all grain-cleaning stations to promote other purely agronomic measures to fight weeds (for instance, by ploughing fallow land, etc.).

The second task of organizing seed improvement – constantly supplying peasant households with excellent seeds – becomes an increasingly important measure that will gradually reduce the peasants' use of homegrown seeds that are non-purebred, mixed, and constantly degenerating. In the future, all work with seeds of some crops should be limited to special seed farms with special conditions of purebred production that will supply all agriculture with seeds. The organization of such farms, the testing of different varieties of seeds, and the selection of new varieties is the third task of agricultural cooperation in seed improvement.

However, it should be noted that today in many regions of the USSR, we still witness large under crops, the reduction of some crops due to the lack of seeds, and intermittent crop failures. Therefore, a simple mass transfer of seeds to the regions with shortages is the primary task of agricultural cooperation.

The organizational work of the agricultural partnership in seed improvement and machinery supply can be adopted in other areas of supplying activities: delivery of fertilizers, pest control agents, etc.

When considering all the operations of the cooperative supply, one should remember that they not only allow savings on purchase but also pursue the much broader task of the most perfect organization of the means of agricultural production on a mass scale and in public form. This is the difference between purchasing cooperation and consumer cooperation, which does not solve agronomic tasks.

Cooperative work in the organization of the means of agricultural production with a persistent, year-to-year plan of compliance opens exceptional perspectives. In five to ten years, it can free the village from backward implements, buildings, and seeds by completely replacing them with the best ones technically. A significant number of complex, large machines and buildings should remain in public use.

These are the supply tasks of agricultural cooperation, but its tasks in the sales of agricultural products are even more significant and important. However, because not only agricultural but also other special cooperatives take part in sales, we believe it is necessary to consider sales cooperation separately in a special chapter.

Therefore, when speaking of the further work of the agricultural partnership, we will focus on the most important part of this work at the present time – small loan operations. We have every reason to consider the restoration of cooperative credit as one of the most important tasks in the development of our agriculture.

During the war and the Revolution, the peasant economy has considerably worn out its production equipment. There are not enough horses, cattle, and pigs, and, in many areas, flocks of sheep have been nearly destroyed, and, in some places, there is a huge shortage of equipment. However, even if the means of production of the peasant economy were now the same as before the war, we would consider them insufficient. Our task is not to restore the previous three-field farming but to create a new agriculture based on new technology and organization.

Such a new agriculture requires more and more financial costs. Now we plan a number of major agronomic reforms. And it is necessary to clearly understand that each of these reforms primarily requires new expenses.

The still weak peasant economy cannot save money from its meagre income and has no source to obtain money. Thus, the only way to satisfy this financial need is to get help. For its development, agricultural production needs loans, and the long history of crediting in the village shows that these loans are possible only on the Raiffeisen principles, which we have already considered.

This credit is so important for the developing agricultural country that, for example, before the war in Russia, credit cooperation was the main branch of the village public works. All other activities of cooperatives were in addition to credit in the small cooperatives.

Today, due to the lack of a stable monetary unit until 1924, credit operations within agricultural cooperations are still underdeveloped, and the main cooperative network consists of general agricultural partnerships. However, this does not reduce the value of cooperative credit. According to the charter, the agricultural partnership can conduct credit operations, and we have no doubt that in the coming years, cooperative credit will be among the key branches of cooperative work.

We will try to study in detail the economic foundations of cooperative credit and its organization.

According to the Raiffeisen basic principle, cooperative credit is primarily a productive loan. Let us find out what this means for our village. When we speak of a productive loan, we want to say that a peasant who took a loan in the cooperative does not spend it on a fur coat or tea and sugar but on economic turnover and, moreover, on such a turnover that ensures an income sufficient not only to repay a loan with interest but also to make a profit for the economy.

A few examples will explain this idea. Suppose that a peasant does not have oat seeds and does not have money to buy them. He takes a loan of 20 rubles, buys 40 *poods* of oats and sows them. In the autumn, he gets a 180-*pood* yield, which he sells for 90 rubles, so he easily takes 20 rubles to repay the loan plus 2 rubles of interest and retains 68 rubles for his labour and other costs. Thus, the loan is fully secured by the expected harvest and is easily repaid by its sale.

Let us consider another example. Due to the very large yield of grass, the peasant gets 600 instead of 400 *poods* of hay. To feed his two heads of livestock, 400 *poods* are sufficient, but to sell the excess 200 *poods* is not profitable, because, under the large yield, the price for hay fell to 15 kopeks per *pood* and is not recouped in harvesting. The peasant takes a loan of 100 rubles to buy a second cow with an autumn calving. During the winter, the cow eats 200 *poods* of hay and gives 80 buckets of milk, which the peasant sells to the dairy for 120 kopeks per bucket; therefore, he gets 96 rubles. In the spring, he sells a cow for the same 100 rubles. From the revenue, he pays 10 rubles of interest and gets 86 rubles for fodder and labour. If he had sold the hay in the autumn for 15 kopeks, he would have received only 30 rubles. But he took a smart loan and used it in the production turnover, which allowed him not only to repay the loan easily but also to increase his income by 56 rubles.

In this example, the loan was secured primarily by using the money for buying a cow, the sale of which always repays the loan, and the payment of interest on the loan is justified by the correct calculation of the difference between the cheap price of hay and the more expensive fodder at the cooperative dairy.

Despite some differences, the examples are very similar. Let us consider a third example that is somewhat different from them. In the autumn, the peasant needs money for his family's food and has the opportunity to sell 100 *poods* of oats at low, autumn prices – 50 kopeks per *pood* or 50 rubles in sum. He considers this revenue to be too small, so he brings his oats to the cooperative warehouse to get a loan of 45 rubles to support his family during the winter. In the spring, the price of oats rises to 70 kopeks per *pood.* The peasant sells his oats in May, earns 70 rubles, of which he pays the 45 rubles of loan plus 4 rubles of interest, and gets 21 rubles of profit. At first glance this loan seems purely consumer but, in fact, it is based on the correct economic calculation of the use of the seasonal price difference and is reliably secured by 100 *poods* of oats harvested.

In all three examples, the economic turnover ensured by the loan did not exceed 6–8 months; the loan was taken for the same period and can be called a short-term loan.

A loan taken for the economic turnover of several years is somewhat different. Suppose that our peasant needs to drain his meadow, which is waterlogged and produces only 120 *poods* of hay from 3 *desiatinas* [1.093 hectare]. Digging ditches, laying down the fascine drainage, levelling the hillocks, ploughing and sowing a mixture of herbs, besides the peasant's own work, would cost 210 rubles or 70 rubles per *desiatina.* As a result, instead of 120 *poods* from 3 *desiatinas,* the meadow gives 330 *poods,* i.e. 210 *poods* more, or, at the price of 40 kopeks per *pood,* 84 rubles more than before the reclamation. Taking into account the increased costs of the larger harvesting per *desiatina,* we can be sure of the increased income of 75 rubles from the meadow's reclamation. Certainly, despite the profitability of reclamation, the loan of 210 rubles taken for it cannot be repaid from one year's income, and it is necessary to distribute the payment on the loan over at least four years. Thus, the loan should be taken for at least four or five years, i.e. this should be a long-term loan. Calculation of the land reclamation costs proves that this loan is quite secure by the increased income from the meadow.

The above examples show perfectly, on the one hand, the benefits that the peasant can get from the proper and reasonable use of a productive loan, and, on the other hand, the grounds for the creditworthiness of the peasant economy, which constitute the small production loan based on the Raiffeisen principles. It is not without reason that in the countries with developed cooperative credit, investments in Raiffeisen partnerships are considered the most reliable ones!

Thus, having identified the economic essence of cooperative credit, we can now consider its technical organization.

The crediting procedure in agricultural partnerships is usually as follows: every member of the partnership who wants to get a loan provides the cooperative board with the information about himself and his economy, such as the number of buildings, equipment, livestock and the size of arable land. This information should be checked to become the basis for issuing loans together with the evaluation of the peasant's personal qualities, his work capacity, ambition, and conscientiousness. The partnership decides on the extent to which it is possible to give a loan to this peasant without risk. Before the war, the average open credit to a member of the partnership was about 80 rubles.

If the partnership has approved giving credit to the member of the cooperative, then, if he needs money, he can ask the cooperative board for a loan by indicating in his application the purpose of the loan, its size, and maturity date. The purpose of the loan should be productive and loss-free, its size should be consistent with the purpose, and, if possible, not exceed the open credit limits, and its period should not exceed six months. A loan for longer terms can be provided only if the partnership has special capital for long-term loans and for a special order.

If the partnership has cash and the peasant's request is economically reasonable, the loan is issued in full or in part, and the interest is deducted in advance for the period declared in the application. For instance, if a peasant gets a loan of 100 rubles for six months at 12 per cent per annum, then he actually receives only 94 rubles but should repay 100 rubles.

The loans are issued under a three-fold collateral: 1) the personal trust of the member receiving the loan, 2) the guarantee of some other member, 3) security of the product or livestock.

Personal trust is enough for relatively small loans indicated at the opening of credit. If the requested loan exceeds this amount, it is issued only if some other member of the partnership gives his guarantee for its return. Under such a guarantee, in case of non-payment, the money is collected primarily from the debtor, and only then from the guarantor, if the debtor cannot repay the loan. It should be noted that, when opening credit, the partnership should set not only the maximum size of the loans available to the member under personal trust and guarantee, but also the size of the loans that this member can guarantee for others.

The amount of a loan issued on bail should correspond to the collateral and be no more than 3/4 or 2/3 of it. Products of agriculture can be accepted as the security of the borrower – bread, flax, leather, etc., or cattle. The pledged agricultural products are usually transferred to the warehouse of the partnership, which often organizes their joint sale; the pledged cattle stay in the stable of the owner but become 'prohibited', i.e. the owner is deprived of the legal right to sell, give away, or take these cattle anywhere without the special permission of the cooperative.

The loan can be issued both in money and in kind in the form of a warrant for the warehouse of the partnership. Such an issue of agricultural machinery, fertilizers, seeds, and other things does not violate the Rochdale principle of trading only for cash, because the necessary amount of money is immediately transferred to the account of the warehouse from the credit department of the partnership, which constitutes a cash payment. Thus, this is a combination of two types of operations – purchase and credit.

Because the loan is provided and the borrower gave a debt receipt to the partnership, its board has the right to check if the money was used for the specified purpose. If the borrower lied, the partnership can demand an immediate return of the loan and exclude an unscrupulous borrower from the partnership. If the economic turnover for which the loan was taken is not over by the time of the repayment, or if the calculations of the borrower were not fully justified, he can ask the board to defer payment. After careful consideration of the circumstances and validity of the request, this can be allowed for usually no longer than six months.

If the borrower delays return of the loan for a few days without notifying the board, a special penalty is imposed on him for each day past due.

This is the crediting technique of credit cooperation.

Where does the partnership get funds for issuing loans to its members? These funds consist of 1) the fixed capital of the partnership, 2) the reserve capital of the partnership, 3) some special capital, such as long-term, loan capital, 4) the partnership's loans for different periods, 5) public deposits transferred to the partnership on different terms, and 6) the money saved by the partnership for different periods. Let us consider each of these sources separately.

The fixed capital can sometimes be made up of the share fees of members of the partnership, but, according to the Raiffeisen principles, it is usually borrowed as a long-term loan, which is gradually repaid by annual deductions from the partnership's profits. Such a method of accumulation ensures that, in a few years, the partnership will turn the fixed capital into the social capital accumulated in the course of its activities.

Today in the USSR, there is no final procedure for small credit organizations to accumulate fixed capital. However, it is most likely that the Central Agricultural Bank of the USSR will take the responsibility for financing the fixed capital of agricultural partnerships and will rely on local agricultural credit communities and local cooperative unions.

The Agricultural Bank as the centre of all agricultural crediting should devote a significant part of its work to issuing all types of loans to the peasant economy through cooperatives. Issuing loans for the fixed capital of local partnerships should become the bank's main activity because of the simplicity of this work, on the one hand. On the other hand, only this bank can solve this task on a mass scale with the help of large and long-term state funds. In all likelihood, a part of state savings banks' funds and some insurance capital will be used to finance cooperative credit.

The reserve capital is accumulated by the partnership gradually – by deducting a part of profits – and serves as collateral for all the obligations of the partnership and as a source to pay accidental damages.

Special capital for different special purposes is accumulated either by special loans or by deductions, fees, and even donations. When it is already on the accounts of the partnership, special capital can be temporarily used for credit purposes. A special long-term loan capital can be used for direct crediting, and its accumulation is extremely important because of the very acute need of our village for long-term loans.

Loans are taken by the partnership when there is a lack of funds: usually these are short-term loans from other cooperative organizations, local banks, and even individuals. Provided the proper organization of the partnership's activities, such loans should not play an important role in its funds, because this is the most disadvantageous and expensive form of getting money.

The main source of funds for the cooperative credit should be the community itself; i.e. the peasants – both members of the partnership and all willing local people – should turn their available funds into the partnership's deposits. Under the developed and trusted cooperative movement and during the noticeable improvement in well-being of the population, the inflow of deposits to cooperative partnerships is usually so great that it ensures their crediting work.

When people are convinced of the strength and complexity of cooperative organizations, they usually transfer to them at a quite low interest rate all their savings 'for a rainy day', which were previously stored in thrift-boxes, stockings, and chests. People make deposits from spare cash that they cannot invest more profitably for some reason, and they temporarily make deposits from their working capital if it is not needed for production purposes for several months during the dead season.

Deposits can be time and non-fixed/on-call. If the person has a non-fixed deposit, he usually pledges to inform the board of the partnership a few days before he will reclaim it, and in the case of a large deposit, a few weeks before reclamation, so that the sudden withdrawal of a large sum will not damage the partnership's business.

The amount of deposits made by the member of the partnership is kept secret. They can be recovered or prohibited to be used only by order of the judiciary. The interest paid by the partnership on time deposits cannot be changed before the maturity of the deposit. The interest on on-call deposits can be changed any time by a resolution of the board.

These are the sources of funds for the crediting work of the partnership.

To finish the description of cooperative credit, we should focus on the very important circumstances of crediting work.

1. When considering the crediting activities of the partnership we said nothing about how the interest rate on its loans is set. We could not explain this without having described the sources of the partnership's funds. Now we can indicate that the interest rate on loans is determined entirely by the interest rate at which the partnership can get funds as loans or deposits. Having received the funds for deposits, for instance at 8 per cent per annum, the partnership adds to this interest another 2 or 3 per cent to pay the board members and to create profit, and issues loans at 10 or 11 per cent per annum. The difference between loan and deposit interests is called 'percentage stress', and, in a well-developed partnership, it should be as small as possible. Profits and funds for salaries of the board should be increased not by higher 'percentage stress' but by the growing credit turnover.
2. When issuing loans, the partnership has to take into account not only the available amount of cash but also the terms on which they were given. Four-month deposits cannot be given for seven months, because, when the time comes to return the deposit, there will be no way to get this money from the borrower. In other words, the terms of loans should always more or less correspond to the terms of deposits and taken loans, because any disparity can put the partnership in an extremely difficult situation.

3. The distribution of profits from credit operations deserves special attention. Because credit partnerships have no shares, their members cannot receive profits on shares. Similarly, there are no profits on the credit or deposited ruble, which is typical for other cooperatives. All profits of the cooperative credit are usually turned into social capital. Before the war, usually in credit partnerships, 40 per cent of profits were deducted for the fixed capital, 20 per cent for the reserve capital, and the remaining 40 per cent for the various agricultural and cultural needs of the local population and sometimes also for special capital.

In short, this is how the cooperative credit works. If you take a deeper look at this work, you will easily see that the cooperative credit is much more important than just helping individual economies. As credit cooperation develops and strengthens, it inevitably absorbs all the spare cash of the village as deposits and supplements them with public funds and capital received from the banks. Thus, a credit cooperation makes loans cheap and accessible for every peasant and introduces them into ordinary life. In agriculture, just as now in industry, most of the working capital will be invested and borrowed mainly from cooperatives. Dairies and potato-grating plants, stud farms, machine and grain-cleaning stations, mills, and other cooperative facilities will be built and organized on cooperative capital, in these cooperative buildings, and all sales, purchases, and processing operations will be implemented on the same cooperative capital. In other words, provided the wide scale of all the above-mentioned operations, we will see a gradual cooperative socialization of all capitals in agriculture and in the marketing of agricultural products.

Contemporary capitalism is usually called financial, because its main owner and organizing and leading force is the bank capital, which finances industry and trade and provides funds for their entire turnover. Provided the development of cooperative credit and a powerful inflow of funds to the peasant economy with its help, the financial capital will gain a governing and all-determining role in the countryside. However, this capital will not be the capital of bankers but rather public, cooperative, and state capital.

The above considerations give an entirely different connotation for the modest work of our cooperative partnerships. Despite their everyday character, they make it the most important work in the creation of a new, social-economic system by providing the whole system of agricultural credit – from local agricultural partnerships and their unions to the Agricultural Bank of the USSR – with an absolutely exceptional value in the socialist construction of our country.

Chapter 5. Cooperative sales of agricultural products

We have already mentioned the benefits of cooperation for peasants in getting cheap loans and purchasing goods. However, cooperation is even more beneficial in marketing the products of peasant labour. Those who visited our northern flax fairs before the Revolution understood quite well the losses of the peasantry from such sales. When the peasant got to the fair with his flax bundles, his flax was pulled and broken, which confused the peasant. By agreement, dealers beat down the price, defamed the goods, and, finally, gave the peasant short weight in the turmoil of the fair. The flax gathered by the dealers was bought by a county trader and then sold at a wholesale price. It was bought by a foreign company and sent to England or other countries by sea to finally appear on factory spindles.

The peasant was selling clean and dry flax at a cheap price; the factory received it damp and with impurities at a high price. Only the dealers and traders profited. It seemed very easy to send flax directly from the peasant to the factories' spindles, and many Russian public figures have long thought and talked about this. However, it is easier said than done. There were much greater obstacles to cooperation in marketing agricultural products than in purchasing them.

These obstacles were primarily determined by the technical organization of marketing. Consumer cooperatives received their goods from factories and wholesale enterprises as sorted, weighed, and packaged. The marketing cooperation dealt with the raw product and had to do all the sorting and packaging by itself, at first without proper skills and knowledge and only gradually learning the technique.

In the most difficult part of trade – the sales – the consumer society had to compete with the small rural shopkeeper, who was quite weak and did not have much capital. But the sales cooperation selling the goods abroad had to compete with the largest, oldest companies in the world with huge capital, many years of experience, and excellent knowledgeable employees.

It was difficult for a cooperation to break into the global market, especially because the buyers had become so used to the low quality Russian flax that, at first, they paid the same price for the pure, cooperative flax as for the flax with impurities, because they did not trust its purity. However, after long efforts, the cooperation managed to win the competition and gradually arrange cooperative sales of flax, eggs, and hemp. Perhaps soon we will manage to arrange the mass cooperative sale of bread, to which serious steps have already been taken.

The grounds of sales cooperation are very simple.

An agricultural partnership or a special sales cooperative, which wants to arrange cooperative sales of, for instance, flax, rents convenient warehouses, gets a press for packing flax into bales, invites an experienced sorter, who knows how to work with the fibre, sets the days and hours for accepting the goods, and proceeds to work.

Every peasant, a member of the cooperative, brings his flax fibre to the cooperative, the sorter examines it, identifies its quality, divides the fibre into varieties if it is not uniform, weighs it and, after accepting it, gives the peasant a receipt stating that the cooperative has accepted from him, for instance, '5 *poods* of the first grade flax at the price of 10 rubles per *pood*, and 10 *poods* of the second grade at the price 8 rubles per *pood*, i.e. in total 15 *poods* for 130 rubles'. The prices are set by the board of the cooperative according to the market situation and are posted for everyone to see together with the samples of sorting.

The flax accepted from the peasant is sorted in special warehouses by specified varieties and mixed with other peasants' flax of the same varieties. Thus, as they say, flax is 'depersonalized', i.e. each strand of the fibre loses its connection with its owner, mixes with other similar strands, and, in the future, the owner has the right not to the flax that he produced and brought to the cooperative, but only to the same amount of the same varieties of flax or rather to the cost of them.

Impersonal flax is pressed by varieties into bales and goes on sale.

Usually the peasant who brought his flax to the cooperative needs money and cannot wait for the cooperative to find a buyer for his goods, which often takes three to four months. Therefore, the cooperative usually provides the peasant immediately with a loan secured by his goods and constituting 60, 75, or even 100 per cent of their estimated price. After the goods are sold, the cooperative takes the amount issued from the proceeds, and the peasant gets all the surplus except for a small commission percentage.

We should never forget that the money given by the cooperative to the peasant for his flax at its acceptance is nothing else than a loan secured by flax and not a payment for flax. We have two operations here: 1) joint sale of flax, and 2) issuance of a loan secured by flax, and not just one operation of purchase and sale. Therefore, if under the confluence of adverse circumstances, the joint sale of flax provides less revenue than the loan issued, and the proceeds from the sale do not repay the loan, the cooperative can and should demand from the peasant payment of the loan balance in cash.

Such a payment is unpleasant for the peasant's empty pockets and can determine distrust in the cooperative. That is why cooperatives do not usually issue the entire loan but only three-quarters or another part of it, so that, even in the case of a cheap sale, the loan will not exceed the amount received from sales. This part will increase if the cooperation does well, and if it can get higher prices in the wholesale market than at the agricultural fair.

It goes without saying that, for the sales cooperation that is striving to sell its goods on the largest foreign market, the transformation of an association of small cooperatives into powerful cooperative unions becomes especially important. Only huge batches of flax of different qualities will allow a cooperation to take a strong position in the market. The larger its turnover, the greater influence it exerts on the level of prices, thus, ensuring the peasant a high payment for his agricultural labour.

In its first years, the flax cooperation united its cooperatives into dozens of unions and merged these unions into its centre called the Flax Centre. It is the All-Russian Union of peasant flax-cultivators and hemp-producers. It meets all the needs of the flax-growing economy, sells peasant flax for tens of millions of rubles, supplies peasants with good seeds, and leads the entire local flax cooperation.

Many peasants followed the path of flax-cultivators: for instance, the hemp-producers in the Chernihiv and Orel Provinces, who organized the hemp cooperation; the peasants of the Kostroma and Vladimir Provinces, who organized the sales of potatoes; the cotton-growers of the Turkestan Province, Voronezh Province peasants, who organized the joint sales of eggs, and, recently, steps have been taken for the joint sale of bread.

Thus, it should be noted that sales cooperation does not only increase the incomes of the peasant by selling his products at higher prices but it also has a great impact on the organization of his production. By paying higher prices for good varieties and by informing the peasant of the market demand, a cooperation sometimes makes him change the whole organization of his economy and develop it on new, improved principles. That is why, although at first glance sales cooperation looks just like a trade, we always consider it the first step in the organization of production and call it production cooperation.

However, it should be noted that many agricultural products have to be processed in order to be sold in a good, distant market at a high price. These are milk, vegetables, potatoes, and fruits. They are very heavy and difficult to transport. They become profitable and non-perishable goods only when processed into cheese or butter, into dry vegetables, starch, or syrup and preserves. Therefore, when arranging a cooperative sale of these products, we should, at the same time, arrange their cooperative processing. The model of such a cooperation for marketing and processing is the most widespread type of cooperative, the dairy, the organization of which will be described in the next chapter.

Chapter 6. Dairy *artels* and other animal husbandry cooperatives

Among all cooperatives, dairy partnerships are of the greatest importance. They are models for cooperation, in which marketing is combined with processing.

The artisanal method of butter-making consists of simply settling the milk in wide cans, and about one-quarter of the butter remains in the skim milk and is lost. If cream is separated by a machine (separator), then only one-hundredth instead of one-quarter of the butter will be lost, and the creaming itself will be much faster. Such a transition from manual creaming to a mechanized process allows one to gain about 10 kopeks per bucket of milk.

The usual milk yield of a good cow is 180 buckets per year, so the replacement of a simple paddle with a separator gives us more than 20 rubles per cow in gold.

It should also be noted that when we use a paddle to make butter at home, we can make only Russian melted butter that is usually quite cheap. Moreover, it is important to note that 1 *pood* of Russian melted butter requires 30–32 *poods* of milk. But when we skim the cream off with a separator and use it to make butter, then we can make the best, so-called Parisian butter, which requires only 21 *poods* of milk per *pood* of butter and is more expensive than the simple Russian butter.

All these advantages encourage the transition from manual creaming and manual bottle-butter-making to the mechanized method. However, to pay off the separator and other machines necessary for mechanical butter-making, we need to process at least 200 buckets of milk per day or most of the time the machines will stand idle, and their work will cost more than manual processing. Thus, for the dairy to operate quite profitably, the owners have to unite in a partnership with at least 200 dairy cows. Obviously, no single peasant economy can have so many cows, so, to take advantage of machine processing it has to unite with its neighbours. Besides the technical benefits of using the separator, such a union allows peasants to sell their butter not in small amounts through the buyer-up but in large quantities and independently in the wholesale market.

In Russia, such dairy unions first appeared in Western Siberia not as cooperative but as private and industrial. Mainly the foreigners built small dairies that quite profitably sold butter to England and other markets. Usually such dairies had small food shops. In fact, it is difficult to understand how these small dairies survived. They bought milk from peasants and paid for it with their shops' food products. You can guess the prices of these goods. Moreover, the shop often traded on credit at high interest rates, which often determined a much higher profit for the dairy's shop compared to the profits of the dairy itself. However, such small industrial dairies played a great educational role in Western Siberia. They allowed the local population to see with their own eyes that technical improvements and the collection of large quantities of milk led to great profits for the dairy and showed the benefits of a cooperative shop. Such private dairies and small shops determined the development of Siberian dairy *artels*.

The *volost* scribes were primarily the first leaders of the Siberian cooperative organizations. They represented the most intelligent group of the population, read a lot, had connections with Russia, and were the first to talk about the possibility of organizing dairies on a partnership basis. The organizer of dairy cooperation in Siberia, [Alexander] Balakshin, began to develop this business. Soon in Western Siberia there were dairies that paid the population 40–50 kopeks per bucket of milk and managed to take the place of private, industrial enterprises.

Entrepreneurs started the Siberian butter-making industry. Now the population has taken this business into their hands in dairy cooperatives, which, from the very first step, followed the path of the partnership. The well-known Siberian Union of Dairy *Artels* was founded and began to develop rapidly.

Following the example of Siberia, dairy cooperation spread into the Vologda, Vyatka, Yaroslavl, Moscow, and other provinces. Today it seems that we will not find any province without some dairy cooperation.

Dairy *artels* are established by a contract of participants or by a charter and its registration.

The necessary machinery and devices for a small factory to process 200 buckets of milk cost about 600 rubles. The premises can be rented; if you want to build your own factory in the forested part of Russia, it will cost about 600 rubles, so the whole factory will cost between 1,200 and 2,000 rubles in gold.

A good icehouse is the main expense. A cellar is to contain at least 2,000 *poods* of ice. According to the practice, the calculation is very simple – 1 *pood* of ice per 5 *poods* of daily milk.

How is the dairy established? Where can we get the necessary 1,000–1,200 rubles? The separator and other machines can be bought on credit through local cooperatives. The loan is usually issued for nine months, and, if the general assembly of the *artel* decides not to take money for milk until its members pay off their debts and the cost of the dairy equipment, then nine months are more than enough for any *artel* to repay this debt with interest.

Let us consider an example of one *artel* in the Vologda Province. It started business with 165 rubles, and, for nine months, none of its members took money for milk. In a year they had produced 1,002 *poods* of butter for 15,000 rubles, which allowed them to repay all the costs of the dairy equipment with interest and gave them a huge profit that was divided between shareholders at the end of the year.

What are the organizational principles of the *artel*? They are the same as in the consumer shop. The *artel* also needs capital, and this capital is also exclusively of service. This means it serves the interests of the united owners. All profits are also not included in the dividends on the capital invested but are distributed according to the amount of milk that each member delivers to the partnership.

In most cases, the partnership does not have any shares. Because of the nine-month loans, almost all partnerships were established on credit. However, sometimes the share capital is collected by members. Equipment on credit is repaid in the very first years, and without any initial capital, the partnership is on its feet.

After the organization of the cooperative, the dairy members of the *artel* begin to deliver their daily milk. Their daily milk is weighed and recorded in a special book. At the end of the week the *artel* pays its members for the delivered milk at the prices set by the board.

These prices are set in such a way that the *artel* gets some profit after the sales of products. As was mentioned above, this profit at the end of the year is calculated in the same way as in the consumer shop, i.e. according to the amount of milk delivered by every member of the *artel*. Suppose that we have 10 kopeks of profit per bucket, and you delivered 200 buckets of milk this year, you get 20 rubles of profit. If you delivered 100 buckets, then you get only 10 rubles.

When delivering milk to a private dairy, it is in the interest of the peasant milk-supplier to sell milk at the highest possible price under the weekly calculations. However, a peasant working for the cooperative dairy can agree to a small payment for each bucket of milk, because he is sure that he will get the profit from his milk in the partnership: the profit will be used to repay all the factory equipment, and the remaining part of the profit will be distributed between members at the end of the year according to the amount of milk they delivered. Thus, eventually you will receive not less but much more for milk than the private entrepreneur gives.

In other words, the income in the *artel* consists of two parts: the member receives one part weekly and the other part at the end of the year. Which of these parts should be larger? Some say that it is better to receive a larger weekly part, and others say that it is better to get a large amount at once at the end of the year, with which one can do much more than with small payouts.

We think that it is better to make weekly payouts at a low price and, at the end of the year, to pay the resulting profit.

This method allows the partnership to always have a large amount of capital in cash for any unexpected extraordinary expenses. If this capital is not sufficient, the partnership deducts 1 or 2 kopeks per bucket from weekly payouts and very soon accumulates a large amount of capital.

These are the general principles of the cooperative dairy's work.

In Western Europe, payouts and distribution of income and expenses are sometimes more complex. In fact, concerning dairies, we are interested not in milk but in butter. But if milk is taken from different cows, then the fat content of milk of each of them is different. The Russian cow gives milk with 4.5 per cent fat, and the Western European cow gives milk with 3.25 per cent fat, although its milk yield is higher. If the cows of the *artel*'s members give different milk by fat content, we should change the method of calculation and take into account not the amount of milk but its fat content.

From the milk delivered by each peasant, small amounts are taken as a sample to identify the fat content. Those who have more butter per bucket get a higher price, because the bucket of their milk gives more butter. This calculation is more correct, although it requires the constant checking of the fat content per bucket of milk. Such checking allows the owner to know for sure which of his cows are profitable and which are not, so he can sell the unprofitable cows and make up his herd of only the most profitable cows.

However, one should not limit oneself to identifying fat content. It is also necessary to know the total amount of milk and of fodder. Sometimes your cow eats a lot of hay, but its yield is small or its fat is very low. Sometimes its yield is large, but the cow is still unprofitable for it eats too much. Sometimes the situation is opposite: the milk yield is small and the cow does not eat much, so the cow is profitable for it gives enough milk for a small amount of fodder.

Today in Western Europe, and after the Revolution the same applies to us, to identify the profitability of cows in peasant partnerships, a special clerk called the control assistant is often hired to calculate milk yields, production of butter, and amount of fodder per each cow based separately on the records and instructions of the owners. Having obtained all these data, the control assistant calculates the profitability of each cow per *pood* of fed hay. If a cow gives little milk per *pood* of hay, it is unprofitable and should be sold. By rejecting such cows and replacing them with better ones the peasant can gradually make up a herd in which each cow ensures high yields per fed hay.

These calculations are also very useful to identify the cheapest and most profitable fodder for the cattle. Unions of owners that hire control assistants for such calculations are called control unions; recently they have spread in Western Europe and now are starting to develop in our country.

Besides control unions, there are also other animal husbandry partnerships in Western Europe, for instance, the so-called 'bull union'. To have a good animal yield, one needs a bull of a good breed. However, such a bull is very expensive, and the individual owner cannot afford it. One bull can service 20 to 25 cows, so a few families can form a partnership to buy a pedigreed bull and have a good animal yield from it. Such unions are widespread in Western Europe and are of great benefit to the peasantry.

Among other cooperative partnerships that are of great importance for animal husbandry, we will focus on livestock insurance partnerships.

One of the biggest disasters for small peasant economies is the death of a horse or a cow. In the annual cash turnover of 150–200 rubles, of which three-quarters are spent on the most urgent needs, 50 rubles for the purchase of a new animal is an extraordinary expense. Especially in the months long before the harvest, such a purchase can destroy peasant economic well-being.

Quite often a peasant economy that lost a horse does not have money to buy a new one and finds itself in a painful situation of a horseless economy, which is difficult to get out of. We believe that every peasant who lost his livestock and cannot afford a replacement will be very happy to be offered the opportunity to buy one on credit for five or six years. We think that no peasant would refuse this, but the problem is that horses and cows are not sold on credit in the market. If this sometimes happens, the trader sets an onerous interest.

Meanwhile, peasants can change the situation in such a way that the money necessary to replace a dead animal would be paid in instalments and not in 2 but in 20 years. This possibility is provided by livestock insurance.

One can confidently say that an economy with one horse will inevitably face at least one unexpected infectious disease and death over 20 years. So, the owner insures his horse just as he insures his house and barn, and pays 2 rubles per year. In case of a death, he will receive 40 rubles from the insuring institution to easily replace the dead farm animal with a new one. Thus, a heavy lump sum is paid in instalments over 20 years.

The profitability of livestock insurance is particularly evident for the Russian peasant economy, whose entire annual cash turnover does not always reach 100 rubles. Therefore, an unexpected lump payment of 40 rubles would almost always destroy its economic well-being.

The only question is how can we insure livestock in Russia?

We believe that cooperation can be of much help to the peasant economy here, because its partnership basis has already played an outstanding role in providing the village with cheap credit and in organizing the sales and purchase of the agricultural means of production. So, we think, and the example of Western Europe completely convinces us, that peasant economies willing to insure their livestock can very successfully unite in a special insurance partnership.

In fact, every peasant knows that the herd of 200 cows loses no more than 5 to 8 cows per year, i.e. no more than 400 rubles (certainly, we do not take into account the years of terrible epidemics). If these 400 rubles are divided by 200 heads, we get 2 rubles per head. If individual owners of these cows unite in an insurance partnership and pay an insurance fee of 2 rubles per head, the owners whose cows will die this year will get new cows bought by the partnership. If the number of dead cows is less than eight, the collected surplus can form the reserve capital to pay the expenses in exceptional years, when the number of dead animals exceeds eight.

In Western Europe, especially in Belgium, such partnerships have become very widespread and contribute greatly to the well-being of animal husbandry. Most of them unite in extensive unions that help partnerships in case of an excessive loss of livestock. Such mutual help is possible due to the collected surplus of the partnerships with insignificant deaths in the same year.

In Russia, the first peasant partnerships for livestock insurance appeared before the war in the Vladimir and Ryazan Provinces. We hope that in the future cooperative insurance will develop rapidly.

Besides the detailed analysis of animal husbandry cooperation, we showed the gradual deepening of cooperation from marketing into production; step by step it penetrated into all its branches, one after another, and introduced the principles of socialization everywhere, where a large form of production has undoubted advantages over a small one, thus, creating new forms of farming.

The value of cooperation in all branches of agricultural production is much more than just a reconstruction of individual peasant economies. By socializing rural capital and the means of production and marketing and by penetrating step by step into the very organization of production, cooperation develops higher forms of large economies in the same way that trusts and financial capital have organized industry in capitalist countries. But it has done so with one difference: our cooperative capitalism from the very beginning had social forms and was under the control of the working masses.

Chapter 7. Conclusion

Our short course on cooperation is about to end. Certainly, in such a small book we could not describe with sufficient completeness all types of cooperation that already exist or can exist. However, we hardly need such a description. We outlined the main principles that cooperative workers use to develop cooperation. We described methods and cooperative enterprises that allow peasants to get a better future.

Everyone looking at the vivid rural life and knowing the great principles of cooperation will easily see where and how cooperation can help the peasantry. In rural life, there are many cases in which cooperation is a true helper to the working man. The same principles that form the basis of dairy partnerships can be used in processing agricultural products – in drying vegetables, canning, potato-grating, and even sugar production. The same cooperative principle as in the bull union can be applied in the partnership for the joint use of machines. Great cooperative principles can help a lot in the handicraft industry, in land issues, and in soil improvement. Thus, almost all aspects of life can take advantage of cooperation.

Sixteen years ago, in 1908, when Russian cooperators first met at the All-Russian Cooperative Congress, our cooperative movement timidly took its first steps, modestly learning from its foreign fellows – cooperators of England, France, and Germany. Today, by the scope of work, Russian cooperation is the first in the world. There are tens of thousands of cooperatives in all regions of the Soviet Union, which unite millions of members – peasants, workers, and townspeople; hundreds of unions have linked cooperatives into a single whole and given it exceptional power.

As of 1 January 1924, the agricultural cooperation of the Russian Soviet Federal Socialist Republic consisted of 12,000 agricultural and credit partnerships, 1,500 dairy *artels*, 500 other types of cooperatives, and about 11,000 agricultural communes – approximately 25,000 cooperatives of all types.

The whole cooperative network includes as members approximately 1.5 million peasant economies representing mainly the middle and poor strata of the village. However, in the general mass of peasant economies, the number of economies participating in the cooperative movement is still small – about 12 per cent. Nevertheless, in some regions, the cooperative movement is much more successful, for instance, in the Kimry district of the Tver Province or in the potato

Shunginsky district of the Kostroma Province, where the overwhelming majority of the local population is involved in cooperation.

To perform large-scale trading operations and technical management, thousands of scattered cooperatives unite in local county or district unions, the number of which is more than 300. For certain operations, especially if they are located remote from the centre, these unions form provincial or even regional unions. All this cooperative structure has a common centre – the All-Russian Union of Agricultural Cooperatives, or *Selsksoyuz*, and a number of special centres, such as the Flax Centre, Soviet Potato, and the very young Butter Centre and the Fruit-Wine Union.

In addition to these special agricultural centres, there are three auxiliary cooperative centres: *Vsekobank* (All-Russian Cooperative Bank), *Strakhsoyuz* (Cooperative Union for Insurance), and the All-Russian Cooperative Publishing House. These centres unite not only agricultural but also consumer cooperation.

This is the complex scheme of the current state and organization of agricultural cooperation, which is nothing but a form of economic organization of 1.5 million peasant economies that make up its basis.

All this represents a strange and unprecedented economic power and promises a bright future to the Russian peasant … provided that he will not change his cooperation for the lentil soup of an obliging shopkeeper or dealer, just like Esau sold his birthright for a mess of pottage.

Russian peasant, your future is in your hands! There is no other way for you to achieve the bright happiness of working life than through cooperation. Know that this way is the only way! To lose it means to die.

In the first chapters of our book, we mentioned that to develop and prosper, the peasant economy should organize its farming and animal husbandry in a new way. Today we see that this new farming, new improved machines, breeding cattle, improved seeds, cheap credit, and profitable sales are accessible to the working peasant only if he unites with other peasants. Only by relying on the union cooperative principle of the socialized economy can the peasantry use all the achievements of agronomic science in their fields and stalls, in order to, indeed, make two ears grow upon a spot of ground where only one is growing now, shake off the burden of usurers and buyers, and take confident steps to a better future.

We see this better future as a complete reorganization of our agriculture. Certainly, today's cooperative undertakings will develop further and further, seizing newer and newer branches of agriculture to organize new forms of social cooperative production. These cooperative undertakings in the form of auxiliary enterprises will gradually and powerfully develop into the main form of agricultural production, which will introduce large-scale production and mechanization principles wherever they can be advantageous.

Thus, we will see a new and unprecedented form of agriculture based on socialization, perfect technology, and the scientific organization of production. This future makes us consider our work (which superficial observers define as only the sale of butter and purchase of ploughs) as the future, grand, social-economic revolution that will turn a scattered, spontaneous, peasant economy into a coherent, economic whole and a new system of organized farming. And this future makes us totally agree with the idea of Lenin's deathbed article that the development of cooperation coincides in many respects with the development of socialism.

CHAPTER 4

A.V. Chayanov on differentiation of the peasant economy

This article by A.V. Chayanov was first published in the journal *Paths of Agriculture* (1927, no. 5, pp. 101–21). This is a revised version of his report presented at the beginning of 1927 in Moscow at a discussion on the social-economic differentiation of the Soviet peasantry. Many prominent scientists participated in this discussion, including representatives of the two most important ideological trends in Soviet agricultural science: on the one hand, Marxist agrarians (L.N. Kritsman, V.S. Nemchinov, Ya.A. Anisimov, I.D. Vermenichev, K.N. Naumov), and on the other hand, the so-called 'agrarian neo-populists' (A.V. Chayanov, N.P. Makarov, A.N. Chelintsev). In the report, Chayanov presents a new interpretation of the social-economic differentiation of the peasantry in Soviet Russia, which differs from the differentiation of the peasantry in pre-revolutionary Russia. According to Chayanov, after the destruction of the landlord and capitalist economies by revolution, the main reasons for the differentiation of the Soviet peasantry in the 1920s were regional contradictions in the peasant population distribution. On the one hand, peasants concentrated in the central, black earth regions, and on the other hand, they moved to the markets of sea ports and large cities. Chayanov argued that in this way, four types of relatively independent family economies emerged from the mass of semi-subsistence peasant economies: farming, credit-usurious, commercial seasonal-working, and auxiliary economies. Moreover, unlike the famous Marxist, three-element, agrarian scheme – 'kulak–middle peasant–poor peasant' – which was developed by the school of L.N. Kritsman, Chayanov developed a more complex, six-element scheme of the differentiation of peasant economies: capitalist, semi-labour, well-to-do family labour, poor family labour, semi-proletarian, and proletarian. Based on this scheme, Chayanov suggested a number of economic policy steps for the systematic development of agricultural cooperation, primarily in the interests of the middle strata of the Soviet peasantry. In the discussion of peasant differentiation in 1927, the arguments of Chayanov and his colleagues from the organization-production school were more convincing and justified than those of their opponents from the Marxist agrarians. However, in 1928, the Stalinist leadership began to inflate the threat of increasing class differentiation in the village. Thus, it initiated the struggle against the kulaks as a class, which became the prologue to forced collectivization during which Chayanov's school was destroyed.

Let me briefly explain my position. I am just starting to study differentiation, and I consider it in a completely different way than it is now interpreted as determined by the production organization of the economy of various social groups. Therefore, I believe that in two or three years, I will present some considerations based on my research. And now I want to make only a few general comments on the formulation rather than the solution of the differentiation problem. I have neither the data of N.P. Makarov nor the experience of A.N. Chelintsev. My ideas will be more deductive and methodological.

First, let us clarify the essence of differentiation. A very unpleasant incident has happened to so many words, especially in economic sciences; they are overloaded with meaning, i.e. a word is associated with many semantic concepts and images. In fact, when someone uses an economic term, he interprets it in one way, whereas another person interprets it differently. Therefore, before considering differentiation, we have to agree on what it is and what problems we face. Otherwise, we will have a whole Noah's ark of various images and terms.

If we consider the history of differentiation, we will see that in the late 19th and early 20th century it was usually defined as a process that accompanied the concentration of production in industry. In other words, it was the struggle of large, medium-sized, and small enterprises under the decisive, technical superiority of large enterprises. They gradually replaced small enterprises, proletarianized artisans, and eventually reorganized industry on the principle of horizontal concentration. The flushing out of medium-sized enterprises, the breaking up of handicraft and small enterprises, and their proletarianization is the process implied by the classical interpretation of differentiation.

Such an interpretation provides us with a solid and clear understanding of the issue and with an accurate classification of economies by size. The middle of this scale was gradually disappearing, and large enterprises were becoming larger and steadily maintaining their position. In contrast, artisans steadily went broke and finally proletarianized and became proletariat. This scheme clearly and accurately explains the nature of the social process under study. Under industrial conditions, differentiation had and has a certain place.

From what perspective should we consider the agriculture of capitalist countries? The recently published work of P.A. Vikhlyaev quite correctly and clearly raises this question. He mentions both the levelling process and differentiation in the countries of Western Europe and America and discusses differentiation not within the peasant economy but within the entire agricultural production. Vikhlyaev notes that in some countries, large, landed estates oppose the entire peasant economy. Medium-sized capitalist farms disappear in the course of history, but some farms from this middle layer integrate and merge to form beet and other landed estates.

Despite such an interesting formulation of the differentiation issue, we have to admit that in 1927 in the USSR this formulation is unacceptable, because we face a completely different problem. We have neither large, nor medium-sized, capitalist farms in agriculture; therefore, we cannot consider differentiation in such a way. The definition of differentiation that is relevant for us is of a different nature. To understand my formulation of the differentiation issue deeply, we have to first reveal the exact conditions of the national economy in which the differentiation that interests us takes place. This question is always crucial for the general understanding and further analysis of differentiation.

If we set ourselves the task of finding out the main types of demographic situations and locations of agricultural production, in most cases we will get two types of countries. One type is countries in which the demographic composition and the *standort*[6] of agriculture developed under the commodity economy, for instance, America, Australia, some other countries of the New World, and some countries of Western Europe. Under such conditions, we always have a very definite type of agricultural *standort* that is entirely determined by the market. The characteristic zones of different systems of the economy are distributed by isocosts. These systems determine the amount of labour required by agriculture, and, respectively, the distribution of population by isocosts. It is enough to look at the line of isocosts in the United States of America to see a clear expression of the described principle. The market creates all agricultural systems, and the population is settled according to the demands of agriculture for workers and exactly according to the heights of isocosts.

There is a different situation in a subsistence economy that excludes the possibility of isocosts; if there are no isocosts, they cannot determine the standard of agriculture. Therefore, in a subsistence economy, we have other types of agricultural production and population distribution.

In most countries, the factors that determine economic systems and population distribution are natural-historical conditions. There are also historical (often strategic) considerations that determine migration flows of subsistence economies. Thus, in the countries with subsistence agriculture, if other strategic things are equal, the distribution of population and agriculture ensures maximums in the most fertile regions.

Let us assume that some countries with a subsistence economy move to a commodity economy. According to natural-historical conditions, because of this transition, the density of population required by the market will not correspond to the density of the population already settled. This is the current situation on our Soviet plains. If you look very carefully at the population density and its distribution, for instance, on the maps of the 19th century – its beginning, middle, and end – you will see that the central concentration of population reflects the subsistence economy. You will see that for some time the population remains concentrated in the places in which it was concentrated before the development of steam transport.

Under commodity forms of economy, the population distribution determined by a subsistence economy is covered by the isocosts system, which determines the commodity production conditions. It goes without saying that the transition to a commodity forms an objective level of intensity, an objective system of economy, and an objective density of population. The need for workers will differ from those who existed before and are now present.

I made a very schematic small map to compare the changes of our grain isocosts with the population distribution. We see on this map that the highest grain isocosts in our country are typical for the ports of the Baltic and Black Seas, the Moscow industrial region, and non-agricultural areas (Turkestan and the far north). The zone with the lowest prices consists of the central agricultural regions and plains of Siberia.

When taking a closer look at the development of the isocosts system, we could assume that the density of population would correspond to the height of isocosts, provided its settlement was in a commodity economy. However, in fact, the distribution of the rural population and partly the standard of agriculture still reflect the conditions of the already obsolete, subsistence economy. The largest density of population is in the central, agricultural region, i.e. the region of the lowest isocosts. This disharmony is the basis of the entire history of our economy in the last century.

We see a complete discrepancy between market requirements and the real distribution of the population. This is the reason for the pressing, agrarian overpopulation in the central and south-western regions of the USSR. It is here that we see migration processes and the development of an enslaving type of relationship between farms. The mass, peasant economy has been reorganized from a natural form into a commodity one and thus has become part of the conflict of an excess of population versus the number of workers required by market-optimal forms of economy. It certainly loses its homogeneity and experiences the most dramatic processes of differentiation and increasing exploitation.

However, these differentiation processes certainly have nothing to do with the struggle of the large capitalist economies of Europe and America with their labour and semi-labour forms, with the differentiation processes in the Volga Region and Kuban, and with the state of things that we observe in the Moscow industrial region, where the processes of differentiation are of a completely different nature and are determined by other factors.

Therefore, I believe that to correctly raise the question and get relevant answers, we have to accurately and thoroughly study every single case to find out what kind of differentiation processes we are observing, how to divide them to identify exactly what we want to study in every single case, to understand how and to what extent we can capture the process of differentiation with statistical measures, and, finally, how to place it in the general system of the national economy of the country under study. When conducting this research, I believe that we can distinguish separate processes that can be included in the concept of differentiation of the economy but have completely different social-economic content.

The most important question is whether, under the transition from the semi-natural forms of our agriculture to commodity forms, there will be a transformation of our main economic form of the peasant family economy into an American farming economy with a semi-capitalist and semi-labour basis. How and with what speed does this process take place, and can we expect it to become large scale in the near historical future under our Land Code and our economic policy in general?

The question is not the size but the social type of economy; the question is not the organization of the production techniques but rather the organization of the social structure of this production. Will we have a farming type of economy or not?

This is the main and most important question in the whole issue of differentiation. Because of how the question is formulated, everything else is somewhat less important. If we are destined to follow the path of the American economy, our way to consider all issues related to agriculture is predetermined; otherwise, our analytical approach should be completely different. That is why I believe it is necessary to give priority to the question of whether our economies' differentiation consists of the crystallization of farming-entrepreneur elements and whether these elements stand out in the total mass of family farms? In addition to this issue, under the pressure of the same basic social factors, we can follow another process. That process is the differentiation of the agricultural population by separating the commercial, seasonal workers from it. This was once brilliantly analysed by N.N. Gimmer-Sukhanov.

For the population that depends on the lowest isocosts because of agrarian overpopulation, this is a question of the type of evolution – either a partial departure from agriculture or the adaptation of their agricultural economy to new, unfavourable market conditions. This question is no less important than the previous one. Among other things, for us it is extremely important to know from which social groups the reserve armies of industrial labour are formed. Under what conditions do the processes of this separation intensify or weaken, and what is the relationship with agriculture of the population that abandons farming? In fact, the most urgent and general question is the type of our proletariat in the next decade. As a result of differentiation, will we have the professional proletariat that completely abandoned agriculture or the new workers who are our old friends – semi-peasants–semi-workers who maintain relationships with their villages. This question is of crucial economic importance.

The third point related to the issue of differentiation is of no less social interest. It is known that the process of agrarian overpopulation in a family community economy always provides the conditions for the development of enslaving forms of exploitation, such as usurious credit, provision of means of production on onerous terms, and commodity exploitation. We have to learn whether this process is taking place in our country, and, if it is, what are the conditions, what are the factors, what are the sizes, and what are the economic consequences of this form of exploitation of one group of the peasantry by the others?

It should be emphasized that this process is completely different from the development of the farming economy. It almost directly implies the absence of the farming economy and becomes the most fruitful process in the subsistence economy.

Finally, the last question about peasant economy differentiation is the differentiation of economies determined by the changes in the structure of production and by the separation of farms for special auxiliary purposes: seed, breeding, primary processing, transport, etc. Very often such separation is determined by the capitalist surplus value; however, this is not an everyday, bonded exploitation but the development of normal, capitalist enterprises.

In this case, I do not mean the local separation of some special crops or the localization of agricultural production in space, but rather the splitting of the agricultural production process within the region – a kind of 'division of labour' between farms. This process is very complex and, unfortunately, often confused with forms of bonded exploitation, which is far from being always right. I will explain my idea with a few examples.

Let us consider elementary forms of pig breeding. They include the processes of mating, growing piglets, fattening, and slaughter all taking place on one farm. In the most developed regions of pig breeding in America, these four processes constitute four types of farms – we see mating stations, pig nurseries, fattening farms, and slaughterhouses.

Furthermore, in Flanders, the process of flax production (which we integrated at one farm) often includes dressing the flax. The process is differentiated into family farms, flax-growing, flax-damping, and flax-scutching enterprises, and also farms for hackling the flax. We see the same type of organization in many branches of primary processing, in livestock breeding, threshing, tractors, etc.

Undoubtedly, when these highly specialized enterprises are based on wage labour, their development is a major step in the development of rural capitalism. Nevertheless, this does not allow us to lump all these farms into one pile with forms of bonded exploitation or to assume that every employed tractor driver, owner of a steam thresher or other large tool, miller, or owner of a breeding bull mating for a fee represents an enslaving form of exploitation.

These are the four processes that we should identify and analyse separately, because each of them has its own specific social-economic nature. So, the first question: is the type of economy created or not created? Is there a transformation of the peasant masses, and if it is created, then under the pressure of what factors, and what is its quantitative scale? The second question: to what extent does the differentiation of the agricultural population resemble an industrial type of seasonal work? The third question: how and under what conditions do enslaving forms of exploitation develop? And finally, the fourth question: how is the production differentiation constituted by the development of individual mono-enterprises?

Actually, these are the questions that we face and that interest us. All these four processes have already been partly described by A.N. Chelintsev, N.P. Makarov, G.I. Baskin, and others. Therefore, after insisting on their separation, I will focus on only one question that has not yet been considered and, in my opinion, is not relevant, but its absence can hinder the study of the four previous questions.

All four processes take place in the context of the usual differentiation of the demographic (family) order, which depends on the relationship inherent in the family economy – between the economy size and the family size. This is the key background of differentiation, and it is especially clearly expressed in sowing groups and family size. Actually, this is not interesting for us because it has been common for centuries and is a common feature of every mass of peasant family economies. It should be taken into account and at the same time eliminated so that it is not confused with the differentiation processes I indicated above.

Already in 1923, in my work *Die Lehre von der bäuerlichen Wirtschaft*, I noted that, even if there were no social or capitalist differentiation in the peasant economy except for ordinary, everyday processes of peasant family development after its separation from the father's household and until its gradual filling of mouths and workers and the final land division starting new development cycles, under community land use and short-term rent, even if this were the case, it would be enough for a strong differentiation by the level of sowing groups and livestock.

This process takes place because of the relationship between the family and economy sizes. It is so important for understanding the social structure of the village that we consider it necessary to focus on it in great detail, especially because other speakers, as far as I know, will not touch upon it at all.

Quite long ago, after the very first cases of *zemstvo* statisticians' application of sowing groups, the relationship between the size of the sown area and family size in the economy was discovered. All research findings of peasant economy studies proved the same relationship of these two variables. For instance, relying on the consolidated work of B.N. Knipovich, Table 4.1 provides the series of data about this relationship by provinces.

Table 4.1 The relationship between the size of the sown area and family size

Groups by sown area, in desiatina	*Per economy*		*Groups by sown area, in* desiatina	*Per economy*	
	Desiatina *of convenient land*	*Peasants of both sexes*		Desiatina *of convenient land*	*Peasants of both sexes*
Vyatka Province			*Poltava Province*		
0	1.2	2.8	0	2.5	4.9
0–1	4.5	3.5	0–1	1.5	4.9
1–2½	8.9	4.4	1–2	2.5	5.1
2½–5	12.6	5.3	2–3	3.6	5.4
5–7½	16.6	6.2	3–6	5.2	6
7½–10	21	7.2	6–9	9.5	6.8

(Continued)

Table 4.1 (Continued)

Groups by sown area, in desiatina	Per economy		Groups by sown area, in desiatina	Per economy	
	Desiatina of convenient land	*Peasants of both sexes*		*Desiatina of convenient land*	*Peasants of both sexes*
10–15	27.7	8.6	9–15	15.8	7.5
15–20	36.5	10.7	15–25	28	8.5
> 20	51.2	12.8	25–50	54.5	9.5
–	–	–	> 50	144	11.2
Vladimir Province			*Yaroslavl Province*		
0	0.2	3.2	0	1.4	2.8
0–3	4.9	5.3	0–1	4.8	4.1
3–6	9.4	6.6	1–2	7.3	5.1
6–9	14.2	8.3	2–3	10.5	6
9–12	20.1	9.8	3–4	14.4	6.9
> 12	31.1	12	> 4	21.2	8.6
Tula Province			*Samara Province*		
0	0	1	0	0	3.5
0–1	0.4	3.4	0–3	1.8	4.4
1–2	1.4	4.4	3–6	4.5	5.2
2–5	3.4	6.2	6–9	7.5	6.1
5–10	6.9	8.4	9–12	10.5	6.9
10–15	11.0	11.0	12–15	13.5	7.5
15–25	17.7	12.6	15–20	17.4	8.2
> 25	23.9	14.4	20–30	24.1	9.4
–	–	–	30–40	34.2	10.9
–	–	–	> 40	65.9	11.3
Kaluga Province			*Vologda Province*		
0	0	3.6	0	9.1	2.5
0–3	2	4.8	0–2	7.4	4.1
3–6	4.3	6	2–3	12	5.3
6–9	7.1	7.3	3–6	16.6	6.2
> 9	11.3	8.4	> 6	19.1	7.5

By tracking the changes of functions, we can prove a significant dependence of family development on the size of land used. The nature of this dependence varies by region according to the differences in the structures of economic life. Thus, in the northern Vyatka, Yaroslavl, and Vologda Provinces with high earnings from developed, seasonal work, the area of land used is directly proportional to the development of the family. In the agricultural regions – Tula, Samara, and Poltava Provinces – the land use curve, as it develops, significantly accelerates its growth.

However, in both cases, the change in the dependence curves is so natural that for many provinces, it can be easily expressed by a mathematical formula. For instance, for the Samara Province: if the family size (number of persons) is x, then the area of convenient land per household in the analysed grouping will be equal to y: $y = 0.36x^2 - 0.52x - 2.6$; and for the Vyatka Province even simpler: $y = 4.38x - 10.5$. Table 4.2 shows the situation, because these formulas accurately express the changes in the curves.

In other words, we can be somewhat certain that the mass observations of the relationship of these two variables in the

Table 4.2 The relationship between Samara Province and Vyatka Province

Samara Province			*Vyatka Province*		
Number of persons in the family (x)	Desiatinas *of sown area per household (y)*		*Number of persons in the family (x)*	Desiatinas *of sown area per household (y)*	
	by formula	*by observation*		*by formula*	*by observation*
4.4	2	1.8	3.5	4.8	4.5
5.2	4.4	4.5	4.4	8.8	8.9
6.1	7.6	7.5	5.3	12.7	12.6
6.9	10.7	10.5	6.2	16.7	16.6
7.5	14.7	13.5	7.2	21.1	21
8.2	17.3	17.4	8.6	27.2	17
9.4	24.3	24.1	10.7	36.3	36.5
10.9	34.5	34.1			

Table 4.3 Correlation coefficients between the sown area and the number of mouths and workers in the peasant family

Provinces and uyezds	*Number of mouths*	*Number of workers*
Vologda *uyezd*	0.43	0.43
Smolensk Province	0.6	0.58
Belsk *uyezd*	0.4	0.4
Starobelsk *uyezd*	0.73	0.6
Novgorod Province	0.46	0.45
Kirgiz farms of Kustanay and Aktyubinsk *uyezds* (number of livestock)	0.59	0.56

peasant economy make them a proven fact. Our calculation of the correlation coefficient between them also proves their significance (for instance, see Table 4.3).

Thus, there is an undisputed fact of relationship. After the recognition of this fact, we must study the content of this relationship. Simply stated, we must identify which of these two interrelated elements is the cause and which is the consequence – which one determines the other. It is well known that there are two opposing points of view. On the one hand, S.N. Prokopovich and some other economists believe that the only determining variable here is the size of the sown area predefined for the family composition. These economists argue that the size of the peasant family is determined by the material living conditions; therefore, the family can increase in size only if it is provided with the proper means of production, in the form of land or in the form of cattle and other means of production in economies of other types.

Many researchers representing the organization-production school oppose this point of view and insist on the reverse relationship. Under the communal economy and rental forms of land mobilization typical for the peasant economy, the land area is much more volatile than the family composition. Therefore, this relationship should most likely be understood as the demographic development of the family being dependent on the distribution of land. I once studied the Starobelsky *uyezd* and tried to prove this position by pointing out that the grouping of the sown area is, at the same time, its grouping by the family age – according to the analysis of the demographic composition of families from different sowing groups. I found that the share of families consisting of a married couple and minor semi-workers reached 76.4 per cent in the economies with up to 3 *desiatinas* of sown area, but it fell to 38.5 per cent in the economies with 3–7½ *desiatinas*, to 4 per cent with 7½–15 *desiatinas* and, finally, to 0 per cent in the economies with more than 15 *desiatinas* of the sown area. In other words, absolutely all peasant economies with large sown areas were the families of older peasants, in which the second generation had already become full-time workers. We also noticed that the transition of some demographic elements from one sowing group to another, for example, the ratio of workers and mouths, provides the same development curves for the sowing grouping as for a direct grouping by family age. However, this decisive remark, not developed on the basis of other budget studies, was completely unnoticed in the literature about the issue. Therefore, the problem still exists with all its tough confrontation and, certainly, is awaiting an objective solution. Without taking on the task of a final solution of the problem posed in the report, we, however, consider it possible to publish one of our new works on the issue.

We believe that if the arguments of S.N. Prokopovich were true and the family size were really and entirely determined by the material living conditions, then these material conditions would affect the family composition primarily by reducing the birth rate or increasing mortality. Only through these two levers that regulate family composition could the material conditions act, because all previous studies defined the family as a composition of assigned families, including industrialists. Thus, the impact of the economic factor on the scale of seasonal activities of the economy was not considered a part of the issues under our study. Therefore, to check the arguments of S.N. Prokopovich in his last work, which aimed to criticize the organization-production school, we started to thoroughly search for the correlation between various elements that could serve

Table 4.4 Correlation coefficients of the share of children under six years in peasant families with various measures of the economy power (per farm)

Provinces and uyezds	*Land tenure (desiatinas)*	*Sown area (desiatinas)*	*Livestock in terms of cattle*	*Fixed capital (rubles)*	*Gross income*	*Personal budget*
Novgorod Province	0.007	–0.1	–0.1	–0.08	–0.13	–0.16
Starobelsk *uyezd*	0.19	0.14	0.21	0.15	0.11	0.16
Kirgiz farms of Kustanay and Aktyubinsk *uyezds*	–	–	–0.1	–0.1	–0.08	–0.09
Belsk *uyezd*	0	0.12	0.11	0	0.07	0.05
Smolensk Province	–0.12	–0.12	–0.18	–0.16	–0.16	–0.17

as indicators of the volume of economic activities: the sown area, number of livestock, etc., on the one hand, and indicators of family demographic dynamics, on the other. Because there were no data on birth rate and mortality in the budget materials available for our calculations, we considered it possible to take the share of children under six years as an indicator of demographic dynamics. We believe this is the indicator we need, because it expresses the birth rate for six years less the mortality of children for the same period. The results are extremely interesting and presented in Table 4.4.

After examining these extremely curious figures, we can absolutely conclude that the correlation coefficients between the elements of the demographic dynamics of peasant families and the measures of economic power of the farm can be negative and positive, but both are so insignificant in size that they can be equated to 0, especially taking into account their opposite signs. In other words, the absolute size of the economy, sown area, capital of the variables that we study has no influence on the birth rate less the mortality of children. We do not want to generalize our conclusion beyond the data that we have or to make any broad generalizations from our calculation. However, we believe that the results of our study are highly significant, especially because, as we showed at the beginning of the article, these are the budgets which provided us with not very high but still noticeable correlation coefficients between family and economy. Thus, we can arrive at certain conclusions: within the examined relationship between the absolute size of the economy and the absolute size of the family, it should be admitted that the first depends on the second, and not vice versa. By the extremely painstaking calculation of correlation coefficients, we did not expand our study to more extensive data and will not do so, because we believe that the 'obligation to provide evidence' is not ours but that of our opponents.

In any case, we have no doubt that: 1) demographic differentiation determines the differentiation of farms by sowing and other quantitative groupings in absolute terms; 2) demographic differentiation itself is not relevant. When studying the actual issues of differentiation (the four issues mentioned above), we should eliminate its influence in every possible way and use indicators that do not correlate with family size for the analysis of these issues.

This is our interpretation of the five processes of differentiation. It goes without saying that all five processes are inextricably linked, mutually determined, and show different forms of interconnection in different regions and different phases of historical development. However, to study them in synthesis, we should consider each process separately and find for each its own most effective measure and indicator.

At the present stage of the empirical analysis, the question of measures is the most important for the development of differentiation studies. Therefore, we will focus only on this question at the end of our report, especially because there is great confusion and little clarity and accuracy in it. As we have already noted, to study the four processes of social differentiation that are relevant for us, first we have to suggest such measures that would not correlate with the processes of demographic differentiation, i.e. those that would not indicate the absolute size of the family or economy. Accordingly, to measure the first process, i.e. the transformation of the family peasant economy into farming forms, as an indicator, we have to take not sowing or any similar groupings but direct measures of capitalist relations in the economy. L.N. Kritsman, V.S. Nemchinov, I.D. Vermenichev, Ya.A. Anisimov and K.N. Naumov developed a synthetic coefficient, or the coefficient of proletarianism/capitalism of the economy, based on the total account of the relations of wage labour and rental of horses and equipment.

The groupings by this coefficient provide very indicative results. However, we should admit that, because of their calculation, they do not distinguish the process of developing farming economies from the process of developing bonded forms of exploitation. We can say that, for example, by observing a farm that rents out equipment or livestock – we cannot conclude that this is certainly the birth of the farming economy. It is very likely that this economy will never become farming. Quite often such a process is the survival of old, bonded forms of domestic exploitation. If we study the differentiation of these methods, we will never answer the question of whether the farming elements in our peasant economy develop or not. It is quite possible that the economy of renting threshers and tractors will turn out to be the farming one.

Therefore, it seems to us much more rational to divide the coefficient of V.S. Nemchinov into two separate ones: the first is based on an accounting rental relationship, and the second expresses bonded domestic forms of exploitation and is based on accounting rental of horses and equipment, credit relations, and rent. However, even in this case, there can be complications and confusion. To eliminate them, we have to avoid confusing bonded forms of exploitation with the emergence of special, capitalist, service enterprises (our fourth type of differentiation) when accounting for the use of equipment and partly of horses. Thus, the integral Nemchinov coefficient is divided into three measures, and each of them is adapted for a special type of social differentiation of economies.

Another favourite measure in the study of differentiation is the economies' capital security. The author of this report and other authors often used the absolute size of fixed capital per economy for groupings. Our analysis shows that it is much more efficient to use the amount of the advanced working capital with the depreciation of fixed capital or even only the annual capital reproduction costs in the economy, although this is less indicative because of the intermittent reconstruction of the fixed capital that is typical for small enterprises.

Our final type of differentiation – seasonal work outside agriculture – is best measured by the share of seasonal work earnings in the gross income and annual wages or the family labour balance.

These are my methodological observations of the study of differentiation in agriculture. As I have already mentioned, I do not have the data of the large-scale, empirical studies of N.P. Makarov, V.S. Nemchinov, A.N. Chelintsev, and others. Therefore, I refrain completely from any comments on the current state of all four types of differentiation I identified. I believe that we will need not only the work already done but also a number of special studies to consider in detail the complexity of the issue we discuss.

The only comment with which I can essentially conclude my report is that the processes of both enslaving and demographic differentiations seem to me a relic of the subsistence economy. We will inevitably take this into account for 10 more years, but the development of this relic does not at all prove the development of capitalist elements. Moreover, the processes of differentiation because of seasonal work and the division of production functions do not always and do not so much indicate the development of capitalism in agricultural production in the narrow sense of the word. Rather they prove the development of the entire national economy towards higher levels of capitalist organization and industrialization. Both are possible without capitalist conditions: for instance, seasonal work can take place at the socialist state industry, and division of the organizational plan of peasant production can lead to the cooperative organization of some separated industries.

Therefore, we should focus mainly on the first type of differentiation: the direct reorganization of labour family economies based on the household form of labour balance into farming economies based on wage labour to get surplus value. It is this type of development of differentiation that constitutes the essence of the problem. In the Soviet economy, this process, which undoubtedly increases agricultural productivity, cannot be considered progressive, because it inevitably causes severe social consequences in rural life and hinders the development of cooperative forms of agricultural concentration that are the mainstream of our economic policy in farming.

CHAPTER 5

Letter from A.V. Chayanov to V.M. Molotov[7] on the current state of agriculture in the USSR compared with its pre-war state and the situation in agriculture of capitalist countries (6 October 1927)[8]

Alexander Chayanov wrote this analytical note to Vyacheslav Molotov in early October 1927 to discuss plans for the agricultural development of the first five-year plan in the USSR. Chayanov begins with a brief review of the history of world agriculture in the early 20th century. He identifies two poles in this evolution: western (American – typically North America and partly South America, South Africa, and Australia) and eastern (Indian-Chinese, typically agrarian overpopulated countries). The American type of agricultural development is based on farms that use machinery and wage labour and are controlled by the vertical system of financial capitalism. The Indian-Chinese type of agricultural development is characterized by agrarian overpopulation of the peasantry under dominant pre-capitalist relations, exceptional labour intensity, and widespread bondage rent and credit. The rest of the world's regions can be placed between these two poles. In the late 19th and early 20th centuries, Russia is a paradoxical, complex mixture of these two types.

Chayanov believed that in the agrarian science of pre-revolutionary and pre-war Russia, these polarized agrarian worlds were reflected in the agrarian-economic disputes of the so-called 'southerners' and 'northerners' about the strategy of agricultural development. 'Southerners' insisted on turning Russia into a 'hundred-per cent America' by the forced development

V.M. Molotov (Minister for Foreign Affairs of the Soviet Union)
Source: https://commons.wikimedia.org/wiki/File:Molotov_(minister_van_Buitenlandse_Zaken_van_de_Sovjet-Unie),_Bestanddeelnr_900-8983.jpg

of farmers' agriculture. The 'northerners' suggested supporting the regional strata of the middle peasantry and its own vertical cooperation to prevent the seizure of the village by trade and financial capital. Chayanov considered himself a 'northerner'. He argued that the post-war, post-revolutionary village has changed significantly. First, the younger generation of peasants who had experienced the World War and Russian Revolution set the tone. Second, the Soviet agronomic science and cooperation of the 1920s contributed to the real progress of peasant farms. Soviet Russia has a unique chance to find a fundamentally new path of rural development, thus avoiding the Scylla of American farmers' dependence on financial capital and the Charybdis of the Indian-Chinese stagnation of peasant overpopulation. Instead of American vertical agrarian integration through the dominance of financial capital over farmers, Soviet vertical integration was to promote the development of diverse forms of peasant cooperation with the support of the socialist state. In the final part of the note, Chayanov considers the ratio of industry and agriculture in the first five-year plan and predicts a radical social-technological change under agricultural industrialization. The Soviet leadership ignored the ideas of this note: Stalin rejected Chayanov's democratic type of vertical cooperation of the peasantry and preferred a horizontal type of cooperation in the form of collectivization.

In response to your questions posed to me by G.N. Kaminsky,[9] I send this brief note.

> Unfortunately, I had only a few hours to write it, which prevented me from concretizing my ideas and providing specific illustrations for them. Moreover, a certain abstractness of the note is also determined by the fact that, for about a year and a half, I have been completely isolated from practical economic work. Therefore, I can assess the situation in the village based only on the data of our academic expeditions.
>
> Nevertheless, if you need it, I can develop any of my ideas with all the necessary detail and provide them with sufficient factual basis. I apologize for somewhat careless editing of the note due to very little time.
>
> Comradely greetings,
> Professor A.V. Chayanov

Basic types of world economies before the war[10]

To most clearly reveal the distinctive features of the present stage of the Soviet agriculture, we must consider it in terms of evolutionary development and compare it with the development of farming in capitalist countries, starting from the pre-war period. When considering the state of world agriculture before the war, we can identify its two polar types.

1. ***American agriculture*** is based primarily on the labour of the farmer who personally works physically on his farm together with two or three wage workers. His economy is medium in size, extensive, highly mechanized, and firmly engaged in the capitalist system of the national economy in the form of so-called vertical concentration. Various banks of land credit, elevator, land reclamation, and trade companies tightly control this economy and extract a significant capitalist profit

from it. Cheap land, expensive labour, extensive low-labour-intensive farming with large capital investments and wide mechanization are foundations of this type of economy.

There are exact opposites of such American forms in the eastern countries – China, India, and some others. In these countries, excessive agrarian overpopulation with a persistent, feudal social order determines the development of family forms of economy, exceptional labour intensity of farming, and widespread enslaving relations in the fields of rent, credit, and employment. Expensive land, cheap labour, hyper-intensive and very labour-intensive farming, lack of both cars and horses, and feudal relations instead of capitalist ones are the national, economic basis of the Chinese forms of agriculture.

Paradoxically, the ***pre-war Russian agriculture*** seems to be a zonal mixture of these two types, or rather a mixture of trends of these two types.

On the eve of the war, the Russian village was at the brutal turn that accompanies the transition from the feudal system to the commodity one. Only a few decades ago, the village managed to get out of true feudalism and had not yet got rid of many of its elements.

For example, the main difference in the agricultural economy of our country from America is that, almost from its very first years, the settlement of America took place under a commodity economy. This determined differences in population density over the territory according to different zones of intensity entirely dependent on market conditions. As for the settlement of our country, for the centuries under the natural, feudal system, regardless of market zones, the majority of the population settled and was concentrated in fertile areas with more or less safe, strategic positions. Such a model of population distribution basically took shape in the 17th century and persisted until the beginning of the rapid development of the commodity economy at the end of the 19th century.

The development of commodity relations presented quite different requirements for the distribution of population by creating new, commodity-concentration zones around the Black Sea and Baltic Sea ports. As a result, 'historically predetermined' distribution became glaringly inconsistent with that required by the market conditions. There were obvious regions of agrarian overpopulation as well as underpopulated agrarian areas. The contradictions between them could not be mitigated by recent migration flows.

In our agrarian overpopulated regions, such an historical process spawned a Chinese-like land regime – family forms of farming, cheap labour, inflated land prices, flourishing slave relations, and pre-capitalist forms of peasant farm differentiation.

In the northern industrial regions, the agrarian crisis was mitigated and at the same time aggravated by seasonal, labour migration and extensive development of local handicraft industries. These hampered the formation of a real class of industrial proletariat and deprived the village of everything above the average level. In contrast, in the extensive, underpopulated areas of the south, south-east, and east, there was a rapid evolution towards American forms of economy. These included the rapid elimination of pre-capitalist forms of family economy, growth of farmer-type elements with machinery, and the active replacement of pre-capitalist and enslaving forms of differentiation with developing forms of truly capitalist differentiation.

Even from the national economy perspective, the economic structure of these regions resembled capitalist America. The high marketability, investment of significant loan capital, and the development of vertical concentration in both capitalist and cooperative forms mimicked the initial stages of all elements that constitute the American organization of agriculture. We have none of these elements in agrarian overpopulated areas, which persistently maintain the pre-capitalist forms of the natural family regime with slowly developing marketability and cooperation.

Before the war, there were two main trends in both the peasantry and agronomic circles. First was to strive for a 'pure America' and to develop farmers' elements in our agriculture in every possible way (the Kharkov group, Sokalsky, Matseevich, etc.).[11] Second was to rely on middle peasants and try to develop cooperative forms of vertical concentration of the economy. This would allow the rationalization and organization of the peasant economy to possibly avoid the seizure of the village by commodity and financial capital and keep control over sales and financing routes in the hands of cooperatively organized masses (Moscow agronomy at the Congress in 1911).

The war caught both trends in their first steps and in the literary forms of the struggle. Such was the situation on the eve of the October Revolution. What changes has the Soviet period of our history brought, and what were the simultaneous changes in the countries of capitalist agriculture?

Contemporary trends in American agriculture

Let us start with foreign countries. In the American-type countries, the rapid development of credit and intermediary cooperation led to the almost complete ousting of private, commercial capital; it fell under the strongest influence and control of financial capital. The cooperatively organized farmer established close relations with a bank to enter a system of a capitalistically organized economy. That farmer is the hero of the day in farming for both Americas, Australia, and South Africa.

The very complicated ideology of this movement can be seen in the attached translation of an article by the Argentine professor, Arano (Buenos Aires).[12] America added a significant set of technical improvements to this system of the organization of agriculture: new sorts of bread led by the Super-*Manitoba*; the melilot exported from the USSR, which promises a significant revolution in forage crops; milk yields of bovine record holders exceeding 1,000 *poods*,[13] etc. In contrast, the organizational-economic relations in the agrarian, overpopulated countries, except for Japan, remained almost the same as before the war.

The current state of agriculture in the USSR

Let us now consider the current situation in our agriculture after 10 years of Soviet power. To study this issue carefully, we must quite sharply divide the problem into two parts.

Changes in the production mechanism of agriculture

First, what changes have occurred in the very production mechanism of agriculture, and, second, what changes have taken place in the structure of agriculture as a whole and as an organized part of the entire national economy of the USSR?

Let us first focus on the first issue. Certainly, one of the major factors determining today's structure of agriculture in the USSR is the agrarian revolution of 1918 to 1920, which eliminated the remnants of the already dying landlord economy. Obviously, specific results of this upheaval differed by region. If the landlord economy was still viable and significant, the agrarian revolution completely transformed the peasant economy. For instance, in 1926, our institute of agricultural economy repeated a research that A. Shingarev[14] had once conducted in two villages in the Voronezh Province. He called them in 1906 hopelessly 'endangered' due to the severe land shortage. In 1920, despite the devastation of Civil War and the tragedy of famine, both villages became 'resurgent' due to a significant increase in the size of land plots. For the most part, the revolution allowed peasants to keep the money for all rent payments up to 20 million *desiatinas*, which they had previously paid to landowners. I consider as even more important the black redistributions[15] in the resurrected land community and dekulakization, which destroyed the farmers' elements of the village.

As a result, our agriculture lost high-commodity enterprises, which inevitably affected the commodity mass of agricultural products and export opportunities. Undoubtedly, they can be restored and even surpassed only by a significant increase in marketability by the mass economy. The liquidation of the landlord economy was so complete that, unfortunately, the state managed to keep only very small, unscattered agricultural lands. Thus, we must admit that our state farms and collective farms did not inherit any mass production capability. The old slogan of 1918 and 1919 – 'From peasant economy through communes to state farms'– has clearly lost its meaning and relevance. The lands of our state farms were seriously scattered during the liquidation period from 1921 to 1923. They are hardly enough even for the auxiliary agricultural activities (experimental fields, breeding farms, state farms, seed plots, etc.) that are necessary for supporting the peasant economy as soon as its massive rise begins. The socialist sector of our agriculture should obviously develop in some other ways.

After the destruction of large forms of the landlord economy and a considerable part of the farmers' economy that had already formed before the war, the production mechanism of our agriculture consisted, to a greater extent than before, of the still persistent pre-capitalist, family-type economy. It also included aggravated, bonded relationships in the rent of agricultural implements and working cattle due to impoverishment. This is clearly shown by the budget-study expeditions of the Institute of Agricultural Economy into the flax and sunflower regions (see corresponding tables in the attached book).[16]

However, since 1921, under the pressure of the developing commodity economy, this set of levelled farms has shown processes of the rebirth of pre-capitalist differentiation and capitalist differentiation of the farmers' type. This is especially true for areas that were accumulating farmers' elements already before the war. For example, according to the Central Statistical Administration of the USSR, in August 1926, there were 11.8 annual, term, and monthly wage workers per 100 households in the North Caucasus, 9.0 in Dnepropetrovsk, and 22.7 in Crimea, whereas in the agrarian, overpopulated, black earth areas, there were 3.2, and on the right bank of Ukraine, 6.2. We have no doubt that if there had been no revolution, in these regions the process of Americanization would have more deeply captured peasant masses. Even now it could have been more significant if it were not restrained by the measures of our social policy.

There was a simultaneous and much deeper second process in the pre-war agriculture – the development of agricultural cooperation. We will discuss it later.

Thus, after the Revolution, formally, in the private-property perspective, the production mechanism of agriculture preserved its pre-war, peasant basis as well as two development tendencies towards farmers' economy and the cooperative concentration of the middle peasant farms. This is naturally reflected in the current, corresponding ideological approaches. However, although the very type of the production mechanism of the economy remains the same, we can identify a number of profound changes in it.

We do not attach much importance to the fears of destroying the means of production of the peasant economy, especially considering draft cattle and implements. Although such fears undoubtedly exist, they do not seem threatening.

First, the huge percentage of non-sowing and horseless peasants must be significantly reduced, because it undermines commercial, peasant activities and seasonal work in the city, i.e. peasant farms are not horseless; they simply do not need implements. Second, before the war and due to the parcelling of farms – not only in agrarian overpopulated areas but also in the north in general – horses and implements were such a heavy burden and were so little used that their reduction did not mean a decline in the production capacity of agriculture in general. It led only to the development of the rent of these means of production, i.e. it had social rather than production consequences. There is an absolute and persistent lack of horses and implements only in the eastern, agrarian, overpopulated areas.

In general, due to the low capital intensity of our pre-war economy, some destruction of the means of production did not have catastrophic consequences. Its capital can be easily restored, as can be seen in the example of a number of regions that were crushed by the famine of 1921.

The positive changes are much more significant. First, we should note the almost ubiquitous and quite complete change of managerial personnel in the peasant economy. Some of the old men who were in control 15 years ago before the war withdrew from business and others were 'overthrown'.

Today in the peasant economy, more than half the 'power' is in the hands of the former soldiers of the World War and Civil War. They were disciplined in the schools of the Revolution and front and have an immeasurably wider outlook than the owners of peasant farms in the period from 1906 to 1915. This new 'staff' of peasant farms is head and shoulders above the former one, more mobile, and open to agro-improvements. Perhaps, this new peasant is more aware of his petty-bourgeois interests, but, undoubtedly, he has already escaped the grip of his grandfather's traditions.

Second, we can already provide this new 'economic entity' with new farming techniques. Our experimental stations and local agronomy, which took their first heroic steps before the war, today already have certain knowledge. In many respects, conclusions about the 10-year research have already been made, and we have considerable results in the rationalization of the economy. The attached diagram-cartogram, made by the Institute of Agricultural Economy on the proposal of the National Commissariat of Agriculture, is based on the data from experimental fields and agro-assistance. It presents a regional picture of our technical proposal for the peasants who are looking for new ways to reorganize their farms (see the large table attached).[17]

This combination of the new peasant with the new achievements of agronomy has already provided many examples of reaching our agronomic goals. Shunga and Ugreshi[18] are known for their 2,000 *poods*[19] of potato harvest per *desiatina;* the fodder grass cultivation is just as well known and is spreading rapidly in the Moscow Province and a number of other regions. Kurovo[20] and other villages are less known although their field crop cultivation is not inferior to the experimental fields of the Timiryazev Agricultural Academy. It is virtually unknown that a few months ago at the Volokolamsk exhibition and competition of cows, the cows with milk yields of 200 buckets[21] per year did not win any awards, because the prize winners' milk yields were much higher. And there are hundreds of such examples. Thus, the peasant economy has moved off dead centre and is developing its own resources.

Undoubtedly, this development would have been much more massive if the incentives to expand the economy were not extremely weakened in our village. One can confidently say that the incentives for expansion are one of the main minima of our economy, especially for production.

It is not so much about price policy but rather about the extraordinary progress of taxation that is sometimes prohibitive in relation to the expansion of the economy. An economically expanded peasant enterprise can pay the highest tax rate but, psychologically for the farm owner, such proceeds do not justify the strenuous efforts necessary to expand the economy.

This is the state of the very production mechanism of agriculture.

Changes in the social-economic organization of agriculture in the USSR

One can say that all the changes listed above contain no socialist elements at all and bring nothing new in social life as compared with the pre-war situation. There are the same petty-bourgeois elements in addition to the obvious trends towards the transformation of the pre-capitalist forms of the family economy [into] capitalist farms in a number of regions. However, this should not confuse us. At the current stage in the transformation of agriculture, the problem is not in the destruction of the peasant economy as such but in completely different forms of the growth of socialist elements. These will not only bring to naught the growth of farmers' elements but will also lead inevitably to the radical social reorganization of the structure of agriculture. At the current stage of agricultural development, these elements should be sought in the vertical concentration of agriculture. Here, and mainly here, the current decisive accumulation of socialist elements takes place.

Just as a crowd of armed people does not make an army, agriculture is not simply the sum of peasant farms. Agriculture, like the army, gets its identity and becomes an active agent when it receives an organization and a sum of known social ties that control individual farms and are drivers of their economic activities.

These social ties have almost no material expression, and this is the only reason for the observers of today's village to maintain that by appearance, it is a completely unchanged village of autocratic Russia. Actually, it is the system of these ties, which are in many respects absolutely different from the pre-war ties, that completely changes the internal essence of our agriculture. At the current stage of development, it is in these ties that one should look for differences from the past. I emphasize the current stage, because at the next stage these differences will extend to the production mechanism itself.

In the newest forms in the development of American agriculture, we saw that capitalism seized it with the financial support of the cooperative system of organized farmers and by introducing all kinds of capitalist auxiliary enterprises into the very heart of the farmers' economy (processing, elevators, refrigerators, etc.). In fact, we are going through the same process in the USSR. The only difference is that instead of financial capital, we have the organizing force and capital of the socialist state under construction.

This is the quantitative expression of the growth of the socialist elements in our economy by 1927: 66,839 primary agricultural cooperatives uniting 7,369,000 peasant farms, 16,962 dairy, potato-grater, handicraft, and other cooperative enterprises; hundreds of millions of loans through the cooperative channel of the Central Agr[icultural] Bank; about 500 breeding farms and state farms; 9,800 rental stores, seed-cleaning and coupling stations; and 7,000 *poods* of the seed fund (for improved seed material). If we add here a near monopoly position and, for some products, quite a monopoly position of state procurers in the market of agricultural raw materials and in foreign trade, then, despite the fact that our agriculture is a spontaneous set of 20 million smallest farms, the question is basically not how to establish state control over this set but what should be the direction and objectives of such control.

Under the further growth of these elements and forms of communication, the issue of the growth of farmers' elements in the village will certainly not lose its social significance but will almost completely lose its organization-production importance. This is because, under the inevitable drawing of the farmers' economy into the system of control described above, farmers' elements in production will eventually accept the role of technical agents of the state regulation of the economic system.

Moreover, in some extensive areas (the left bank of the Volga river and Akhtuba) and in the regions of special cultures (Crimea, etc.), the farmers'-type farms can be the only mechanism capable of coping with the production tasks in those areas, which cannot be solved by one- or two-horse farms of the middle peasant. They are almost incapable of organizing production cooperative associations in today's village. If such farmers'-type farms are included in the system of controlled agriculture, they are absolutely safe provided there are restrictions on territorial distribution and a spontaneous increase in the elements of the public economy.

The foregoing with sufficient clarity answers the question about the difference between the old village, the new village, and the village of capitalist countries of the American type. Today's village preserved the old, family-organized production mechanism in its peasant part and has received a new system of social-economic ties that allow the gradual accumulation of cooperative and other elements of the public economy in the very heart of peasant farms. This new system of social ties is growing stronger every year and organically enters the system of the planned state economy, thus, turning agriculture itself into an element of the national economy of the USSR under socialist reconstruction. In the countries of the American-type agriculture, there are also changes in the system of social ties, but this system in its cooperative part is linked with the bank financial capital and, thus, subordinates all agriculture to the control of capitalist centres. In our opinion, this is the essential difference in the current historical processes.

Challenges for the evolution of agriculture in the USSR

Today our Soviet agriculture faces two main acute problems posed by life itself.

1. The danger of a farmers' transformation of the peasant economy

First, given all the socialist-type ties described above, will the pre-capitalist family forms of the peasant economy rapidly turn into the farmers' type of economy, thus, changing the social basis of our whole system of control and support of agricultural production? Undoubtedly, there is a danger of this kind of transformation, and many contemporary figures who prefer to follow the line of least resistance would consider this transformation among the most desirable ways of developing our agriculture. However, we consider such a direction of evolution and assistance to it, if it is rather a rule than an exclusion, as a movement along the line of least resistance on the verge of liquidation.

We are convinced of the complete possibility of developing a quantitative accumulation of the socialist elements of agriculture in our farming in the form of a much more essential support than the current purely intermediary form. We believe that cooperation and elements of the public economy can follow the links and stages of the development of capitalism in the manufacturing industry. The gradual development of the public economy elements must go along the line: credit – purchase – sales – enterprises auxiliary for agriculture – organization of primary processing – joint organizations of draft and joint cultivation of land, and socialization of a number of branches of agriculture into large cooperative enterprises. This is the only form of accumulation of socialist elements in our village that can resist the development of the farmers' economy trends.

The simultaneous development of electrification, all kinds of engineering facilities, a system of warehouses and public premises, and a network of improved roads and cooperative loans lead to such a fast quantitative growth of the elements of the public economy that the whole system qualitatively transforms from a system of peasant farms into a system of public, cooperative economy of the village. This economy is based on public capital and leaves the technical implementation of certain processes for the private farms of its members practically in the form of a technical assignment.

Certainly, in such a system of organization of agriculture, there is no place for the farmers' economy. The system itself can hardly be called a petty-bourgeois type, for it undergoes such deep processes of transformation that it must be considered a form of consistent, socialist, public economy. This system can further develop and replace the remaining individual plots with larger enterprises of the collective-farm type organized as agricultural production mechanisms of the optimal size.

All the above is somewhat abstract. However, when visiting Shunga, Kurovo, and a number of our other regions, we saw first-hand the trends of this kind, albeit underdeveloped.

2. The place of agriculture in a system of the industrialization of the national economy of the USSR

Another issue of the same urgency as the issue of overcoming the farmers' forms of economy is the place of agriculture in the industrialization process that is currently carried out in the national economy of the USSR.

If we consider the industrialization of the national economy of the USSR as the most important among the immediate tasks of economic policy, we should specify the concept 'industrialization' in more detail. It would be incorrect to define industrialization as exclusively the development of

'Only a close, inseparable alliance of workers and peasants will save Russia from ruin and starvation'
Source: Moscow: Gosizdat, 1920. www.rsl.ru

the manufacturing industry and power plants, because industry cannot develop without simultaneous changes in those branches of agriculture that are connected with it. Therefore, we should always speak and think of industrialization as the restructuring of the entire national economy to make it more industrial. The growth of the share of industry in the national economy should imply the largest changes in the agricultural basis of industry. Specifically, when developing industry, we must completely modify the structure of its raw materials base and, in every possible way, promote commodity forms of agriculture as a market for other products of future industry.

Undoubtedly, we must start industrialization of the country with industry, and, in the first years of work, the greatest material resources should be invested in industry. Certainly, for some time, the rapidly developing manufacturing industry and transport and power plants can be supported by the old agricultural basis. But it is equally certain that in a few years, there will be an inevitable and predictable gap between the already restructured industry, on the one hand, and the corresponding agricultural base, on the other. Then, and I believe that this 'then' can come within the next five years, we will have to use most of the efforts and means to organize such an agricultural sector of the industrialized economy that will ensure sustainable existence and development of all its industrial elements.

Therefore, already in the coming years in the most important costs in manufacturing, transport, and energy sectors, we must systematically foresee the above-mentioned turning point and plan in advance all the activities that we will eventually have to implement.

These are my main thoughts of your questions in a few hours at my disposal and without the possibility to refer to any research and samples from the actual material, due to lack of time.

CHAPTER 6
Organization of agricultural production at the local level

This typescript was found in the fund of the Soviet party economist Lev Natanovich Kritsman in the Archive of the Russian Academy of Sciences, and has never been published before. The typescript consists of 16 sheets without an autograph or any handwritten corrections and marks. The typescript does not have any direct indications of the time of its creation. There are two more documents: a letter to Kritsman of 26 December 1929, and a fragment of the text written by Chayanov's hand, which is very close to this typescript and seems to be one of its drafts.

One of the most important questions of our economic policy is how and in what forms our agriculture, almost entirely peasant, can be integrated into the system of state capitalism, and whether such forms can become the basis for the further development of socialist economy and for the transformation of this transitional system of state capitalism.

One cannot but admit that this issue receives enough attention. It has been and is still considered by many authors; however, they tend to consider it in the most general terms – pointing either to the system of state regulation and cooperation or to the state trade and credit as forms for linking agriculture with urban industry; foundations of state capitalism are the most evident in the organization of the latter.

As a rule, there is no clear development of these provisions and no details; thus, it is impossible to imagine how different authors interpret the 'molecular' structure of the new Russian village, the specific everyday economic and social behaviour of Ivans, Sidors, Pankrats, and Emelyans – each of them separately and all of them together.

Certainly, this specification forms the heart of the matter; this specification can reveal those 'molecular' shifts and processes that transform the entire social array of peasant economies and completely change its quality as a fabric for all kinds of social constructions.

In the current situation, the question can be formulated as follows – should we consider the peasant economy as an element of dispersed dwarf family farms, in relation to which the system of state capitalism has to adopt the same methods of work as the system of ordinary capitalism, i.e. to organize the peasant economy with the methods of market pressure, to draw it into the orbit of its influence, and to make it a source of primary accumulation by the usual means of trading and financial capitalism. Or should we admit that in the thick of the peasant economy, there are historical processes which, provided their further development, lead to the elimination of the spontaneity and dispersal of peasant economies and introduce principles of the large-scale social economy, thus, allowing us to organically integrate our agriculture into the planned economy of the state capitalism system.

In the first case, the further path leads to the destruction of the peasant economy and to its gradual replacement by large grain and meat factories; in the second case – to the ever-increasing strengthening among the small commodity producers of the elements of the social large-scale economy to its optimal size under agricultural production, and to the organic combination of the resulting new system of agricultural organization with the large-scale urban industry.

It goes without saying that the question cannot be decided by the cabinet-style logical reasoning – only by the historical process of rural development.

However, even today we can and have to admit that in the surrounding rural reality, there are economic and social elements, the development of which can lead to the second decision of our main question, i.e. to the gradual organic rebirth of the peasant element into higher forms of production organization.

We have already considered in great detail the theoretically conceivable forms of such development in the articles on the production significance of agricultural cooperation and on the forms of industrialization in agriculture; it seems that we have succeeded in proving the theoretical possibility of this form of the peasant economy evolution.

However, for the current practical policy, it is not the theoretical possibilities that are important, but the actual presence of the described processes in the peasant economy, their share in the current stage of the historical development of the Russian village, and the state influence methods that can strengthen and accelerate these processes.

Today, this is precisely the heart of the matter.

Before the Revolution and especially in its first years, the development of the Russian economic and political thought was to a large extent limited to a number of urban issues. The countryside was considered only a factor that put pressure on national and urban interests, which explains our little awareness of the state of affairs in the depths of the countryside; the revival of interest in it made us almost send special expeditions to the countryside similar to expeditions to Central Africa.

However, for local agronomists, cooperators, and other rural workers, it is clear from their daily impressions that, under the developing monetary-commodity relations and the favourable global market conditions for agricultural products, our countryside is reorganized relatively quickly and is filled with those elements of social economy which determine a higher level of its organization.

The village organization is expressed in the development in the very heart of the village, partly in infancy and often to a large extent, of the following elements of social economy and life, which were completely unknown in the village before 1905.

1. Proper organization of settlements by territory, allocation of settlements, and in general proper, rational land management
2. Organization of water supply by engineering means

3. Organization of roadworks and equipping highways and other access roads to railway stations
4. Equipping the local commodity circulation with commercial premises, scales, warehouses, elevators, refrigerators, etc.
5. Providing the population with postal, telegraph, telephone, and other means of communication
6. Development of a cooperative network and related local facilities for the primary processing of agricultural products (dairy, potato-grating, drying, canning, and other plants)
7. Development and rationalization of the local industry auxiliary to agriculture (repair shops, forges, etc.)
8. Development of a network of agronomic centres and other auxiliary agricultural facilities (cattle breeding and seed farming, grain-cleaning, coupling and rental points, etc.)
9. Power organization of the region, i.e. its electrification and supply with tractors
10. Organization of public medicine, veterinary medicine and sanitation
11. Development of a network of schools, village reading rooms, local museums, folk houses, theatres, and other forms of cultural work
12. Organization of regional social life, its linking with cultural centres, and providing equipment for this work.

It is clear that this organizational work, which is ever-increasing quantitatively due to the developing cooperative collectivization of individual peasant farms, will lead to the inevitable qualitative rebirth of the countryside and to its historical transition to new forms of social life.

The development of the above-mentioned elements – imperceptible, routine, but gradually increasing for local workers – was clear already from 1911; however, it seemed self-evident and was not given any fundamental importance[22] despite its historical significance.

By way of proof, we would take the liberty of providing information about the current development of these elements in the village organization based on the Moscow *uyezd* data, i.e. the region without a special agricultural organization.

The main responsibility for the local economy reorganization is taken by land departments of local councils, and its key part is undertaken by the apparatus of the so-called 'agronomic assistance to the population'.

In the Moscow *uyezd*, this apparatus, in addition to the central *uyezd* group of specialists and agronomists, is divided into 12 groups – each serves one small-district *volost*, has a small plot of land, and is headed by the district agronomist. We will provide information based on the handwritten reports of these agronomists.

From 1 October 1923 to 1 October 1924, with the significant participation of agronomists and specialists, 14 single-plan settlements were allotted, and 11 settlements were divided into farmsteads (*khutors*) and land allotments. Most importantly, in 80 villages, intra-communal land management was carried out, and land was divided into wide strips. The number of strips owned by one peasant in each field before the land management was 3.5, after, 2.0; thereby, the average size of the strip increased from 222 square *sazhens*[23] to 648. With the transition to wide strips, there was a transition to the improved crop rotation. Before the transition to wide strips, 89 per cent of 80 villages had the three-field system, after the transition, only 1.3 per cent; the rest chose other, mainly rational crop rotation.

Eighty villages that reorganized their territory in 1924 accounted for 14 per cent of 569 villages in the *uyezd*; together with the settlements that switched to wide strips in previous years, they accounted for 278, or 48 per cent of the villages that rationally organized their territories. As the reader can see, the pace of the reform is striking. Even more surprising is the pace of the grass-sowing development.

By 1924, there were 134 villages (23 per cent) with grass-sowing; during 1924, 85 villages switched to grass-sowing, i.e. 219 (38 per cent) in total; out of 350 villages without grass-sowing, in 130 it was economically irrational (horticulture and other more intensive areas); 200 villages kept the three-field system, but, provided the same pace of transition, they would switch to grass-sowing in three to four years at most.

In addition to land management, 13 associations were engaged in land improvement: more than 30 *versts* (31.8 km) of drainage channels were dug in a year, and extensive measures were taken to improve meadows.

The scope of organizational and social work of 12 agrarian points can be seen from the following data:

- agrarian staff had 613 conversations on agriculture in 419 villages – 16,340 listeners, 1,226 hours;
- gave 347 lectures on agriculture in 264 villages – 15,968 listeners, 1,101 hours;
- taught 35 general and special advanced courses – 1,472 people, 1,271 hours;
- held 4,395 individual consultations;
- organized three agricultural exhibitions attended by 21,000 people, mostly peasants.

Thus, peasants contacted agrarian staff in the form of lectures, conversations, and consultations 38,175 times, or 49,000 if we count visits to exhibitions. This work was of a truly mass nature.

In addition to oral propaganda, more than 3,000 copies of agricultural books were distributed free of charge; 33 libraries with 15,000 volumes were engaged, which, however, were considered by agronomists to be far from complete.

Besides this usual methodology of agrarian propaganda, its new forms were used quite successfully – agrarian plays and trials, agricultural holidays, and all other kinds of campaigns.

Methods for the objective influence on the peasant economy deserve even more attention. In 95 villages, on the land of 110 households, 124 demonstration plots were organized for various comparative experiments on agricultural improvements; in 100 settlements, experiments with crop variety testing caused a massive demand for pedigree seeds.

At 74 rental points of 12 agricultural plots, there were 929 agricultural machines serving 1,811 households; 26,905 *poods* of oats, rye, and wheat were threshed and cleaned. It should be noted that this does not include the work of numerous rental points of agricultural cooperation.

Eight coupling points with 18 stallions impregnated 27 peasant horses; the work on other types of animal husbandry is being organized. Pest control is carried out on a large scale. In total, in 1924, agrarian staff made 5,205 working trips from agricultural bases.

The above-described work of 12 agrarian points is supplemented by the work of 189 agricultural cooperatives (according to the Moscow Land Department's data as of 1 October 1924). The nature of the work of this cooperative network can be seen from its composition. As of 1 October 1924, there were 6 communes, 33 *artels*, 16 partnerships for joint ploughing; 19 land improvement, 18 animal husbandry, 13 electrification, 22 credit, 8 agricultural, 3 dairy, 1 seed breeding, 2 beekeeping, and 7 handicraft *artels*; 13 machine associations; and 28 consumer societies.

The provided information on only one branch within only one *uyezd* precincts is completely sufficient to prove that our village is in the state of rapid economic fermenting and organization. In the place of the routine rest of disunited, isolated local farms, we see, perhaps, the first steps, but they are impressive enough to admit those processes of our village rebirth, which we spoke about at the beginning of the article, and this predetermines the second decision for our main question.

Due to the importance of this question, we have to examine in more detail the main organizing principle of the above-described agronomic apparatus and its agronomic assistance to the population.

Certainly, we know that far from everywhere things are going just as well as in the Moscow *uyezd*. However, as one can judge from the comments of local agronomists visiting Moscow, from the impressions of agronomic conferences, and from all kinds of printed materials, reports, articles, and even books, in recent years, the local agronomic work has gradually woken up from the almost 10-year stagnation that began in 1914. For many years, this stagnation has torn agronomic workers from their plots to send them to the front, food production, state farms, schools, commercial trade, land department offices, agricultural bases, i.e. everywhere except peasant fields and stalls.

Today, this difficult period has ended or, more precisely, is ending. A new agronomy is developing and starting to work. The observer and participant of this process would strive to identify the main direction of this new agronomic work and what is happening – the revival of the old agronomy or the emergence of something new.

There are fierce debates about this issue, which sometimes become of a sharp, almost political nature: the 'young' and the 'old' butt heads – the latter admit the continuity of the Soviet culture from the Russian pre-revolutionary culture, while the former do not accept anything from the obsolete world.

In any case, this issue is on the agenda and requires, if not a solution, then at least clarification or, perhaps, abolition.

We believe that if we consider this issue with some composure, both sides – 'revivalists' and 'originators' – will turn out to be both right and wrong. If we define 'revival' as the restoration of the old agronomic work in general, 'revivalists' are clearly wrong and historically naive ... In 1921, the old village, the old *zemstvo*, and the entire old social-political atmosphere, in which the old local agronomy had developed and existed, were gone, never to return.

On the other hand, completely wrong are those who want to build the new from scratch and declare the entire experience of the old *zemstvo* agronomy to be obsolete and to be thrown overboard with other elements of the obsolete system. This would be an organizational blunder. Neither Lenin nor other leaders of the October Revolution have ever denied the fact that in its smallest forms our Soviet culture is a successor of the Russian pre-revolutionary culture, and that many of the Soviet cultural elements and ideas were inherent in the Russian public consciousness long before 25 October 1917.

The very basic ideas of communism and dictatorship of the proletariat, which determine our contemporary existence, were born many decades before this historical date.

The same applies to agronomic work. Our pre-war social agronomy cannot be regarded as something unified, established, and firmly connected with the foundations of the old pre-revolutionary society. Agronomic community and agronomic work were a part of the Russian community and Russian life, i.e. showed a similar diversity of ideas and views of agriculture, the struggle of the most diverse approaches, and a large variety of methods. At the same time, it should be noted that most of the guiding agronomic ideas have been formulated for the first time very recently and have not been realized yet in a more or less noticeable form.

Therefore, the only right attitude to our old agronomic experience is a careful analysis of its working ideas and technical methods, and a selection of those vital and practically useful ones that can be applied in our current work.

The whole task is not to deny the old but to identify those elements of the old that can be practically useful in the new.

What has been said is enough to understand the wrong opposition of the 'old' and 'new'. The solution to the dispute lies in the formulation of our tasks as organizing a new system of agronomic assistance to the population, which will correspond to the new political and social-economic situation, provided the indispensable use of all those elements of the old social agronomy that can be practically useful; as we will show further, there are many such elements.

Let us try to find out what will be 'new' and 'old' in our tomorrow's work.

For anyone familiar with our current national economic life, it is clear that the new will mainly consist of realizing the political essence of agronomic work and its social-economic tasks, while the old will primarily provide some organizational principles, a significant part of pedagogical and technical methods, and the huge agronomic-technical experience that our science has accumulated for decades.

Indeed, we have to consider as new the following elements of agronomic work:

1. The old agronomy was not connected with the state policy of old Russia; moreover, it was mainly hostile to it and in many respects represented 'a state within the state'. This explains why agronomists often tried to heal the deepest ulcers of our pre-revolutionary agriculture with technical reforms by 'tale' and 'show'. It goes without saying that in a significant part of work, this led to helpless marking time, since in a significant number of cases, the desired agronomic effect could not be achieved by either 'tale' or 'show', but needed completely different measures of the agrarian, trade, tax, and tariff state policy.

   Today, when agronomic measures have merged with all other state measures into a unified system of the state economic policy, such isolation is no longer acceptable. The spontaneous development of peasant economies should be provided not with agrotechnical propaganda but with a system of economic policy and with agronomic assistance as an organic part of this system.

   In other words, at each point of its programme, agronomic work has to be supported by measures of the agrarian, trade, tax, and other state policy. On the other hand, agronomic work should not leave the general course of the state policy or contradict it, because agronomic work is only a service part of the whole.
2. As an organic part of the whole, agronomic work has to pursue the same tasks and goals as this whole. Since the USSR economic policy strives to create a system of state capitalism and to include the scattered agriculture in it, agronomic work has to accept these tasks.

   Concerning the peasant economy, penetration of capitalism took place primarily in the forms of trading and financial capitalism, which means the capital's seizure of the peasant commodity circulation and its crediting in usurious forms. Then, the capitalist forms of economy seized the primary processing of agricultural products, which separated primary processing from agriculture into special industrial enterprises (dairy, potato production, canning, flax-scutching, etc.).

Thus, the system of state capitalism primarily strives to occupy these positions of capitalism in order to command these branches of the local economy in the state forms, mainly cooperative trade, credit, and production. Thereby, the agronomy's task is to connect its work with these strongpoints, but mainly to organize the population and connect it with local agricultural cooperatives in such a way that each peasant household would establish a certain, though not direct, organizational connection with the planning bodies of our republic.

This statement may seem utopian, but we feel certain that in the Russian Soviet Federal Socialist Republic, in the potato, dairy, and partly flax cooperation, the planned coordination of centres has already covered peasant economies that form the basis of the cooperative system.

In addition to linking peasant economies with the economic bodies of the state capitalism system (mainly in the form of cooperative organizations), agronomy has to ensure their development around agrarian bases, seed and breeding farms, grain-cleaning, rental and coupling points, thus, increasing the elements of social economy in the composition of peasant economy.

3. Some changes should take place in the social foundations of agronomic work. First and most likely, we would have to stop misusing the expression 'an object of agronomic influence', because our peasant, having passed through the mill of the war and Revolution, outgrew 'object' and managed to turn into a 'subject' building the contemporary village. No matter how hurtful for our well-being, we must admit that the peasantry (its Soviet and cooperative organizations) becomes the master of

> the agronomic progress in the countryside after the Revolution.
>
> The era of the agronomic 'enlightened absolutism' is over. If in some places it is not over yet, it must end. The social factor will inevitably affect the identification of the village strata which the agronomic work will serve. As a rule, when developing its programme, local agronomy prepares its own plans. Often, as, for instance, the southern agronomists noted, small peasants were unable to implement this programme, which threw them out of agronomic work.
>
> Already in 1911, the northern agronomists noted the abnormality of this situation and suggested a differentiated programme, i.e. the agronomic programme that anticipates the social-economic stratification of the village and finds forms of the progressive evolution for each village strata. However, before the war, this idea was not realized in any noticeable form. Certainly, under the current agricultural policy, this idea is mandatory.
>
> In new circumstances, these are the principles of agronomic work, which to a large extent change its social-economic content and significance.

Let us turn to the second part of our topic in order to assess whether the new tasks require new organizational and technical methods of agronomic work, or they can be performed with methods of the old *zemstvo* agronomy.

There are different points of view on this issue. It is unlikely to be remembered today, but in 1921, one of the speakers of the Moscow Society of Agriculture suggested to organize peasant economies into groups (30–50 units) headed by managing agronomists with strong administrative powers. Such a system would need tens of thousands of agronomists, whom we do not have; therefore, the speaker proposed to concentrate the available agrarian personnel in two or three provinces leaving the rest up to chance. Such a radical project for the abolition of peasants provoked objections from all those present, including two members of the

Board of the People's Commissariat for Agriculture; the project was not developed.

A much more realistic project was the state regulation suggested by N. Osinsky in the last months of war communism: peasant economies were to receive quantitative assignments for various crops and to use new elementary farming methods tested on experimental fields: autumn ploughing, and so on.

With the transition to the New Economic Policy, this project was significantly cut and, when implemented, reduced to a memorable sowing campaign of 1921–1922 with almost no element of administrative interference. Nevertheless, the idea of 'agronomic regulation' cannot be considered abandoned, and there are still lively disputes about it in agronomy.

Strangely enough, we do not regard this issue as fundamental – in the life of our village, elements of 'agronomic regulation' are not new; there have always been such elements in the form of mandatory 'crop rotation', orders for meadows and mowing, and so on. All kinds of forest protection, land improvement, and veterinary measures have always been of a 'regulation' nature. Therefore, the point is not in principle but in feasibility. It is necessary to identify in a detailed study which methods can ensure the same mass results with the least material resources and organizational forces. After all, it is about the price that the result is bought at.

We believe that with the combined efforts of the agrarian, trade, tax, tractor, and other economic policy, on the one hand, and cooperative and agronomic work, on the other, we can do everything or almost everything without measures of the visible non-economic coercion. To do what is not included in this 'almost everything', we can use administrative interference, provided that it really ensures an inexpensive goal achievement, does not destroy anything in the economic life incidentally, and does not cause social complications.

Thus, the entire methodology of agrarian propaganda and the whole arsenal of techniques and methods, with which the old agronomy awakened peasant independent activity and directed it to the path of the agronomic progress, to a large extent remain in force.

One may say that in our understanding of things, there is nothing new, and the district agronomist will continue to do almost everything he used to do, say, in 1913. We will answer that, when fighting for Perekop, the three-line rifle in the hands of the Red Army soldier fired in exactly the same way as in the battles of the Bzura and Prasnysh; however, in the former, it was a weapon of the Revolution, and in the latter, it was a rifle of the old army.

The point is in the rifle's aim, and we set the social-economic aim of agronomic work with sufficient clarity.

It should be noted that in 1924, the district agronomist works very differently from the way he used to work in 1913: due to the revolution in our village, his possibilities expanded significantly, and, in addition to 'tale' and 'show', there are many means of influence. He selects machines in all cooperative and state warehouses and sets the composition of the improved seeds for peasant economies; he has at his disposal all breeding farms and centres; he can regulate technical requirements for accepting agricultural goods and marketing; he sets all other ways for a direct economic intervention in the depth of peasant economies.

Speaking figuratively, agronomy has always tried to organize agricultural life by influencing the peasant consciousness, and today agronomy has an additional opportunity to change it – by directly influencing the being of the peasant economy.

That is all the author wanted to say. Readers familiar with our agronomic assistance policy can see that we are not so much criticizing as asserting. The only thing I cannot agree with is the widespread local oblivion of the basic zootechnical rule: to get high outputs, all livestock including agronomists should be kept on productive rather than survival feeding.

Selected works of Chayanov and about Chayanov in English

Banaji, J. (1976) 'Chayanov, Kautsky, Lenin: Considerations towards a synthesis', *Economic and Political Weekly* 11(40): 1594–607.

Belykh, A.A. (1989) 'A note on the origins of input-output analysis and the contribution of the early Soviet economists: Chayanov, Bogdanov and Kritsman', *Soviet Studies* 41(3): 426–29. https://doi.org/10.1080/09668138908411823

Bernstein, H. (2009) V.I. Lenin and A.V. Chayanov: Looking back, looking forward. *Journal of Peasant Studies*. 36(1), pp. 55–81.

Bourgholtzer, F. (1999) Aleksandr Chayanov and Russian Berlin. *Journal of Peasant Studies*. 26(4), pp. 13–53.

Brass, T. (1996) 'Popular culture, populist fiction(s): The agrarian utopiates of A.V. Chayanov, Ignatius Donnelly and Frank Capra', *Journal of Peasant Studies* 24(1–2): 153–90. https://doi.org/10.1080/03066159608438634

Chayanov, A. (1991) *The Theory of Peasant Co-operatives*, transl. by D.W. Benn, London, New York: I.B. Tauris and Co. Ltd; Columbus, OH: Ohio State University Press, pp. XI–XXXV.

Chibnik, M. (1984) 'A cross-cultural examination of Chayanov's theory', *Current Anthropology* 25(3): 335–40. https://doi.org/10.1086/203141

Coleman, W. and Taitslin, A. (2008) 'The enigma of A.V. Chayanov', in V. Barnett and J. Zweynert (eds), *Economics in Russia: Studies in Intellectual History*, pp. 91–105, Farnham: Ashgate.

Cook, S., Binford, L. 1986. 'Petty Commodity Production, Capital Accumulation, and Peasant Differentiation: Lenin vs. Chayanov in Rural Mexico'. *Review of Radical Political Economics*. 18(4), pp. 1–31.

Durrenberger, E.P. (ed.) (1984) *Chayanov, Peasants, and Economic Anthropology*, Orlando, FL: Academic Press.

George L. (2021) Interpreting Alexander Chayanov's Peasant Utopia since 1991. *Istoria i Polityka*. No. 38(45)2021, pp. 9–34. http://dx.doi.org/10.12775/HiP.2021.031.2021.031

Harrison, M. (1975) 'Chayanov and the economics of the Russian peasantry', *Journal of Peasant Studies* 2(4): 389–417. https://doi.org/10.1080/03066157508437947

Harrison, M. (1977) 'The peasant mode of production in the work of A.V. Chayanov', *Journal of Peasant Studies* 4(4): 323–36. https://doi.org/10.1080/03066157708438028

Harrison, M. (1979) 'Chayanov and the Marxists', *Journal of Peasant Studies* 7(1): 86–100. https://doi.org/10.1080/03066157908438093

Hedican, E.J. (2009) 'Ways of knowing in anthropology: Alexander Chayanov and the perils of "dutiful empiricism"', *History and Anthropology* 20(4): 419–33. https://doi.org/10.1080/02757200903219621

Hunt, D. (1979) 'Chayanov's model of peasant household resource allocation', *Journal of Peasant Studies* 6(3): 247–85. https://doi.org/10.1080/03066157908438075

Kremnev, I. [Chayanov, A.V.] (1976) The Journey of My Brother Alexei to the Land of Peasant Utopia. *The Journal of Peasant Studies*, 4(1), pp. 63–108. DOI: 10.1080/03066157608438004

Krishnaji, N. 1995. 'Family Size and Wealth–Standing Chayanov on his Head in the Indian Context'. *The Journal of Peasant Studies*. 22(2), pp. 261–278.

Lehmann, D. 1982. 'After Chayanov and Lenin. New paths of agrarian capitalism'. *Journal of Development Economics*. 11(2), pp. 133–161.

Millar, J.R. (1970) 'A reformulation of A.V. Chayanov's theory of the peasant economy', *Economic Development and Cultural Change* 18(2): 219–29. https://doi.org/10.1086/450420

Monday, C. (2015) 'An intellectual's revolt against the Sun: Alexander Chayanov and Abram Bragin's Albidum (1928)', *Russian History* 42(3): 304–42. https://doi.org/10.1163/18763316-04203003

Nikulin A. (2011) *Tragedy of a Soviet Faust: Chayanov and Central Asia 1917–1937*. Soviet Era in Anthropology of Eurasia. Halle Studies, vol. 4, pp. 211–219.

Nikulin A.M. (2017) An omitted Intellectual Tradition: The Chaianov School on Collective Farming. *Jahrbucher fur*

Geschichte Osteuropas. 2017. Vol. 65. No. 3. pp. 423–444. https://www.jstor.org/stable/26381389

Özveren, E. (2005) 'Polanyi, Chayanov, and lessons for the study of the informal sector', *Journal of Economic Issues* XXXIX: 765–76. https://doi.org/10.1080/00213624.2005.11506844

Patnaik, U. (1979) 'Neo-populism and Marxism: The Chayanovian view of the agrarian question and its fundamental fallacy', *Journal of Peasant Studies* 6(4): 375–420. https://doi.org/10.1080/03066157908438083

Raskov, D. (2014) 'Socialist agrarian utopia in the 1920s: Chayanov', *Oeconomia: History, Methodology, Philosophy* 4(2): 123–46. https://doi.org/10.4000/oeconomia.836

Roberts, R. and Mutersbaugh, T. (1996) 'On rereading Chayanov: Understanding agrarian transitions in the industrialized world', *Environment and Planning A* 28: 951–56. https://doi.org/10.1068/a280951

Schmitt, G. (1992) 'The rediscovery of Alexander Chayanov', *History of Political Economy* 24(4): 925–65. https://doi.org/10.1215/00182702-24-4-925

Schulman, M.D.; Newman, B.A. 1991. 'The Persistence of the Black Farmer–The Contemporary Relevance of the Lenin–Chayanov Debate'. *Rural Sociology*. 56 (2), pp. 264–283.

Schulze, E. (ed.) (2003) *Alexander Vasilievich Chayanov – the Tragedy of an Outstanding Agricultural Economist*, transl. by M. Schlichter, Bergen an der Dumme, Germany: Agrimedia.

Shanin, T. (2009) 'Chayanov's treble death and tenuous resurrection: An essay about understanding, about roots of plausibility and about rural Russia', *Journal of Peasant Studies* 36(1): 83–101. https://doi.org/10.1080/03066150902820420

Smith, A.E. (1979) 'Chayanov, Sahlins, and the labor-consumer balance', *Journal of Anthropological Research* 35(4): 477–80. https://doi.org/10.1086/jar.35.4.3629542

Stanziani, A. 2004. 'Chayanov, Kerblay and the shestidesiatniki: A global history?' | [Čajanov, Kerblay et les šestidesjatniki: Une histoire « globale »?]. *Cahiers du Monde Russe*. 45(3–4), pp. 385–406.

Tannenbaum, N. (1984) 'The misuse of Chayanov: "Chayanov's rule" and empiricist bias in anthropology', *American Anthropologist* 86(4): 927–42. https://doi.org/10.1525/aa.1984.86.4.02a00060

Thilakarahtne, L. and Yanagita, Y. (1996) 'The Chayanov concept of a peasant farm economy', *Research Bulletin of the Faculty College of Agriculture Gifu University* 61: 45–59.

Thorner, D., Kerblay, B., and Smith, R.E.F. (eds) (1966) *A.V. Chayanov on the Theory of Peasant Economy*, Homewood, IL: R.D. Irwin.

Thorner, D., Kerblay, B., and Smith, R.E.F. (eds) (1986) *A.V. Chayanov on the Theory of Peasant Economy*, with a foreword by T. Shanin, Madison, WI: Wisconsin University Press.

Uleri, F. (2019) 'Capitalism and the peasant mode of production: A Chayanovian analysis', *Russian Peasant Studies* 4(3): 43–60. https://doi.org/10.22394/2500-1809-2019-4-3-43-60

van der Ploeg, J. D. (2013). *Peasants and the Art of Farming: A Chayanovian Manifesto*. Halifax and Winnipeg: Fernwood Publishing.

White, B. 2018. 'Marx and Chayanov at the margins: understanding agrarian change in Java'. *Journal of Peasant Studies,* pp. 1–19, http://doi.org/10.1080/03066150.2017.1419191

Endnotes

1. *Desiatina (desyatina)* – a Russian unit of area measure: 2.7 acres or 1.1 hectares.
2. Province (*guberniya*) – a major administrative unit of the Russian Empire. European Russia was divided into 49 such units.
3. Sazhen: a Russian unit of length: 3 arshins (0.71 m) or 2.13 m.
4. Agricultural cooperatives usually include the so-called 'complete agricultural cooperatives', i.e. agricultural communes in which individual farms are completely dissolved in the social economy. Due to their importance, a special book is devoted to 'complete agricultural cooperatives', and we do not consider them at all in this essay.
5. The Russian pound (*funt*), weight 0.9 pounds avoirdupois, 0.4 kilograms.
6. Standort: word of German origin meaning 'location', 'position', or 'site'.
7. V.M. Molotov (1890–1986) – a famous Soviet party leader, one of the closest associates of I.V. Stalin, a member of the Politburo of the Central Committee of the Communist Party of the Soviet Union (CPSU) from 1926 to 1957, the prime minister of the Soviet government from 1930 to 1941.
8. As the Head of the Commission of the Central Committee of the CPSU, while preparing theses about the work in the countryside for the XV Congress of the CPSU, V.M. Molotov asked A.V. Chayanov to write his ideas and suggestions on the development of agriculture in the USSR. This text is A.V. Chayanov's answer to the request of V.M. Molotov.
9. G.N. Kaminsky (1895–1938) – a prominent figure in the Bolshevik Party, Head of the Trade Union of Agricultural and Forestry Workers, Deputy Head of the Board of the Union of Agricultural Cooperation of the USSR.
10. The headlines underlined in the typescript are given here in bold italics.

11. Agrarian economists from the south of Russia, especially those who published the *Agronomic Journal* in Kharkov (K.A. Matseevich, S.A. Sokalsky), are the main representatives of agronomist southerners who primarily support the liberal, capitalist farmers' development of rural Russia.
12. This article by Professor Arano was not found in the archive.
13. *Pood* is an old Russian measure of weight. One *pood* is equal to 16.38 kg; 1,000 *poods* are equal to 16.38 tonnes.
14. A.I. Shingarev (1869–1918) – a liberal public figure, doctor, publicist, author of the book *Endangered Village: A Sanitary-Economic Study of Two Villages of the Voronezh* Uyezd' (Saint Petersburg, 1907).
15. Black or radical redistribution was the system of land redistribution in peasant communities: all communal land was divided into plots of approximately similar quality, and land units of different quality were allocated to families (according to the number of ploughmen, family members, etc.). Thus, each peasant family received a certain number of land strips of different quality, and strip farming increased.
16. The book was not found in the archive.
17. There was no attachment in the archive.
18. Villages of the Kostroma Province of Russia.
19. 2,000 *poods* are equal to 32.7 tonnes.
20. A village in the Tula Province of Russia.
21. 200 buckets are equal to 2,460 litres.
22. Underlined in the original.
23. Square *sazhen*: a Russian unit of area: 4.5 m^2.

www.ingramcontent.com/pod-product-compliance
Ingram Content Group UK Ltd.
Pitfield, Milton Keynes, MK11 3LW, UK
UKHW061932100926
8556IPUK00007B/878